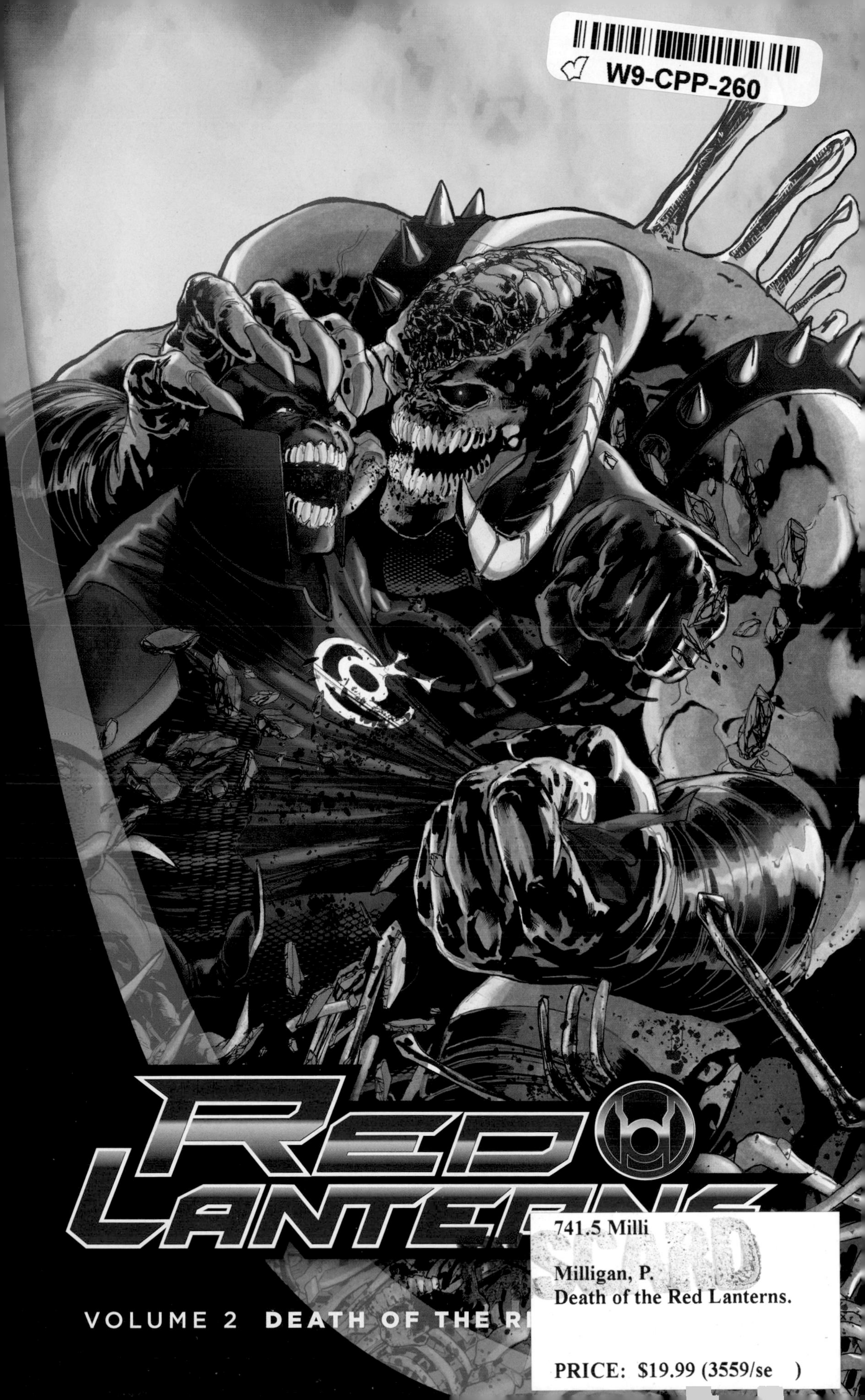
RED LANTERNS
VOLUME 2 DEATH OF THE

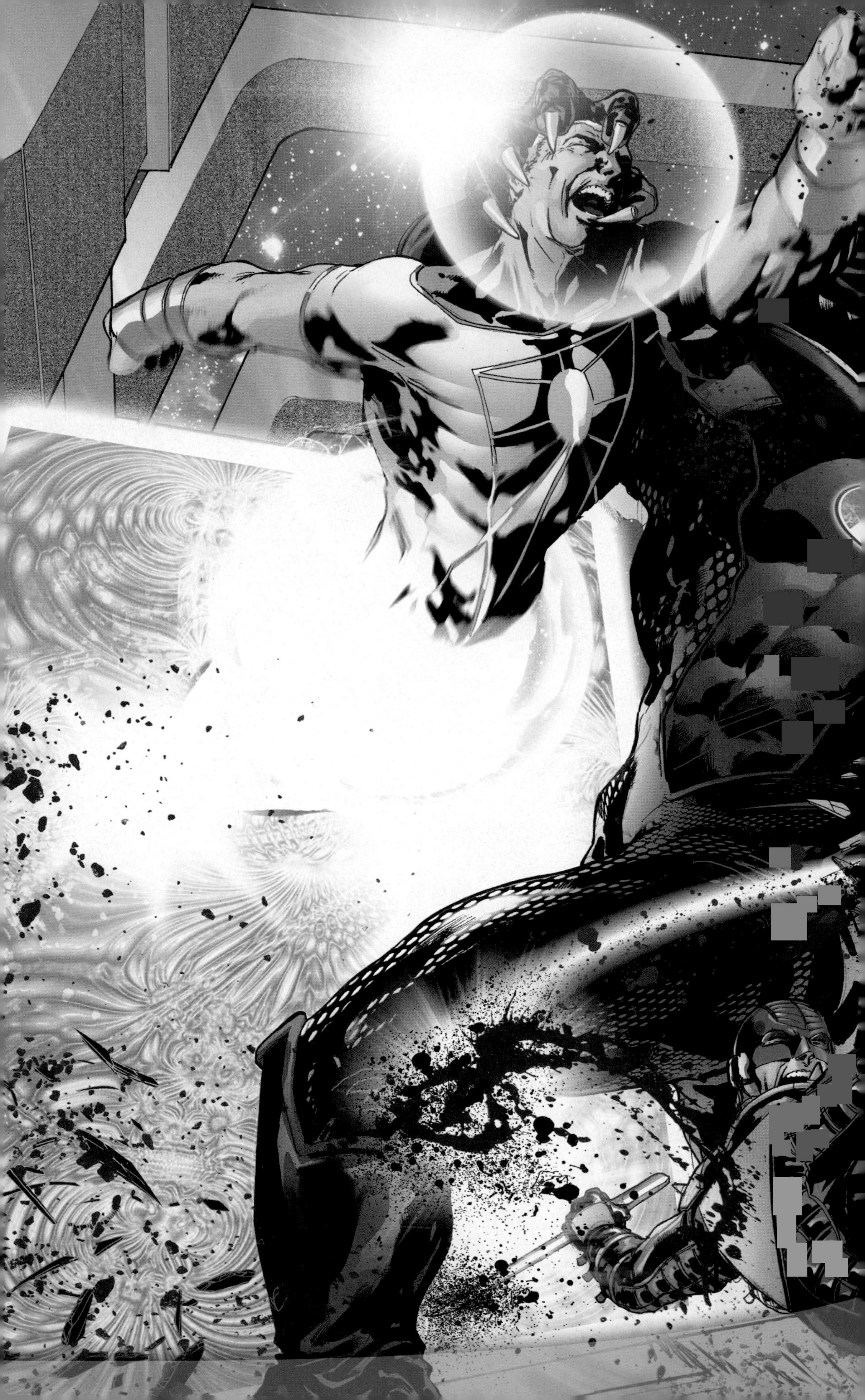

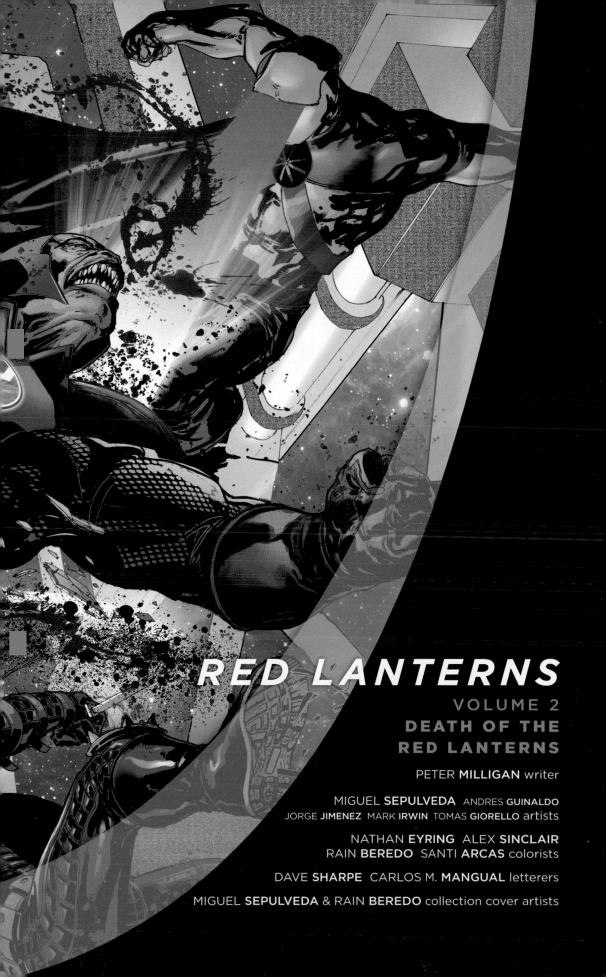

RED LANTERNS

VOLUME 2
DEATH OF THE
RED LANTERNS

PETER **MILLIGAN** writer

MIGUEL **SEPULVEDA** ANDRES **GUINALDO**
JORGE **JIMENEZ** MARK **IRWIN** TOMAS **GIORELLO** artists

NATHAN **EYRING** ALEX **SINCLAIR**
RAIN **BEREDO** SANTI **ARCAS** colorists

DAVE **SHARPE** CARLOS M. **MANGUAL** letterers

MIGUEL **SEPULVEDA** & RAIN **BEREDO** collection cover artists

PAT MCCALLUM Editor – Original Series SEAN MACKIEWICZ Assistant Editor – Original Series ROWENA YOW Editor
ROBBIN BROSTERMAN Design Director – Books ROBBIE BIEDERMAN Publication Design

BOB HARRAS VP – Editor-in-Chief

DIANE NELSON President DAN DIDIO and JIM LEE Co-Publishers
GEOFF JOHNS Chief Creative Officer
JOHN ROOD Executive VP – Sales, Marketing and Business Development
AMY GENKINS Senior VP – Business and Legal Affairs NAIRI GARDINER Senior VP – Finance
JEFF BOISON VP – Publishing Operations MARK CHIARELLO VP – Art Direction and Design
JOHN CUNNINGHAM VP – Marketing TERRI CUNNINGHAM VP – Talent Relations and Services
ALISON GILL Senior VP – Manufacturing and Operations HANK KANALZ Senior VP – Digital
JAY KOGAN VP – Business and Legal Affairs, Publishing JACK MAHAN VP – Business Affairs, Talent
NICK NAPOLITANO VP – Manufacturing Administration SUE POHJA VP – Book Sales
COURTNEY SIMMONS Senior VP – Publicity BOB WAYNE Senior VP – Sales

RED LANTERNS VOLUME TWO: DEATH OF THE RED LANTERNS

DC Comics, 1700 Broadway, New York, NY 10019
A Warner Bros. Entertainment Company.
Printed by RR Donnelley, Salem, VA, USA. 2/1/13. First Printing.

ISBN: 978-1-4012-3847-6

Library of Congress Cataloging-in-Publication Data

Milligan, Peter, author.
Red Lanterns. Volume two, Death of the Red Lanterns / Peter Milligan, Miguel Sepulveda.
pages cm
"Originally published in single magazine form in Red Lanterns #8-12, Stormwatch #9."

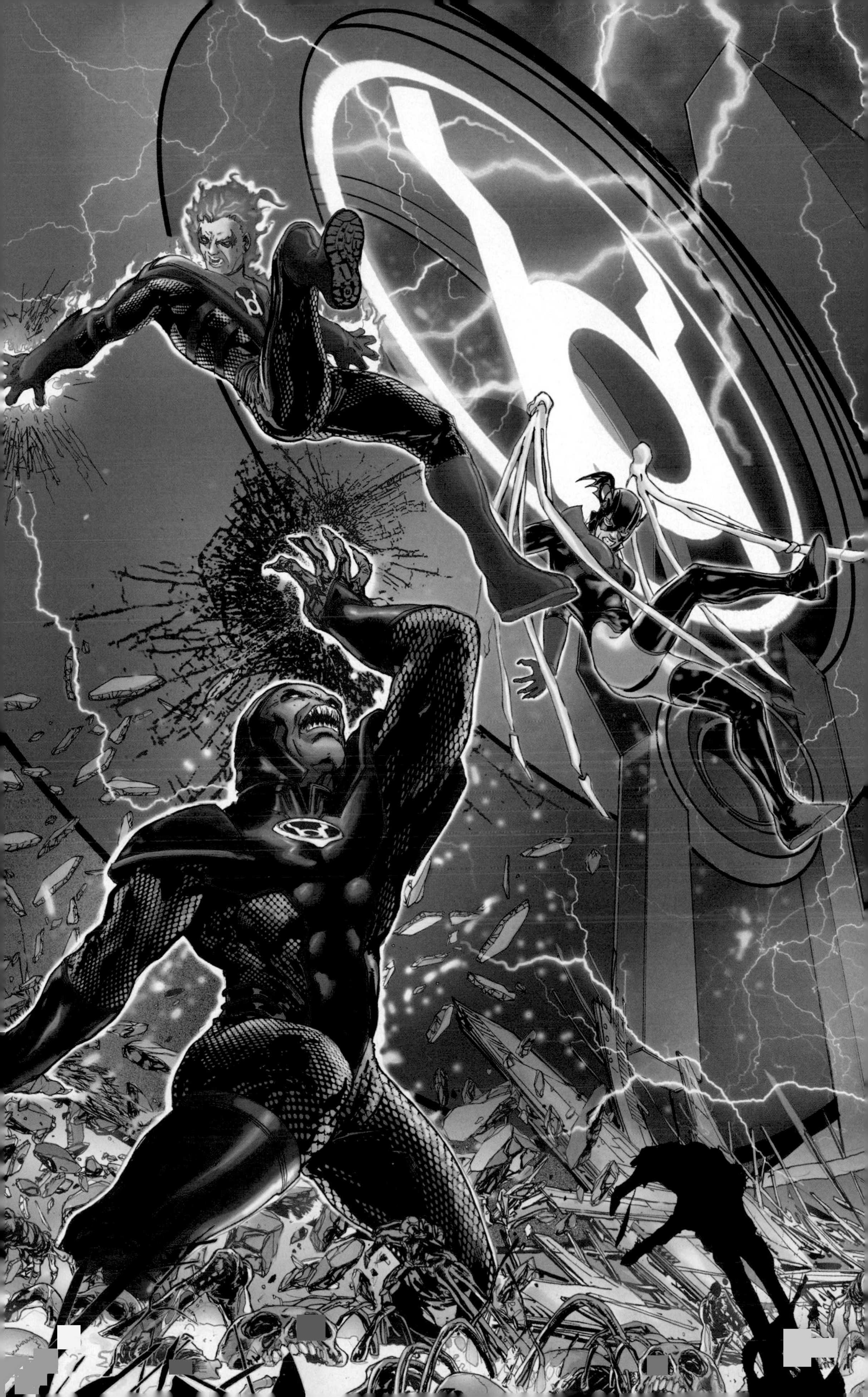

DEATH ON YSMAULT

PETER MILLIGAN
writer

ANDRES GUINALDO
JORGE JIMENEZ
pencillers

MARK IRWIN
JORGE JIMENEZ
inkers

cover art by MIGUEL SEPULVEDA

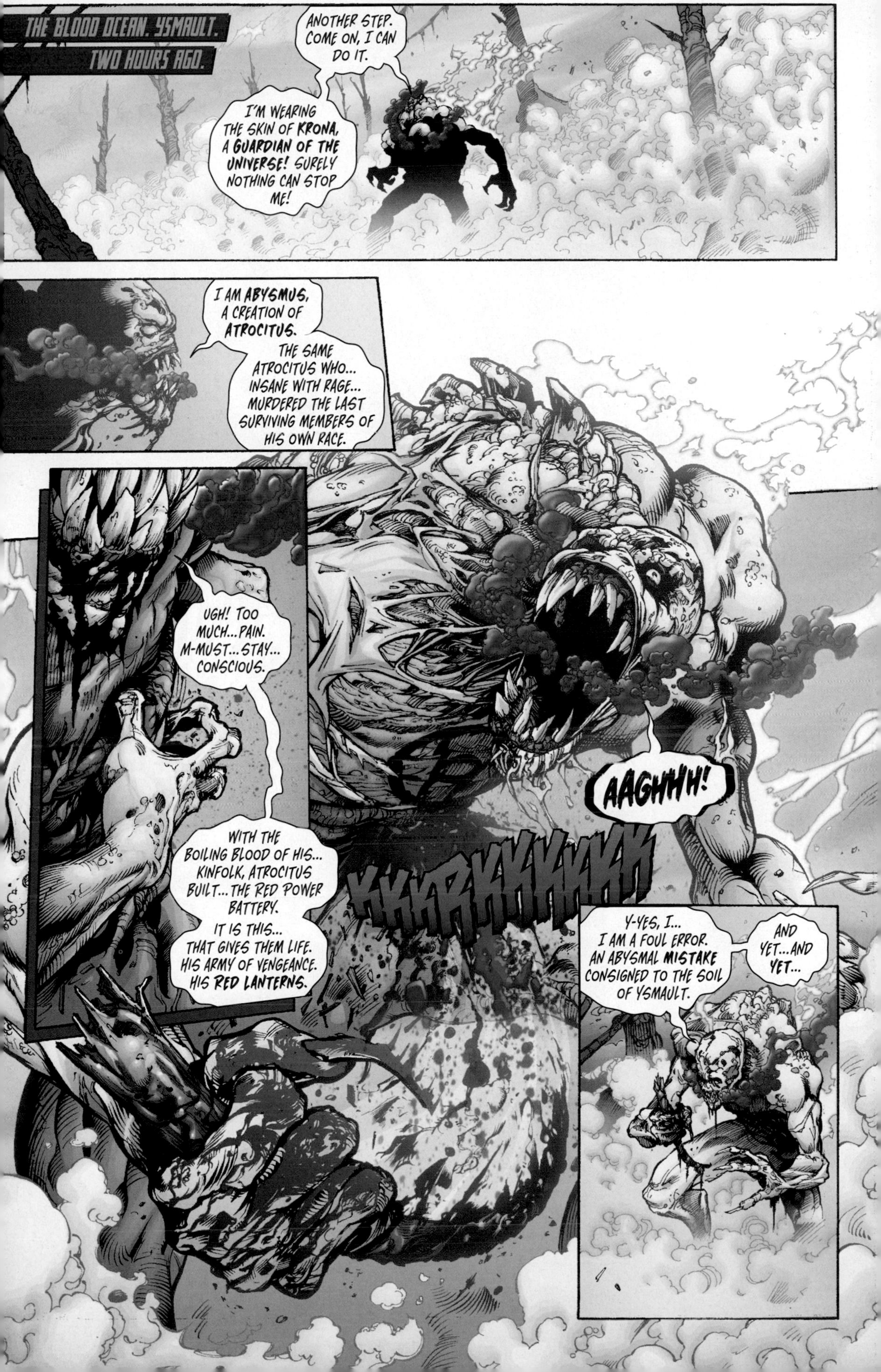
THE BLOOD OCEAN. YSMAULT.
TWO HOURS AGO.
ANOTHER STEP. COME ON, I CAN DO IT.
I'M WEARING THE SKIN OF KRONA, A GUARDIAN OF THE UNIVERSE! SURELY NOTHING CAN STOP ME!
I AM ABYSMUS, A CREATION OF ATROCITUS.
THE SAME ATROCITUS WHO... INSANE WITH RAGE... MURDERED THE LAST SURVIVING MEMBERS OF HIS OWN RACE.
UGH! TOO MUCH...PAIN. M-MUST...STAY... CONSCIOUS.
AAGHHH!
WITH THE BOILING BLOOD OF HIS... KINFOLK, ATROCITUS BUILT...THE RED POWER BATTERY.
IT IS THIS... THAT GIVES THEM LIFE. HIS ARMY OF VENGEANCE. HIS RED LANTERNS.
KKKRKKKKKK
Y-YES, I... I AM A FOUL ERROR. AN ABYSMAL MISTAKE CONSIGNED TO THE SOIL OF YSMAULT.
AND YET...AND YET...

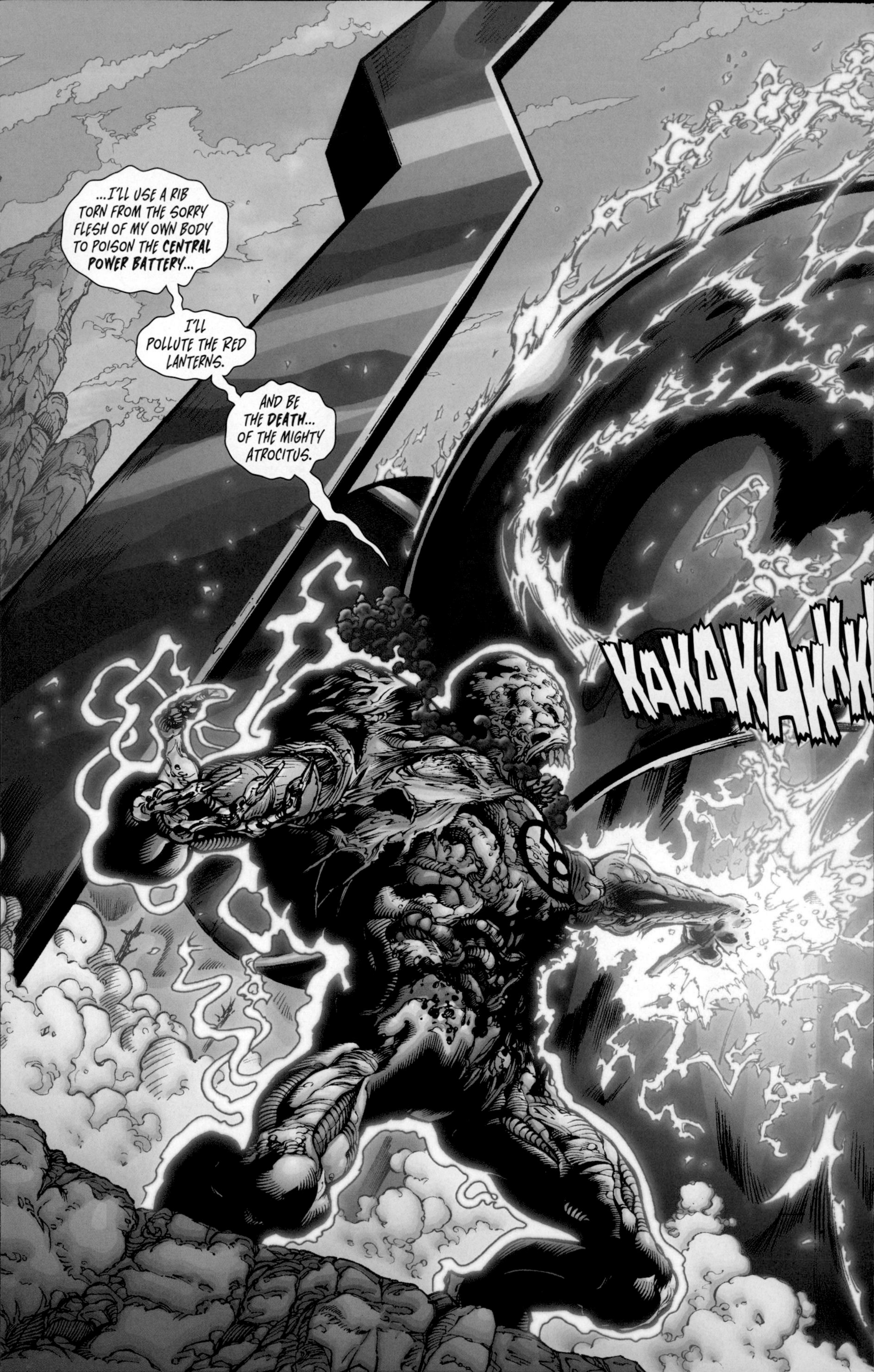
...I'LL USE A RIB TORN FROM THE SORRY FLESH OF MY OWN BODY TO POISON THE CENTRAL POWER BATTERY...
I'LL POLLUTE THE RED LANTERNS.
AND BE THE DEATH... OF THE MIGHTY ATROCITUS.
KAKAKAKKK

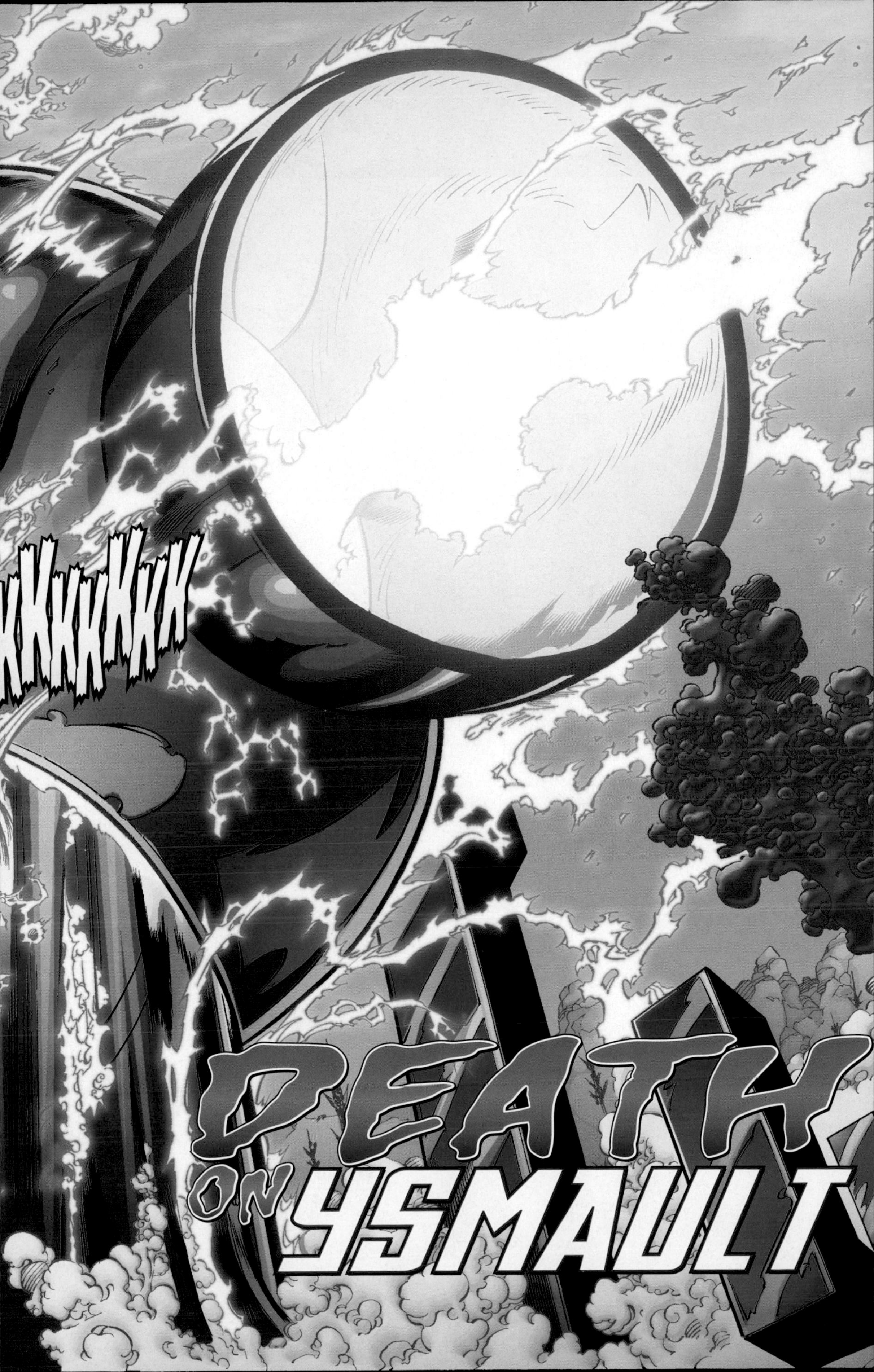
KKKKKKKK
DEATH ON YSMAULT

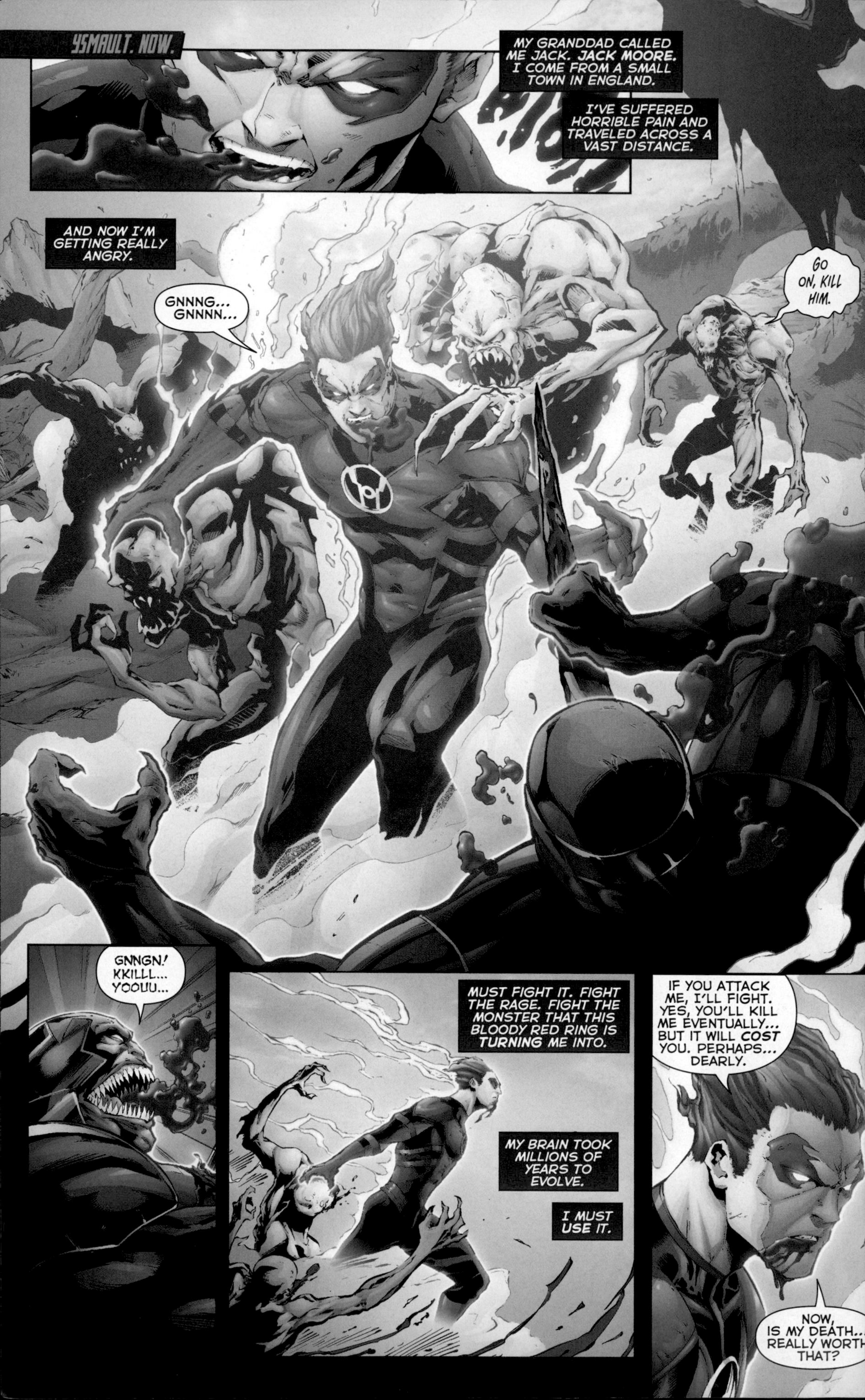
YSMAULT. NOW.
MY GRANDDAD CALLED ME JACK. JACK MOORE. I COME FROM A SMALL TOWN IN ENGLAND.
I'VE SUFFERED HORRIBLE PAIN AND TRAVELED ACROSS A VAST DISTANCE.
AND NOW I'M GETTING REALLY ANGRY.
GNNNG... GNNNN...
GO ON, KILL HIM.
GNNGN! KKILLL... YOOUU...
MUST FIGHT IT. FIGHT THE RAGE. FIGHT THE MONSTER THAT THIS BLOODY RED RING IS TURNING ME INTO.
MY BRAIN TOOK MILLIONS OF YEARS TO EVOLVE.
I MUST USE IT.
IF YOU ATTACK ME, I'LL FIGHT. YES, YOU'LL KILL ME EVENTUALLY... BUT IT WILL COST YOU. PERHAPS... DEARLY.
NOW, IS MY DEATH... REALLY WORTH THAT?

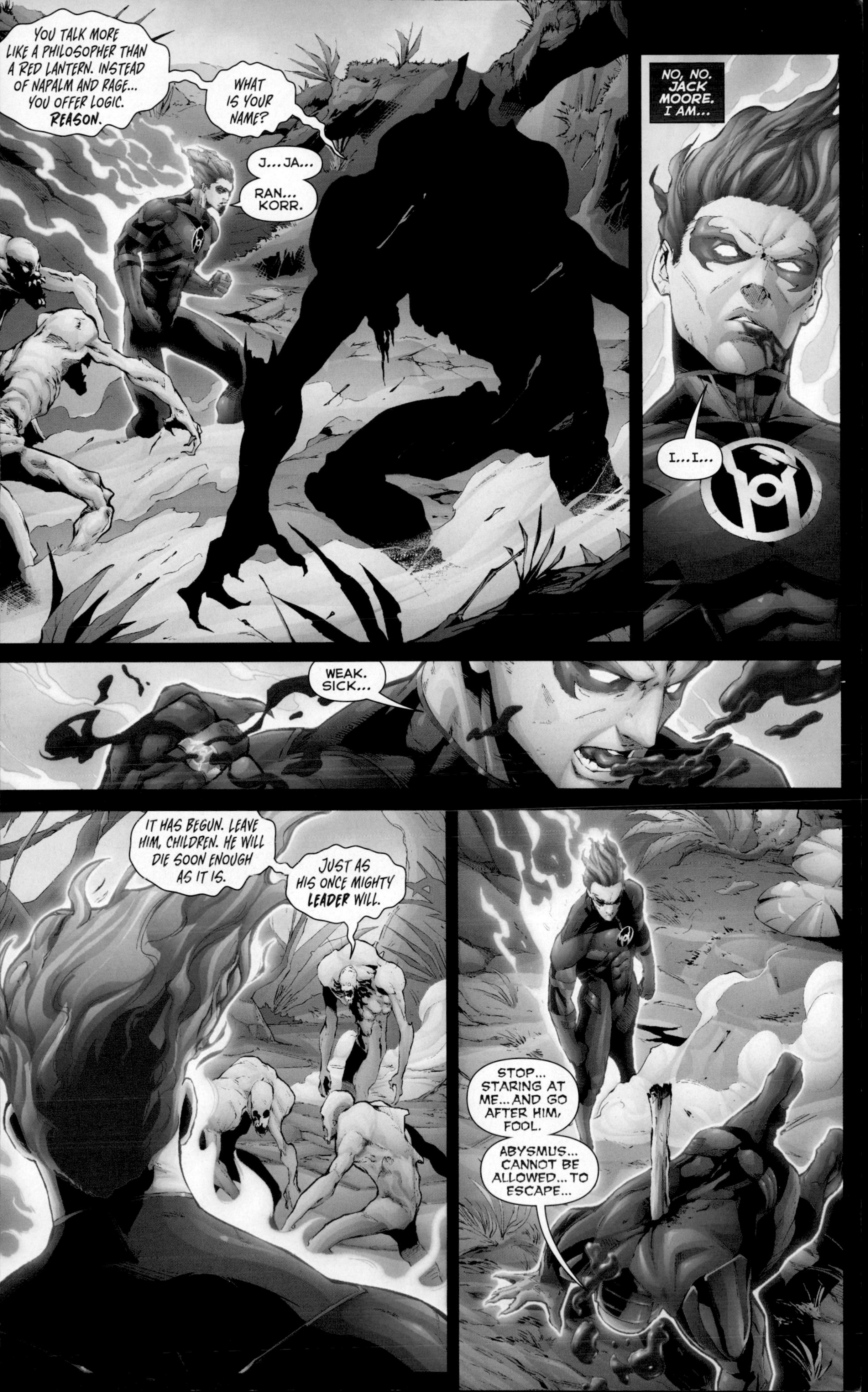

YOU TALK MORE LIKE A PHILOSOPHER THAN A RED LANTERN. INSTEAD OF NAPALM AND RAGE... YOU OFFER LOGIC. REASON.
WHAT IS YOUR NAME?
J... JA...
RAN... KORR.
NO, NO. JACK MOORE. I AM...
I...I...
WEAK. SICK...
IT HAS BEGUN. LEAVE HIM, CHILDREN. HE WILL DIE SOON ENOUGH AS IT IS.
JUST AS HIS ONCE MIGHTY LEADER WILL.
STOP... STARING AT ME...AND GO AFTER HIM, FOOL.
ABYSMUS... CANNOT BE ALLOWED...TO ESCAPE...

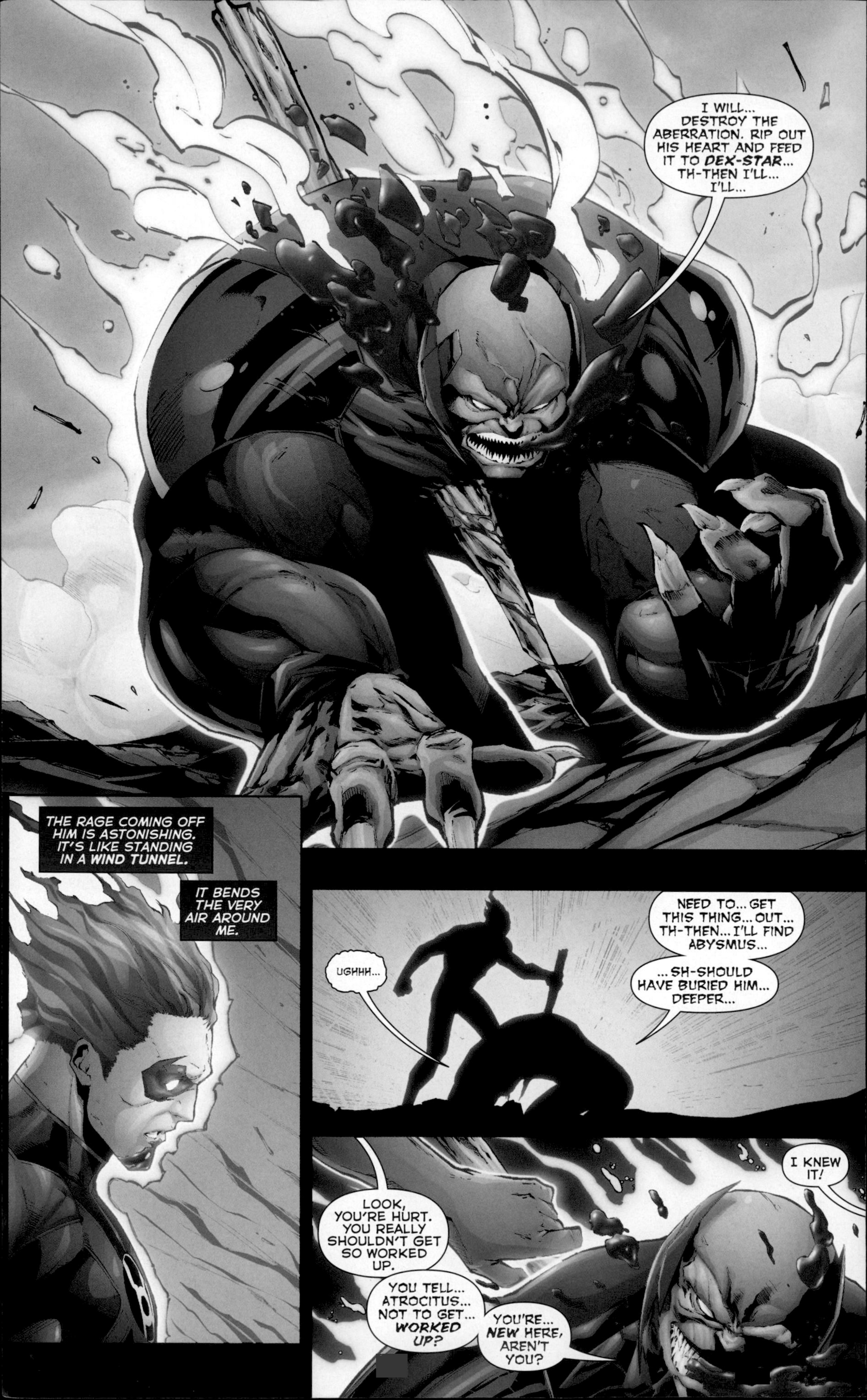
I WILL... DESTROY THE ABERRATION. RIP OUT HIS HEART AND FEED IT TO DEX-STAR... TH-THEN I'LL... I'LL...
THE RAGE COMING OFF HIM IS ASTONISHING. IT'S LIKE STANDING IN A WIND TUNNEL.
IT BENDS THE VERY AIR AROUND ME.
UGHHH...
NEED TO... GET THIS THING... OUT... TH-THEN... I'LL FIND ABYSMUS...
...SH-SHOULD HAVE BURIED HIM... DEEPER...
LOOK, YOU'RE HURT. YOU REALLY SHOULDN'T GET SO WORKED UP.
YOU TELL... ATROCITUS... NOT TO GET... WORKED UP?
YOU'RE... NEW HERE, AREN'T YOU?
I KNEW IT!

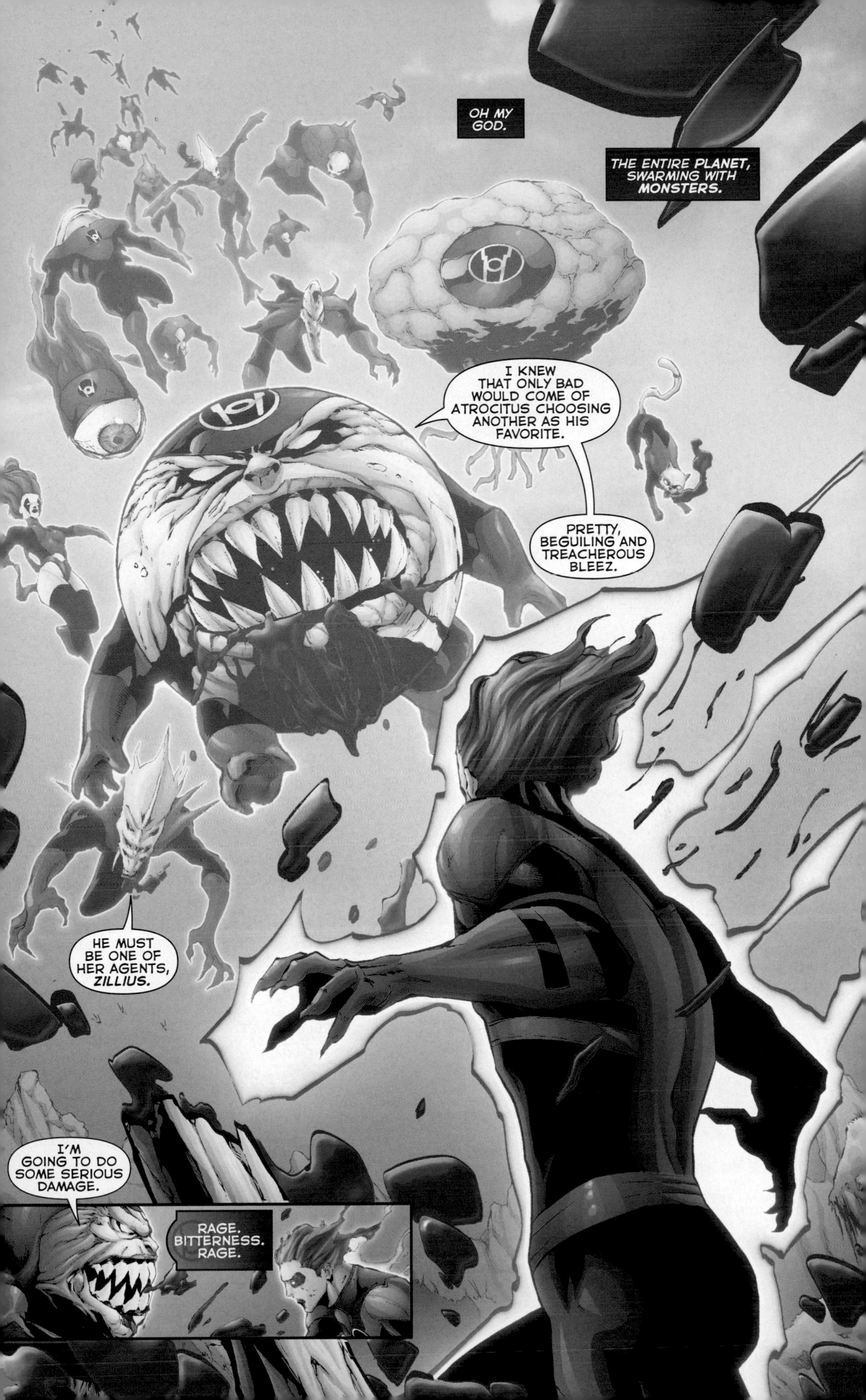
OH MY GOD.
THE ENTIRE PLANET, SWARMING WITH MONSTERS.
I KNEW THAT ONLY BAD WOULD COME OF ATROCITUS CHOOSING ANOTHER AS HIS FAVORITE.
PRETTY, BEGUILING AND TREACHEROUS BLEEZ.
HE MUST BE ONE OF HER AGENTS, ZILLIUS.
I'M GOING TO DO SOME SERIOUS DAMAGE.
RAGE. BITTERNESS. RAGE.

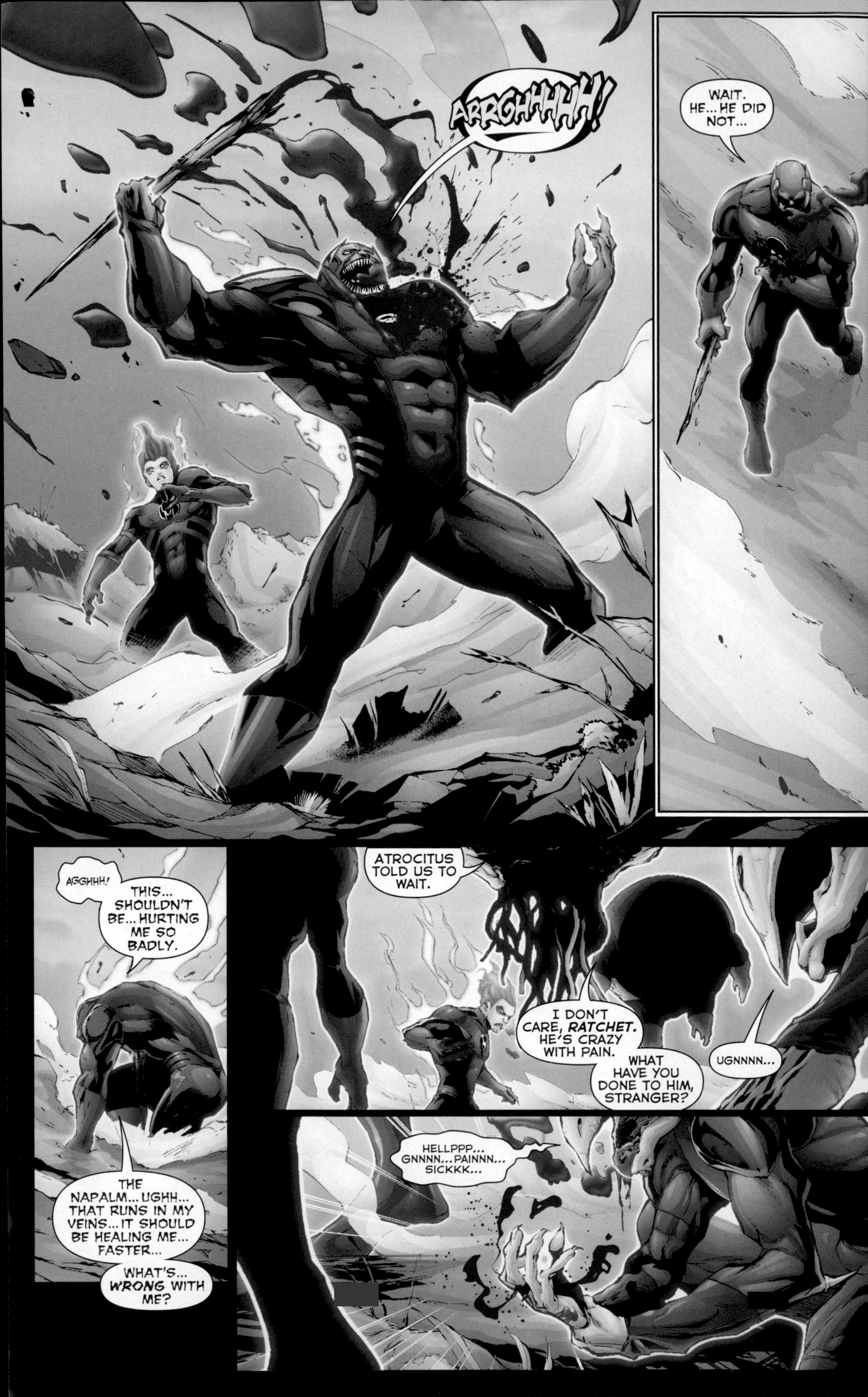
ARRGHHHH!
WAIT. HE... HE DID NOT...
AGGHHH!
THIS... SHOULDN'T BE... HURTING ME SO BADLY.
THE NAPALM... UGHH... THAT RUNS IN MY VEINS... IT SHOULD BE HEALING ME... FASTER...
WHAT'S... *WRONG* WITH ME?
ATROCITUS TOLD US TO WAIT.
I DON'T CARE, *RATCHET.* HE'S CRAZY WITH PAIN.
WHAT HAVE YOU DONE TO HIM, STRANGER?
UGNNNN...
HELLPPP... GNNNN... PAINNN... SICKKK...

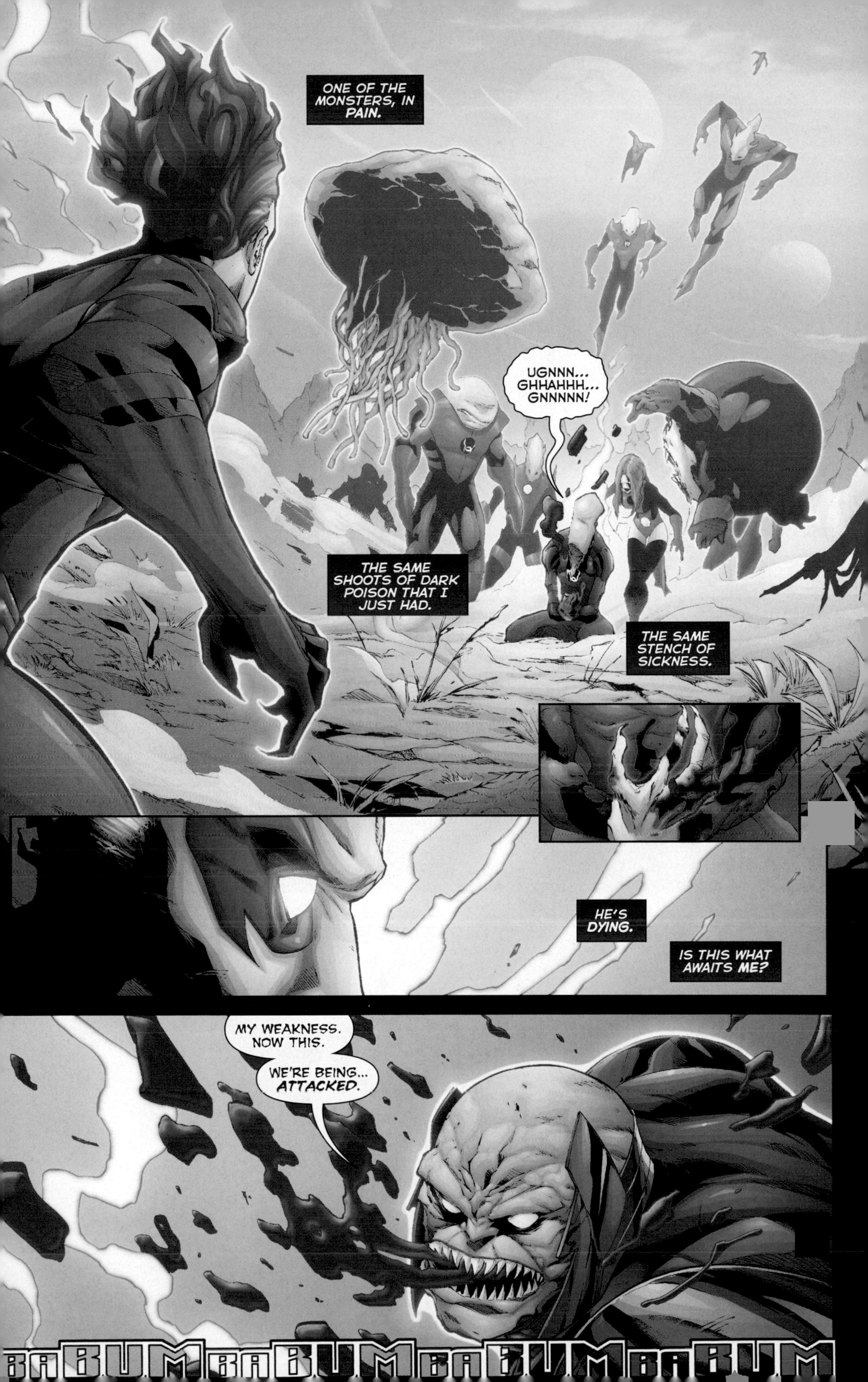
ONE OF THE MONSTERS, IN PAIN.
UGNNN... GHHAHHH... GNNNNN!
THE SAME SHOOTS OF DARK POISON THAT I JUST HAD.
THE SAME STENCH OF SICKNESS.
HE'S DYING.
IS THIS WHAT AWAITS ME?
MY WEAKNESS. NOW THIS.
WE'RE BEING... ATTACKED.
BA BUM BA BUM BA BUM BA BUM

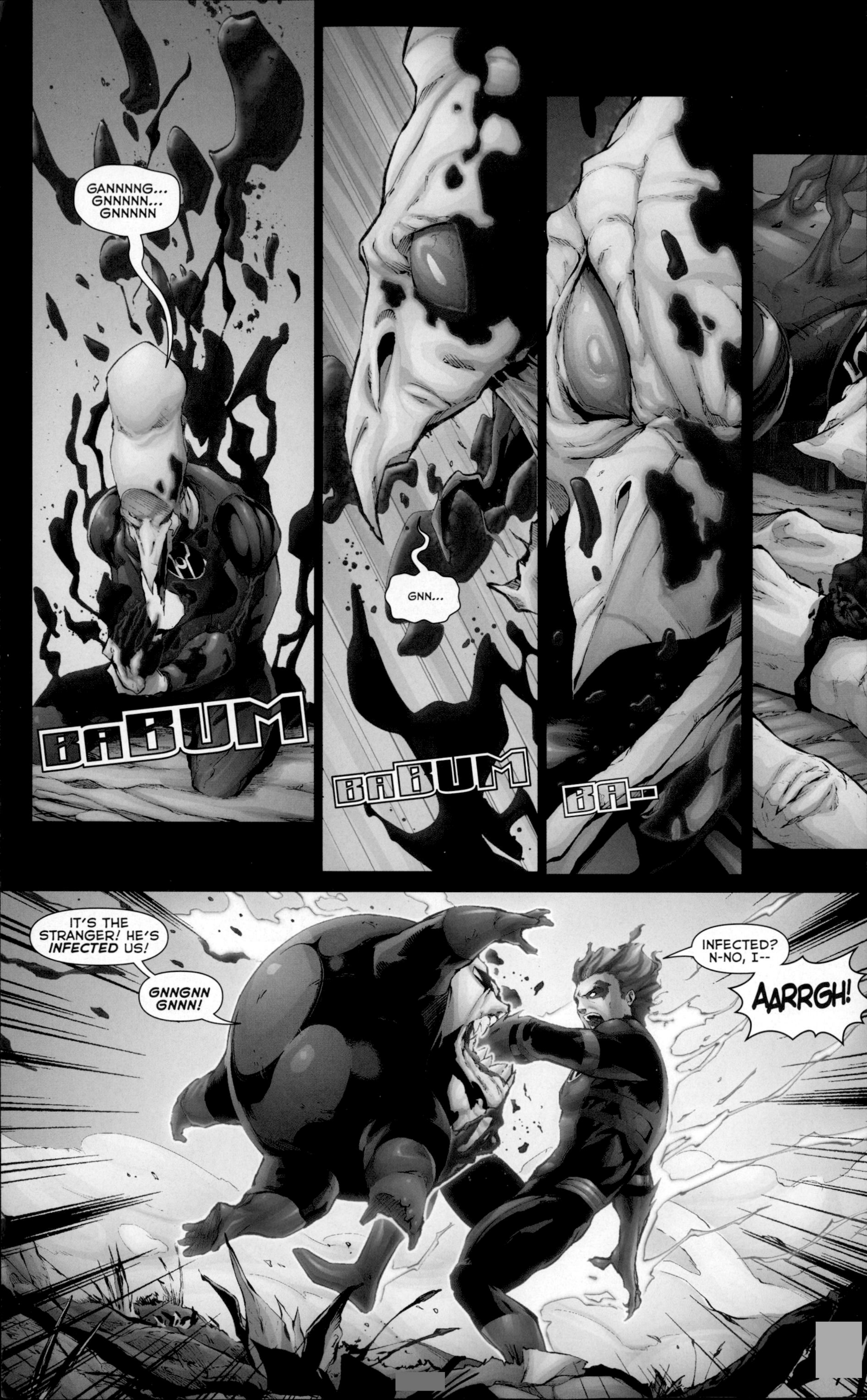
GANNNNG...
GNNNNN...
GNNNNN
BABUM
GNN...
BABUM
BA--
IT'S THE STRANGER! HE'S INFECTED US!
GNNGNN GNNN!
INFECTED? N-NO, I--
AARRGH!

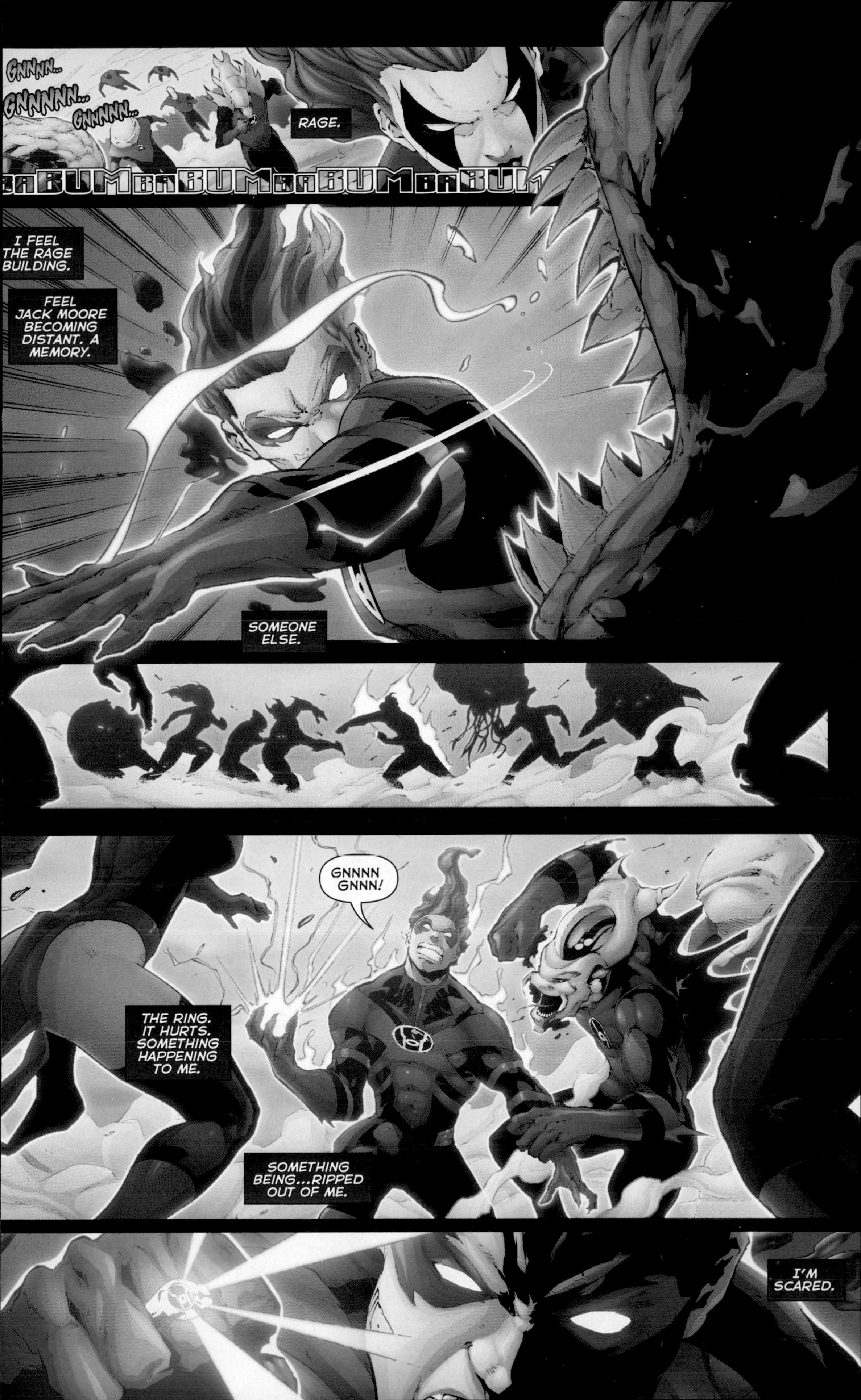
GNNNN...
GNNNNN...
GNNNNN...
RAGE.
BABUMBABUMBABUMBABUM
I FEEL THE RAGE BUILDING.
FEEL JACK MOORE BECOMING DISTANT. A MEMORY.
SOMEONE ELSE.
GNNNN GNNN!
THE RING. IT HURTS. SOMETHING HAPPENING TO ME.
SOMETHING BEING...RIPPED OUT OF ME.
I'M SCARED.

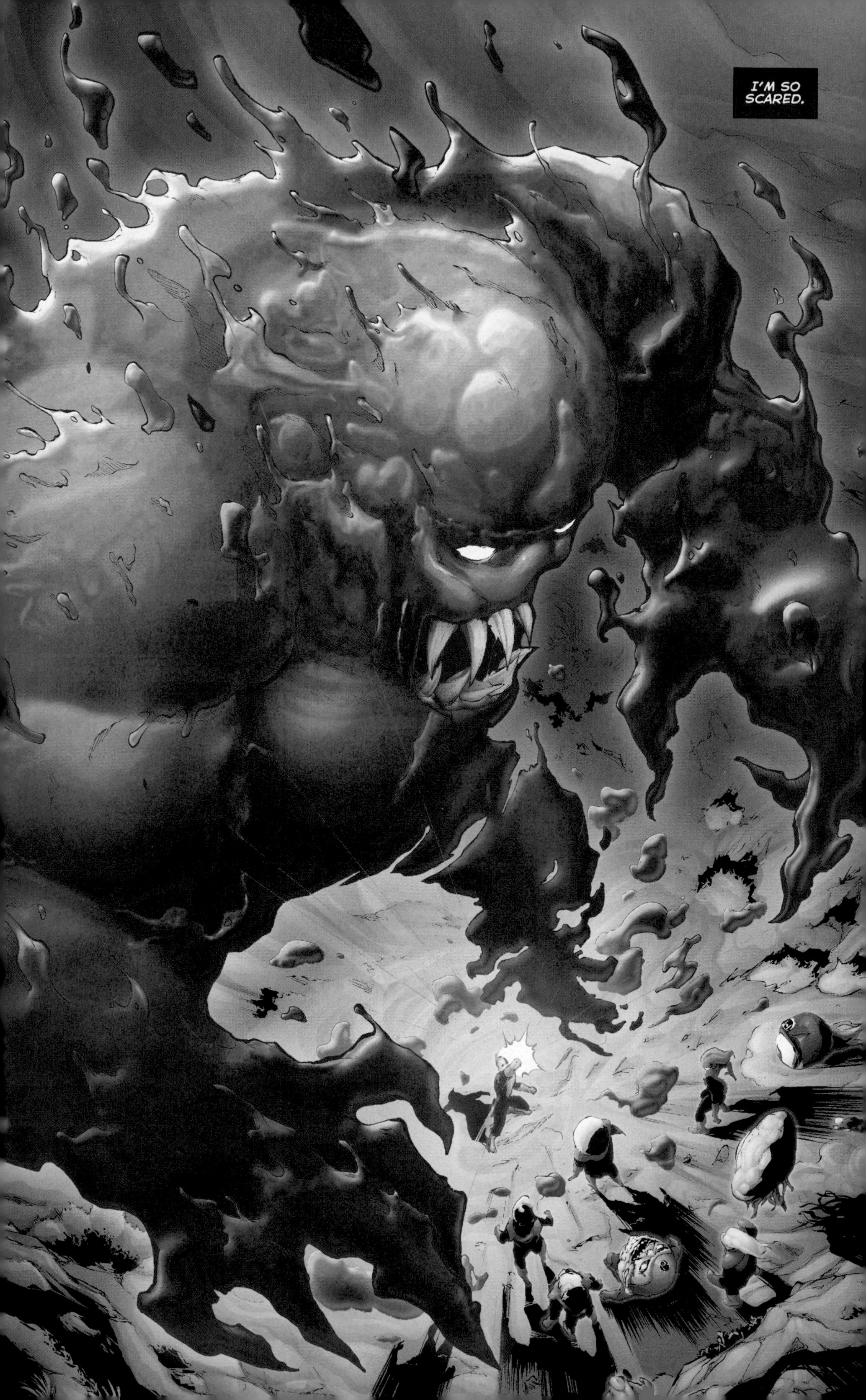
I'M SO SCARED.

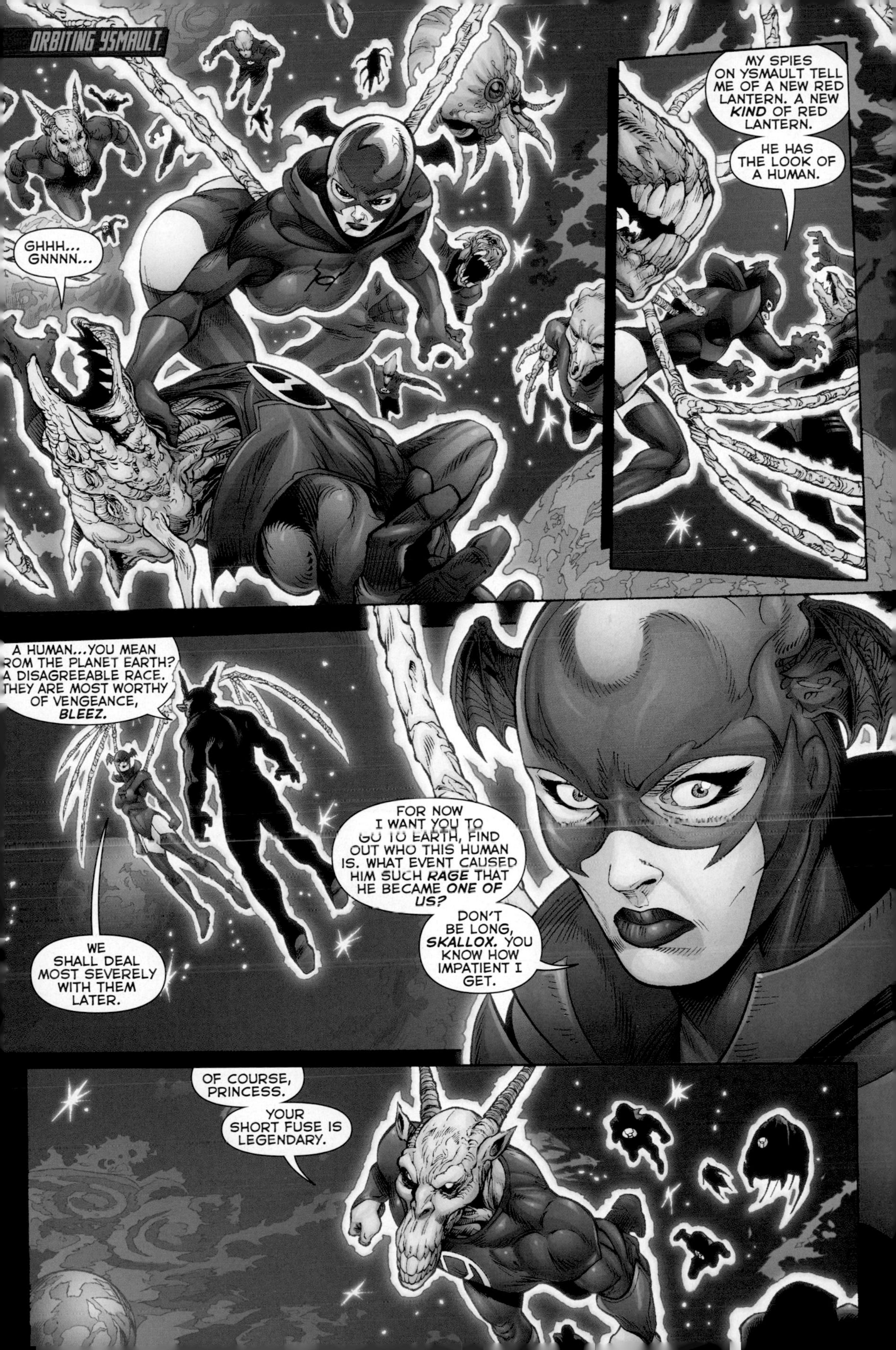
ORBITING YSMAULT.
GHHH... GNNNN...
MY SPIES ON YSMAULT TELL ME OF A NEW RED LANTERN. A NEW KIND OF RED LANTERN.
HE HAS THE LOOK OF A HUMAN.
A HUMAN...YOU MEAN FROM THE PLANET EARTH? A DISAGREEABLE RACE. THEY ARE MOST WORTHY OF VENGEANCE, BLEEZ.
WE SHALL DEAL MOST SEVERELY WITH THEM LATER.
FOR NOW I WANT YOU TO GO TO EARTH, FIND OUT WHO THIS HUMAN IS. WHAT EVENT CAUSED HIM SUCH RAGE THAT HE BECAME ONE OF US?
DON'T BE LONG, SKALLOX. YOU KNOW HOW IMPATIENT I GET.
OF COURSE, PRINCESS.
YOUR SHORT FUSE IS LEGENDARY.

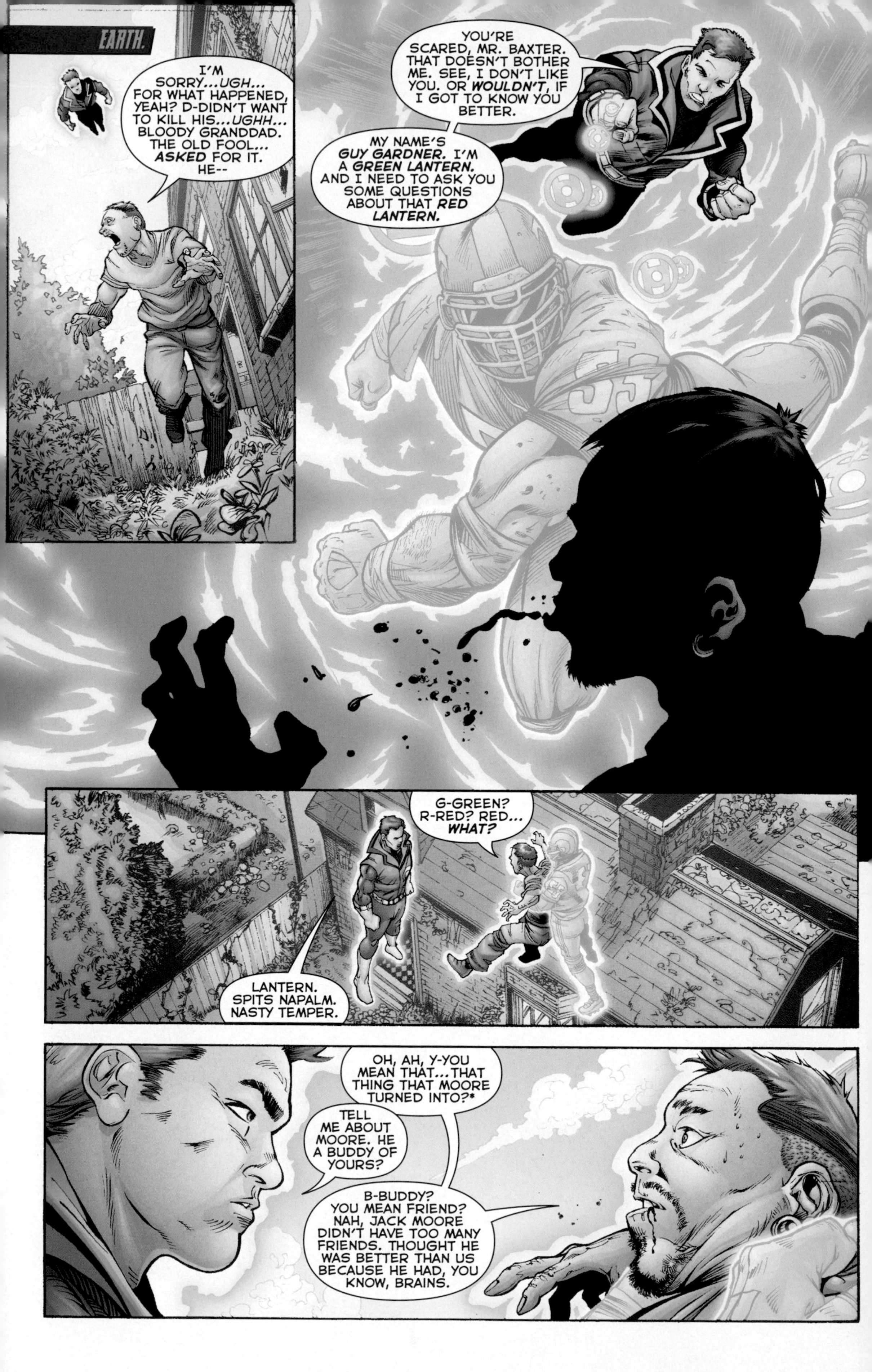
EARTH.
I'M SORRY...UGH... FOR WHAT HAPPENED, YEAH? D-DIDN'T WANT TO KILL HIS...UGHH... BLOODY GRANDDAD. THE OLD FOOL... ASKED FOR IT. HE--
YOU'RE SCARED, MR. BAXTER. THAT DOESN'T BOTHER ME. SEE, I DON'T LIKE YOU. OR WOULDN'T, IF I GOT TO KNOW YOU BETTER.
MY NAME'S GUY GARDNER. I'M A GREEN LANTERN. AND I NEED TO ASK YOU SOME QUESTIONS ABOUT THAT RED LANTERN.
G-GREEN? R-RED? RED... WHAT?
LANTERN. SPITS NAPALM. NASTY TEMPER.
OH, AH, Y-YOU MEAN THAT...THAT THING THAT MOORE TURNED INTO?*
TELL ME ABOUT MOORE. HE A BUDDY OF YOURS?
B-BUDDY? YOU MEAN FRIEND? NAH, JACK MOORE DIDN'T HAVE TOO MANY FRIENDS. THOUGHT HE WAS BETTER THAN US BECAUSE HE HAD, YOU KNOW, BRAINS.

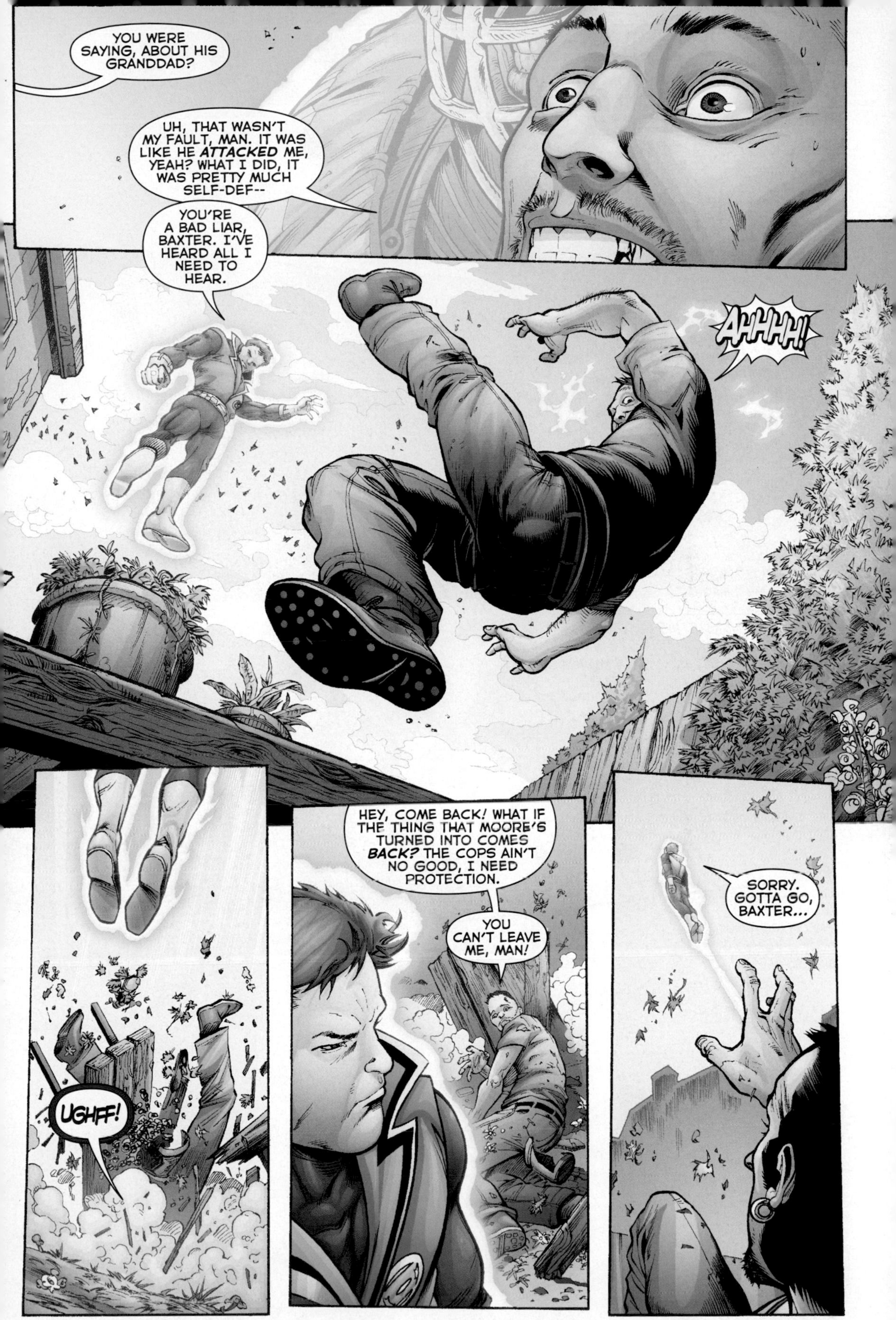
YOU WERE SAYING, ABOUT HIS GRANDDAD?
UH, THAT WASN'T MY FAULT, MAN. IT WAS LIKE HE ATTACKED ME, YEAH? WHAT I DID, IT WAS PRETTY MUCH SELF-DEF--
YOU'RE A BAD LIAR, BAXTER. I'VE HEARD ALL I NEED TO HEAR.
AHHHH!
UGHFF!
HEY, COME BACK! WHAT IF THE THING THAT MOORE'S TURNED INTO COMES BACK? THE COPS AIN'T NO GOOD, I NEED PROTECTION.
YOU CAN'T LEAVE ME, MAN!
SORRY. GOTTA GO, BAXTER...

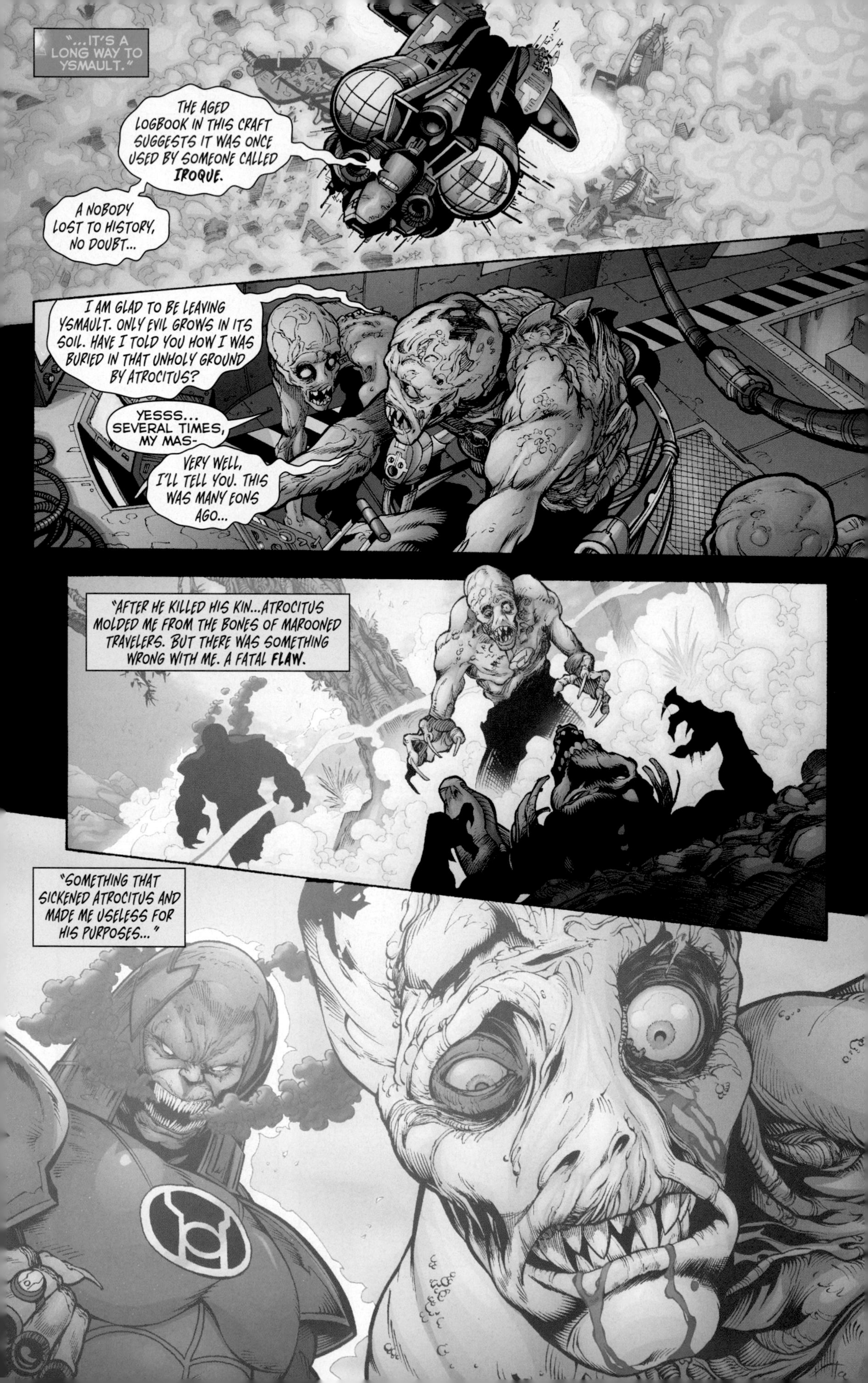
"...IT'S A LONG WAY TO YSMAULT."
THE AGED LOGBOOK IN THIS CRAFT SUGGESTS IT WAS ONCE USED BY SOMEONE CALLED IROQUE.
A NOBODY LOST TO HISTORY, NO DOUBT...
I AM GLAD TO BE LEAVING YSMAULT. ONLY EVIL GROWS IN ITS SOIL. HAVE I TOLD YOU HOW I WAS BURIED IN THAT UNHOLY GROUND BY ATROCITUS?
YESSS... SEVERAL TIMES, MY MAS-
VERY WELL, I'LL TELL YOU. THIS WAS MANY EONS AGO...
"AFTER HE KILLED HIS KIN...ATROCITUS MOLDED ME FROM THE BONES OF MAROONED TRAVELERS. BUT THERE WAS SOMETHING WRONG WITH ME. A FATAL FLAW.
"SOMETHING THAT SICKENED ATROCITUS AND MADE ME USELESS FOR HIS PURPOSES..."

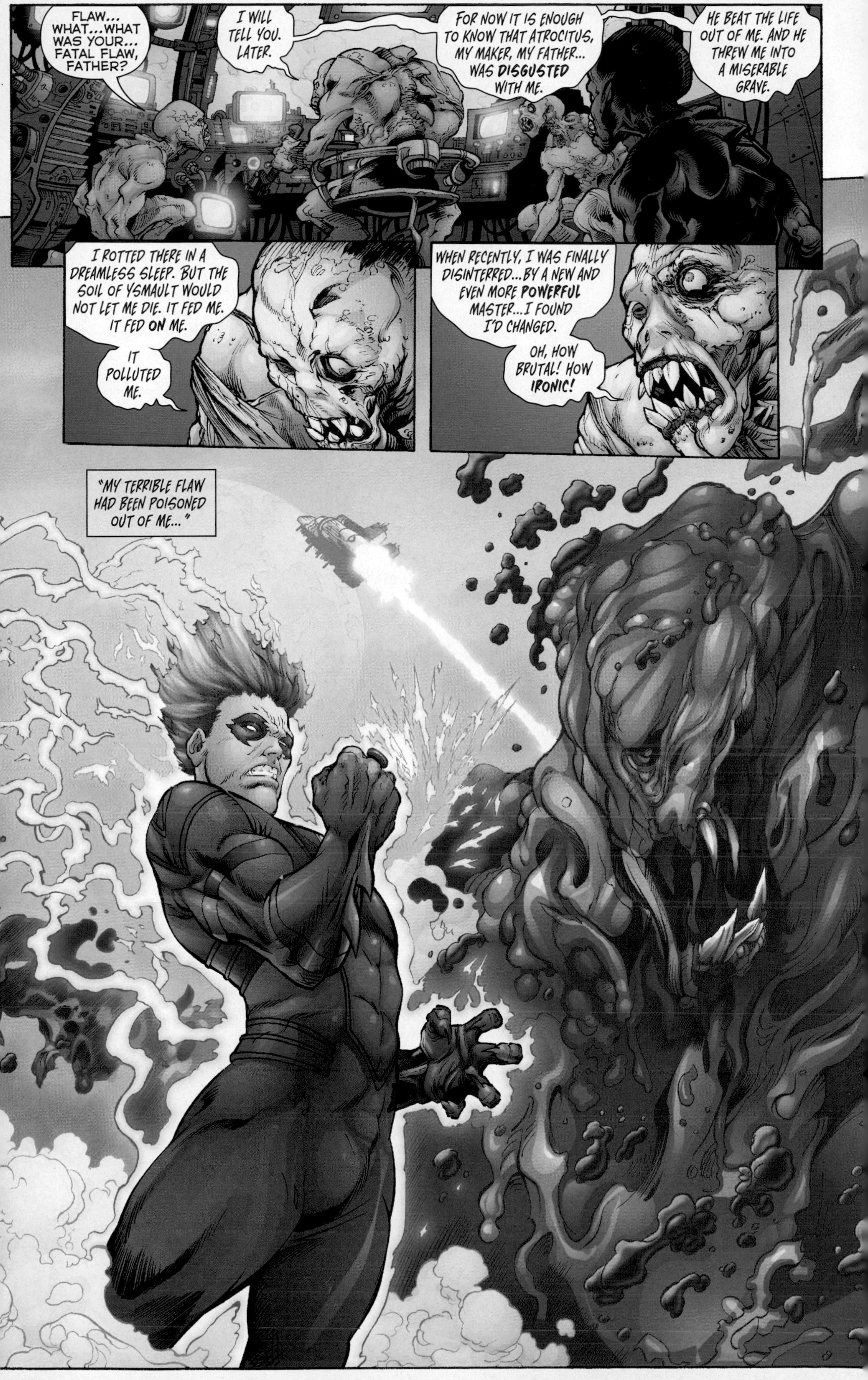
FLAW... WHAT...WHAT WAS YOUR... FATAL FLAW, FATHER?
I WILL TELL YOU. LATER.
FOR NOW IT IS ENOUGH TO KNOW THAT ATROCITUS, MY MAKER, MY FATHER... WAS DISGUSTED WITH ME.
HE BEAT THE LIFE OUT OF ME. AND HE THREW ME INTO A MISERABLE GRAVE.
I ROTTED THERE IN A DREAMLESS SLEEP. BUT THE SOIL OF YSMAULT WOULD NOT LET ME DIE. IT FED ME. IT FED ON ME.
IT POLLUTED ME.
WHEN RECENTLY, I WAS FINALLY DISINTERRED...BY A NEW AND EVEN MORE POWERFUL MASTER...I FOUND I'D CHANGED.
OH, HOW BRUTAL! HOW IRONIC!
"MY TERRIBLE FLAW HAD BEEN POISONED OUT OF ME..."

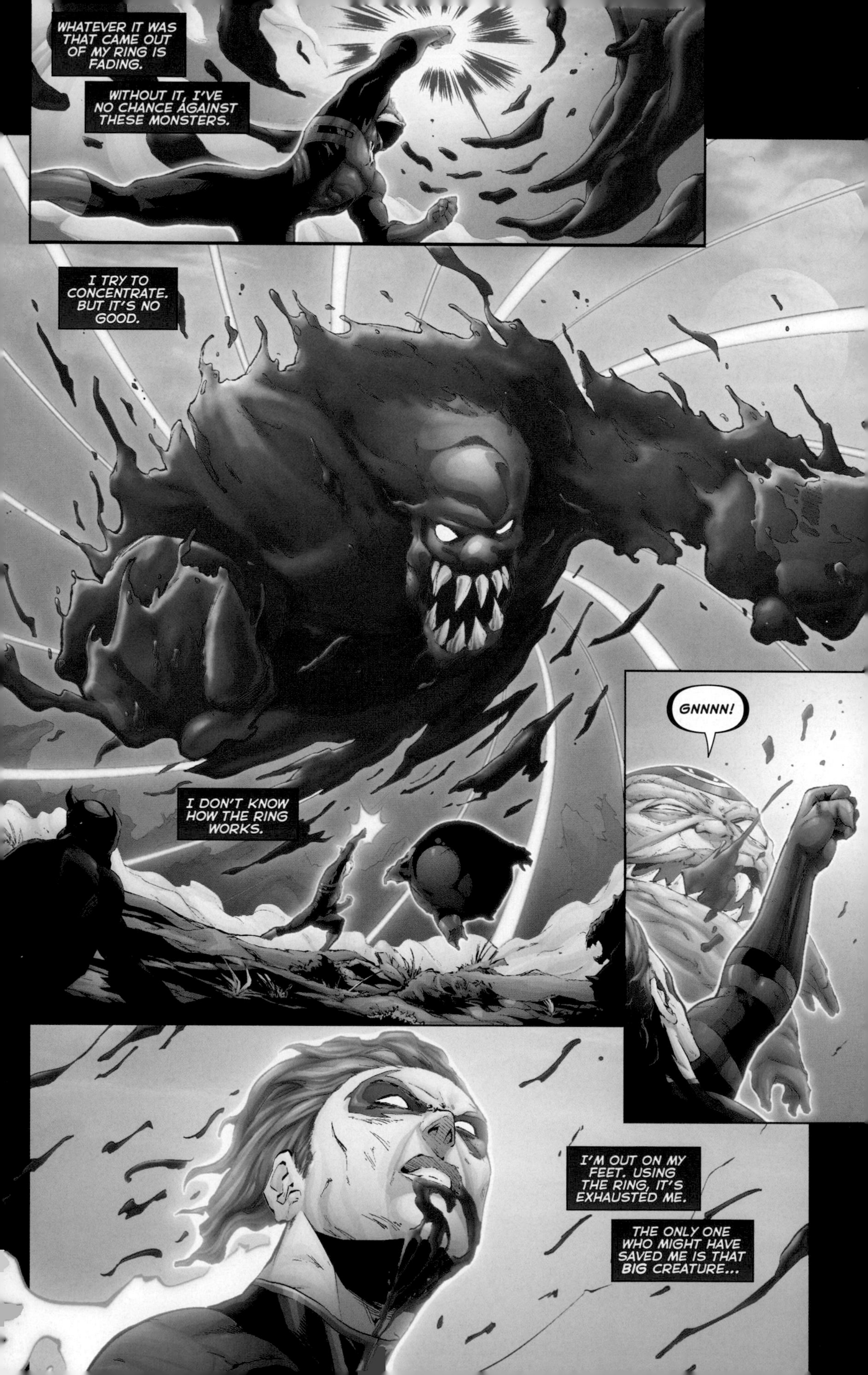
WHATEVER IT WAS THAT CAME OUT OF MY RING IS FADING.
WITHOUT IT, I'VE NO CHANCE AGAINST THESE MONSTERS.
I TRY TO CONCENTRATE. BUT IT'S NO GOOD.
I DON'T KNOW HOW THE RING WORKS.
GNNNN!
I'M OUT ON MY FEET. USING THE RING, IT'S EXHAUSTED ME.
THE ONLY ONE WHO MIGHT HAVE SAVED ME IS THAT BIG CREATURE...

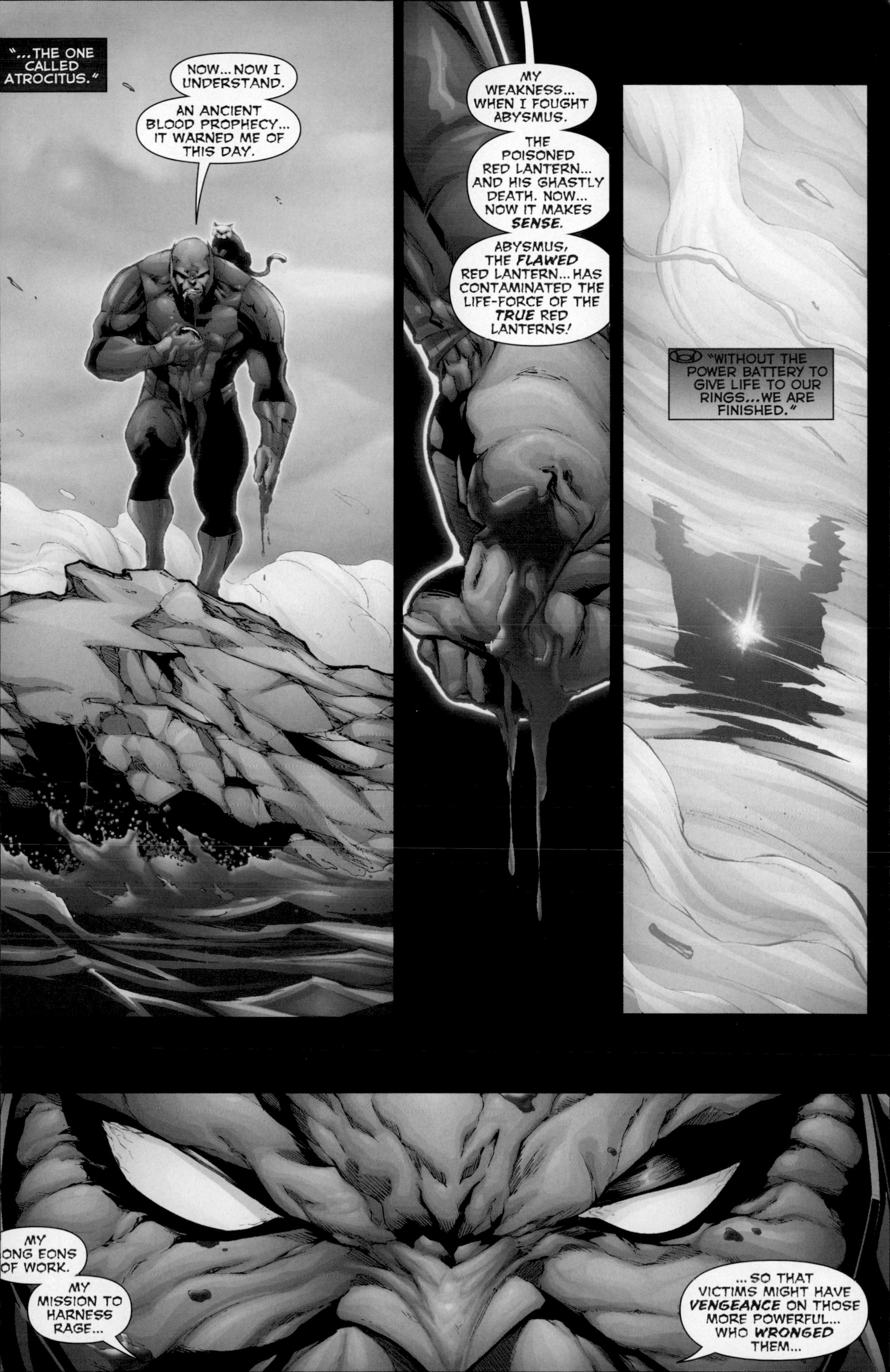
"...THE ONE CALLED ATROCITUS."
NOW... NOW I UNDERSTAND.
AN ANCIENT BLOOD PROPHECY... IT WARNED ME OF THIS DAY.
MY WEAKNESS... WHEN I FOUGHT ABYSMUS.
THE POISONED RED LANTERN... AND HIS GHASTLY DEATH. NOW... NOW IT MAKES SENSE.
ABYSMUS, THE FLAWED RED LANTERN... HAS CONTAMINATED THE LIFE-FORCE OF THE TRUE RED LANTERNS!
"WITHOUT THE POWER BATTERY TO GIVE LIFE TO OUR RINGS...WE ARE FINISHED."
MY ONG EONS OF WORK.
MY MISSION TO HARNESS RAGE...
...SO THAT VICTIMS MIGHT HAVE VENGEANCE ON THOSE MORE POWERFUL... WHO WRONGED THEM...

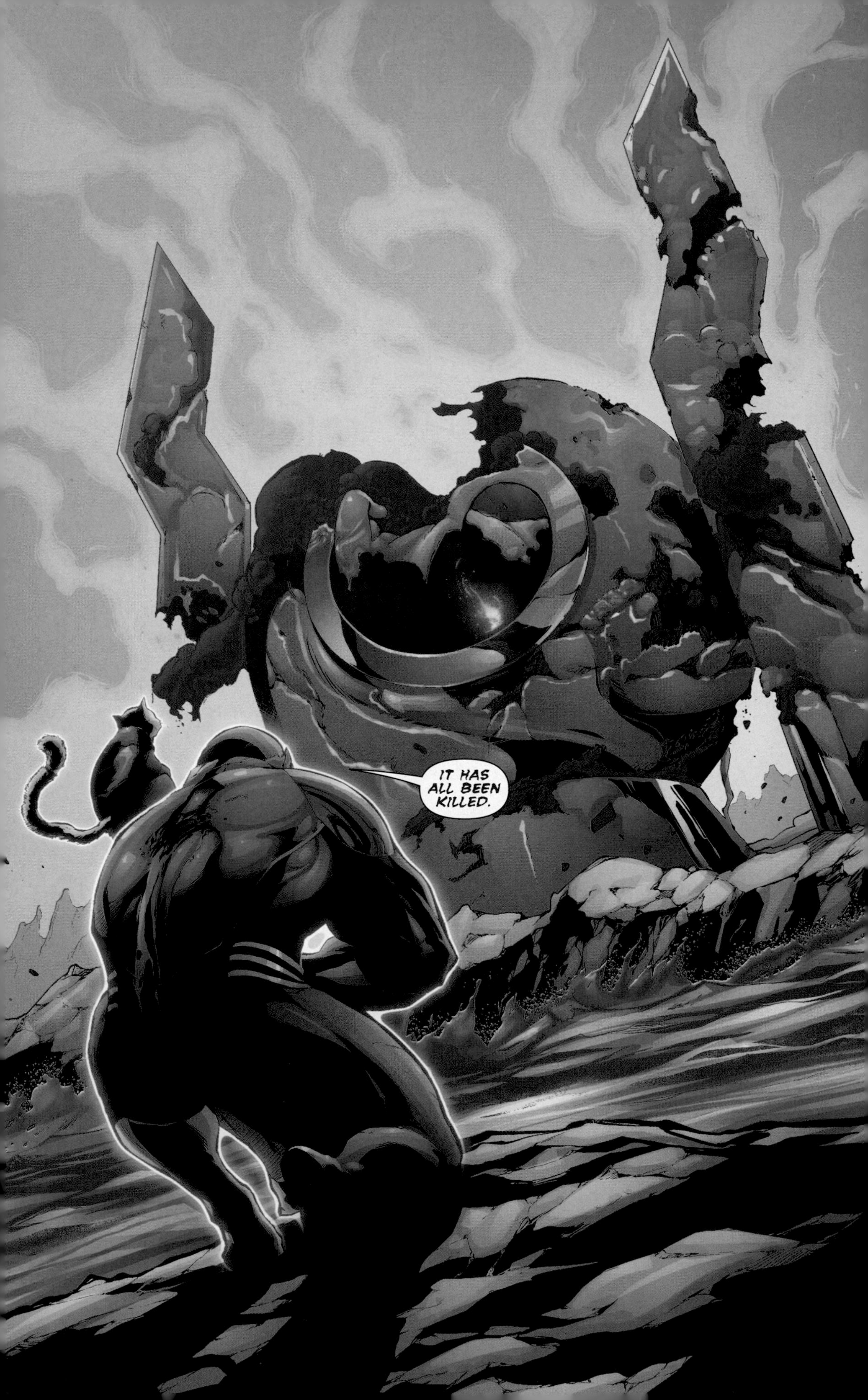
IT HAS ALL BEEN KILLED.

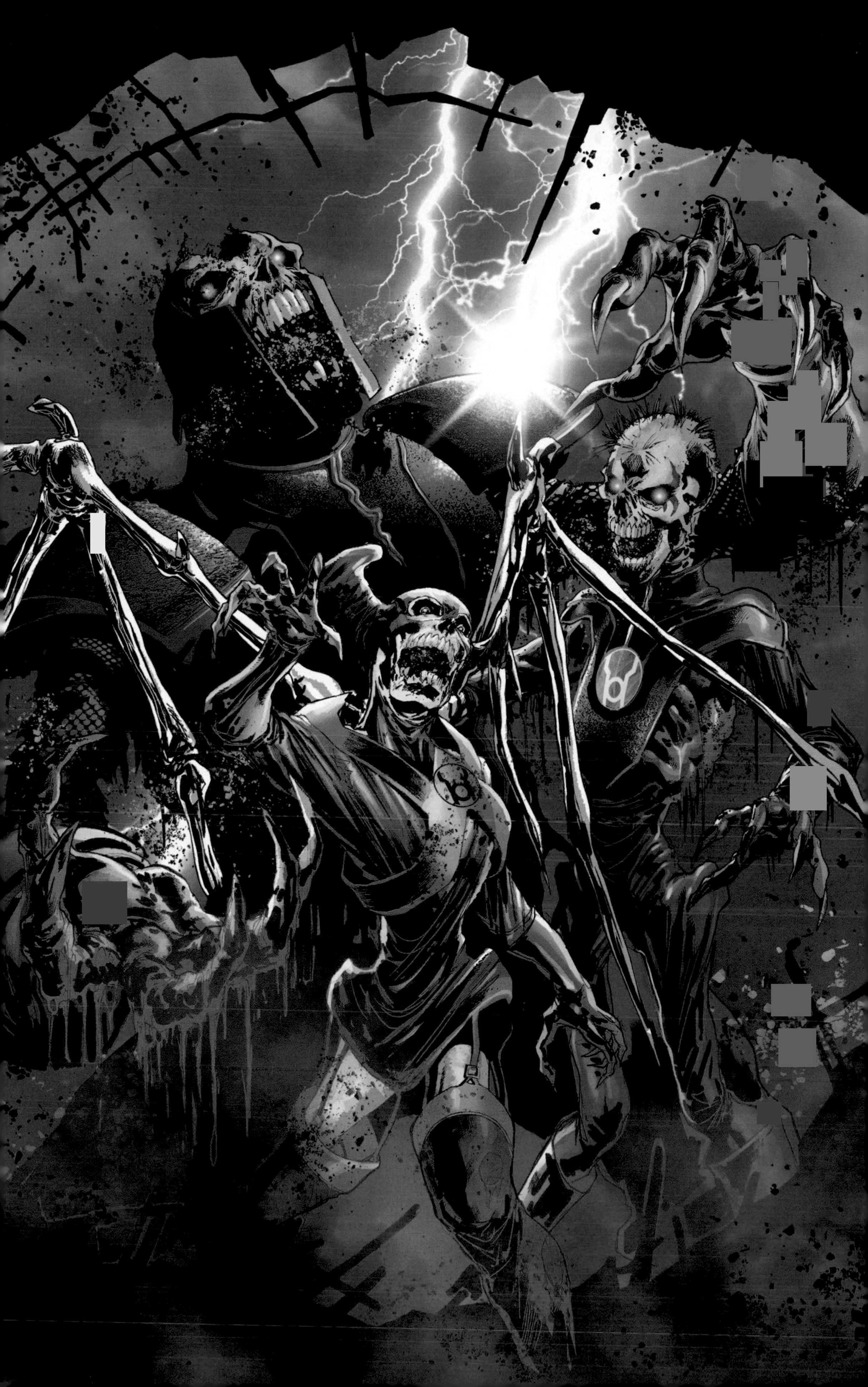

EXODUS

PETER MILLIGAN
writer

TOMAS GIORELLO
penciller

cover art by MIGUEL SEPULVEDA & RAIN BEREDO

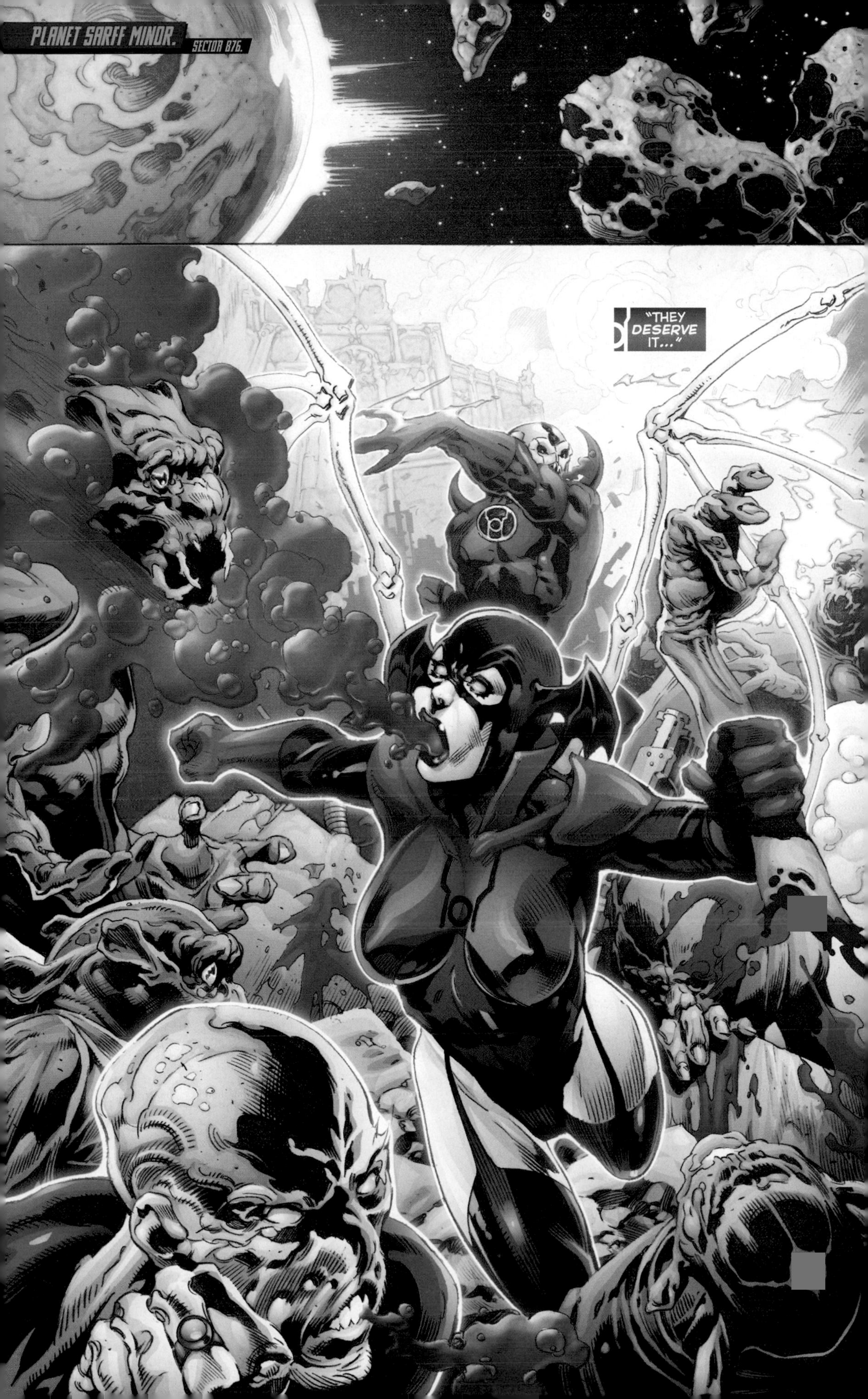
PLANET SARFF MINOR.
SECTOR 876.
"THEY DESERVE IT..."

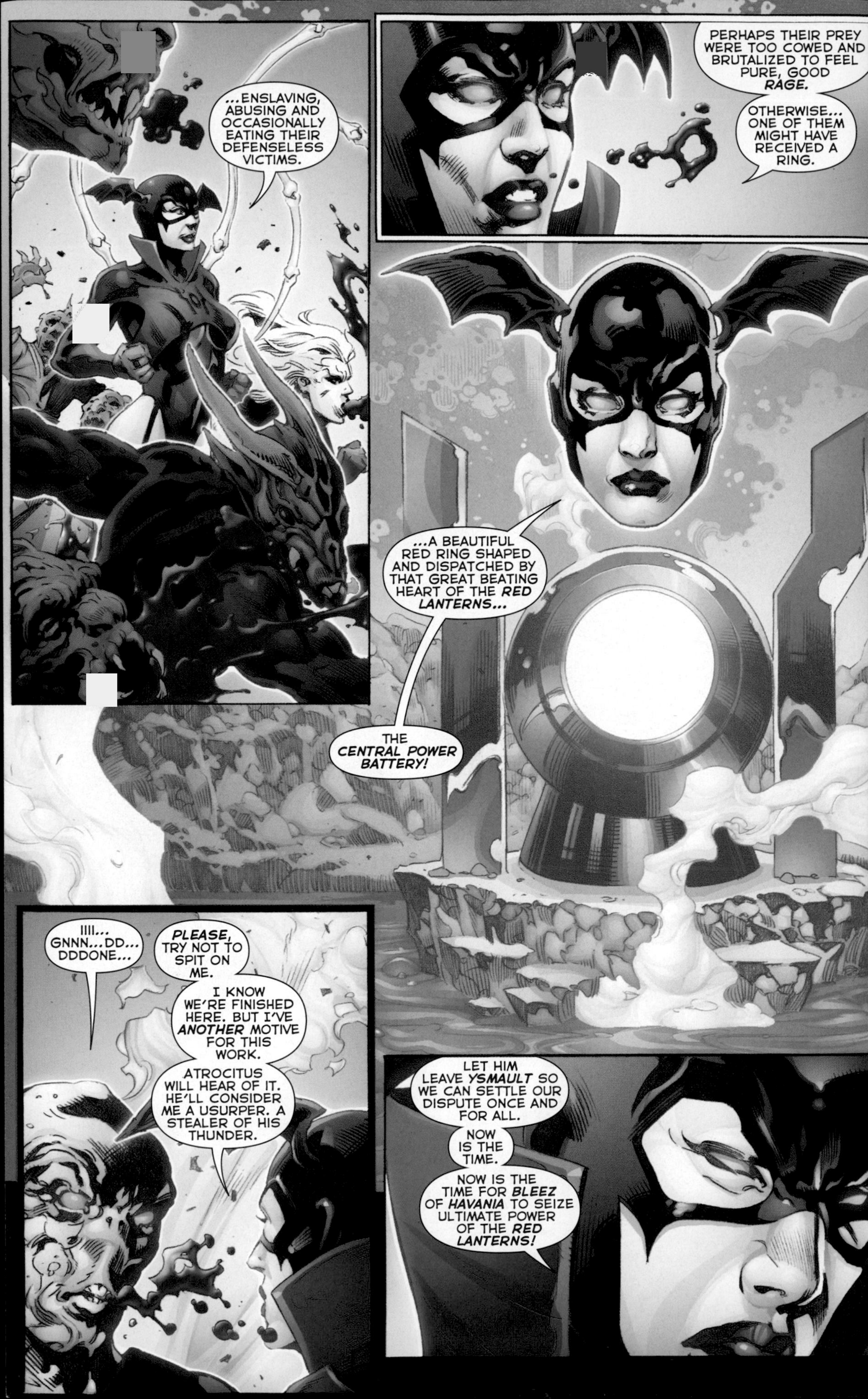
...ENSLAVING, ABUSING AND OCCASIONALLY EATING THEIR DEFENSELESS VICTIMS.
PERHAPS THEIR PREY WERE TOO COWED AND BRUTALIZED TO FEEL PURE, GOOD RAGE.
OTHERWISE... ONE OF THEM MIGHT HAVE RECEIVED A RING.
...A BEAUTIFUL RED RING SHAPED AND DISPATCHED BY THAT GREAT BEATING HEART OF THE RED LANTERNS...
THE CENTRAL POWER BATTERY!
IIII... GNNN...DD... DDDONE...
PLEASE, TRY NOT TO SPIT ON ME.
I KNOW WE'RE FINISHED HERE. BUT I'VE ANOTHER MOTIVE FOR THIS WORK.
ATROCITUS WILL HEAR OF IT. HE'LL CONSIDER ME A USURPER. A STEALER OF HIS THUNDER.
LET HIM LEAVE YSMAULT SO WE CAN SETTLE OUR DISPUTE ONCE AND FOR ALL.
NOW IS THE TIME.
NOW IS THE TIME FOR BLEEZ OF HAVANIA TO SEIZE ULTIMATE POWER OF THE RED LANTERNS!

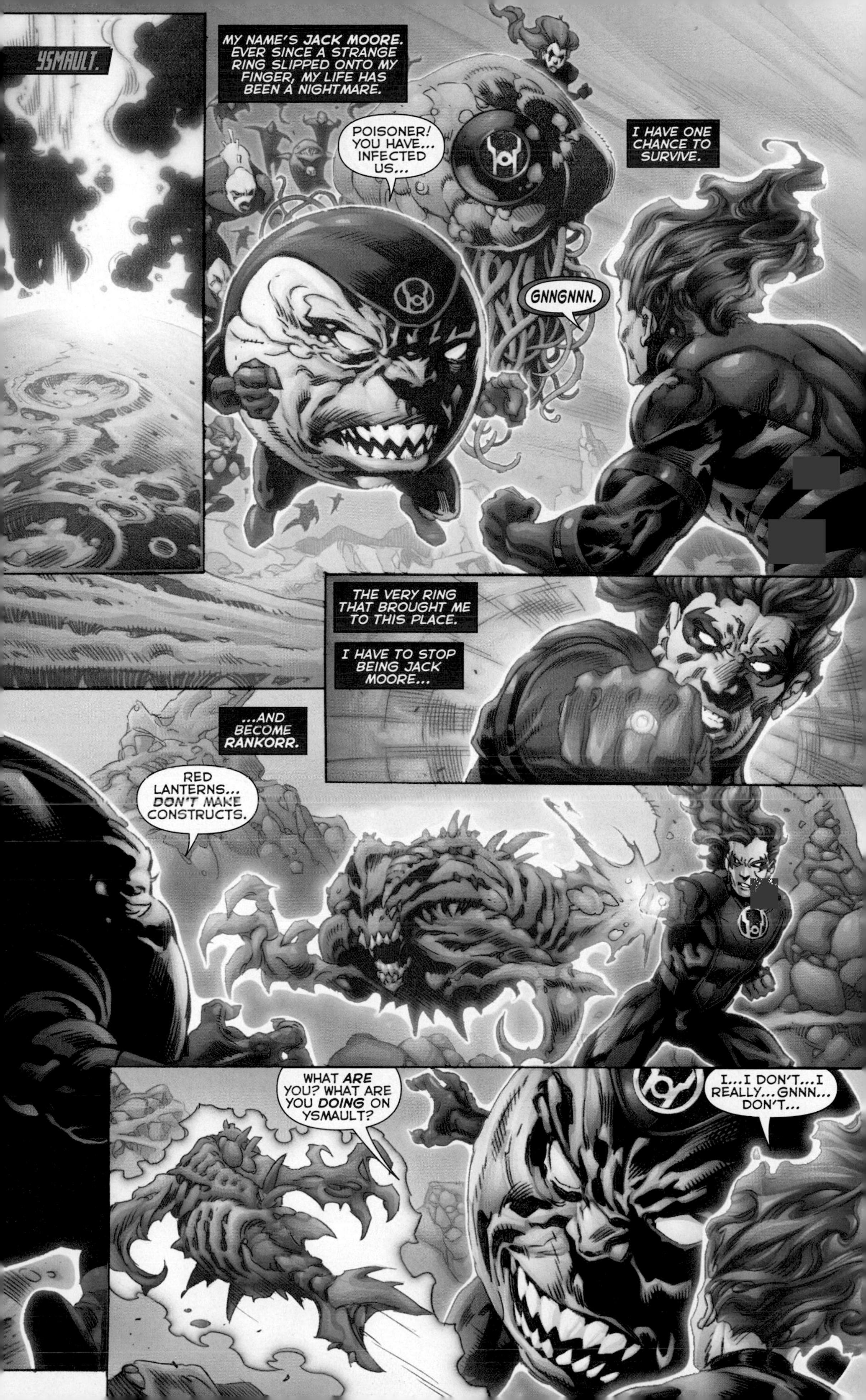
YSMAULT.
MY NAME'S JACK MOORE. EVER SINCE A STRANGE RING SLIPPED ONTO MY FINGER, MY LIFE HAS BEEN A NIGHTMARE.
POISONER! YOU HAVE... INFECTED US...
I HAVE ONE CHANCE TO SURVIVE.
GNNGNNN.
THE VERY RING THAT BROUGHT ME TO THIS PLACE.
I HAVE TO STOP BEING JACK MOORE...
...AND BECOME RANKORR.
RED LANTERNS... DON'T MAKE CONSTRUCTS.
WHAT ARE YOU? WHAT ARE YOU DOING ON YSMAULT?
I...I DON'T...I REALLY...GNNN... DON'T...

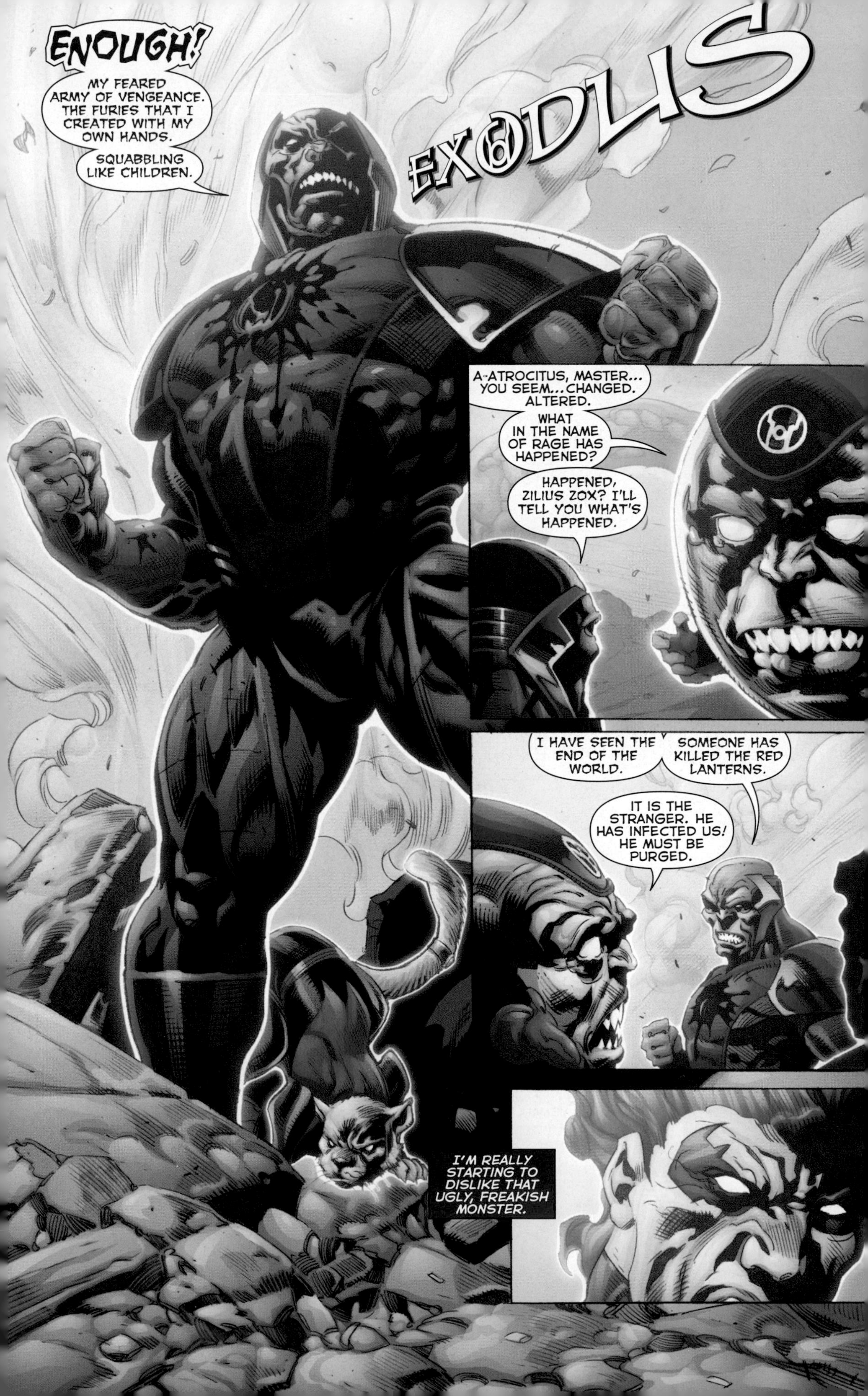
ENOUGH!
MY FEARED ARMY OF VENGEANCE. THE FURIES THAT I CREATED WITH MY OWN HANDS.
SQUABBLING LIKE CHILDREN.
EXODUS
A-ATROCITUS, MASTER... YOU SEEM...CHANGED. ALTERED.
WHAT IN THE NAME OF RAGE HAS HAPPENED?
HAPPENED, ZILIUS ZOX? I'LL TELL YOU WHAT'S HAPPENED.
I HAVE SEEN THE END OF THE WORLD.
SOMEONE HAS KILLED THE RED LANTERNS.
IT IS THE STRANGER. HE HAS INFECTED US! HE MUST BE PURGED.
I'M REALLY STARTING TO DISLIKE THAT UGLY, FREAKISH MONSTER.

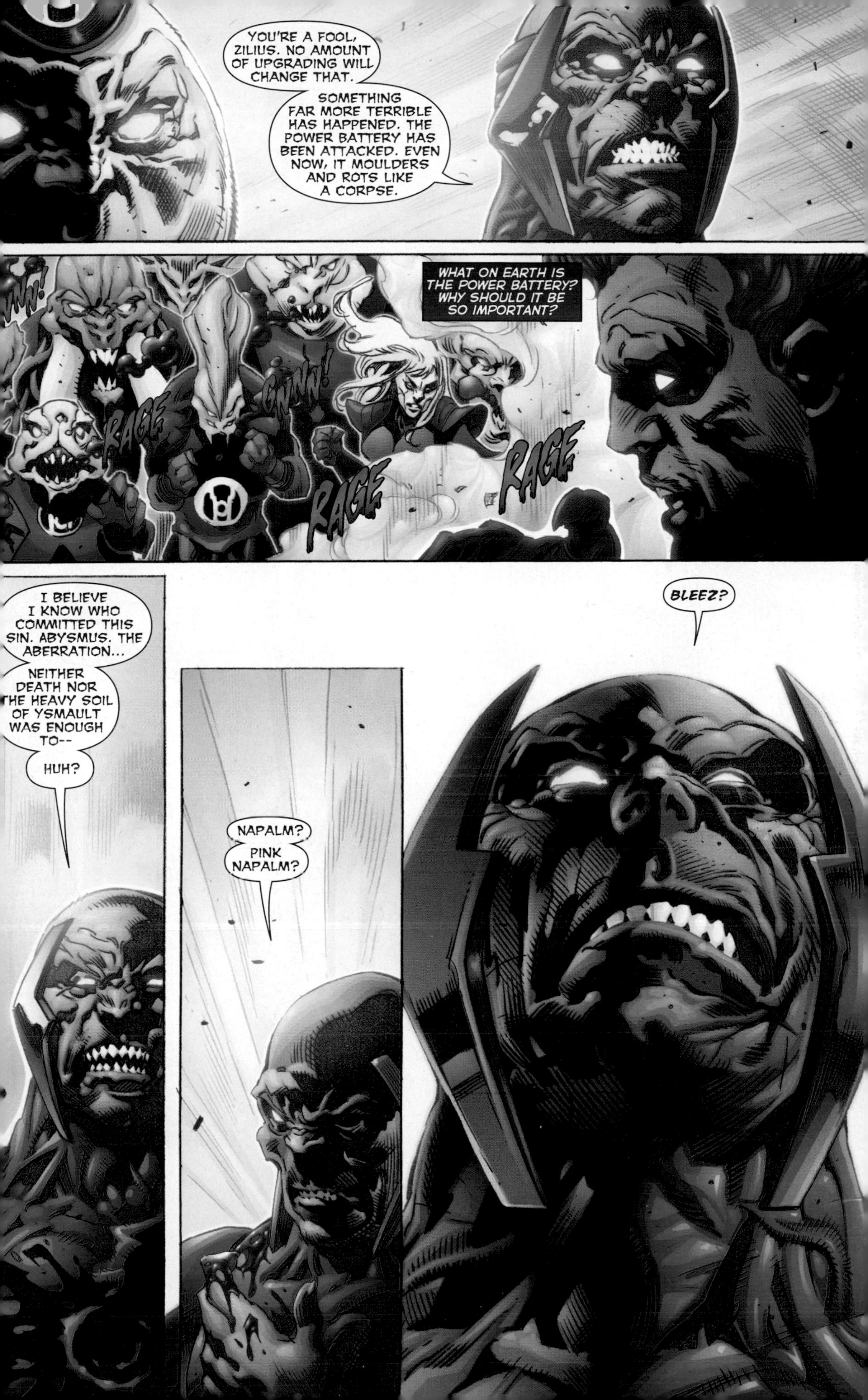

YOU'RE A FOOL, ZILIUS. NO AMOUNT OF UPGRADING WILL CHANGE THAT.
SOMETHING FAR MORE TERRIBLE HAS HAPPENED. THE POWER BATTERY HAS BEEN ATTACKED. EVEN NOW, IT MOULDERS AND ROTS LIKE A CORPSE.
WHAT ON EARTH IS THE POWER BATTERY? WHY SHOULD IT BE SO IMPORTANT?
GNNN!
RAGE
GNNN!
RAGE
RAGE
I BELIEVE I KNOW WHO COMMITTED THIS SIN. ABYSMUS. THE ABERRATION...
NEITHER DEATH NOR THE HEAVY SOIL OF YSMAULT WAS ENOUGH TO--
HUH?
NAPALM?
PINK NAPALM?
BLEEZ?

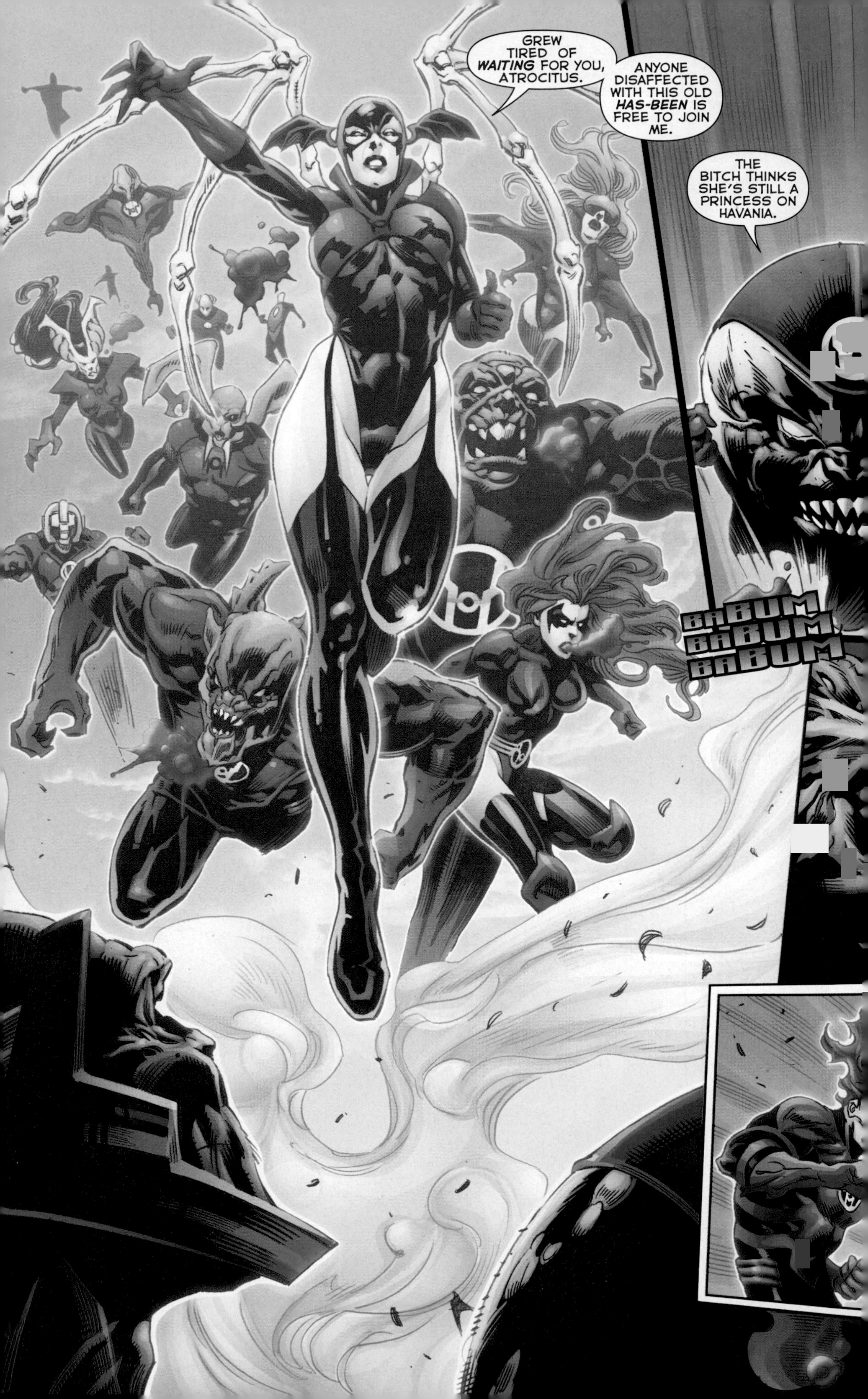
GREW TIRED OF WAITING FOR YOU, ATROCITUS.
ANYONE DISAFFECTED WITH THIS OLD HAS-BEEN IS FREE TO JOIN ME.
THE BITCH THINKS SHE'S STILL A PRINCESS ON HAVANIA.
BABUM BABUM BABUM

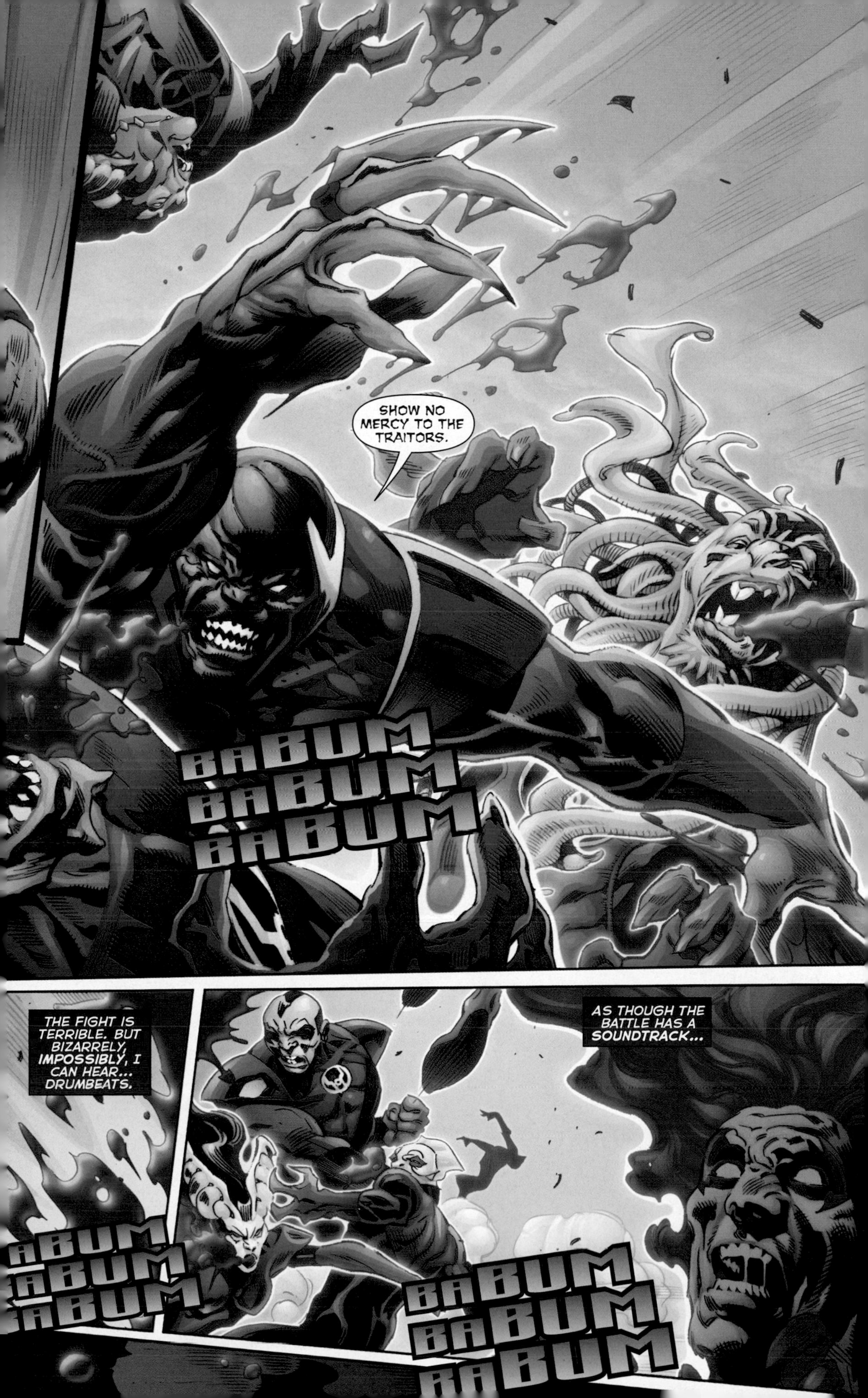
SHOW NO MERCY TO THE TRAITORS.
BABUM BABUM BABUM
THE FIGHT IS TERRIBLE, BUT BIZARRELY, IMPOSSIBLY, I CAN HEAR... DRUMBEATS.
AS THOUGH THE BATTLE HAS A SOUNDTRACK...
BABUM BABUM BABUM
BABUM BABUM BABUM

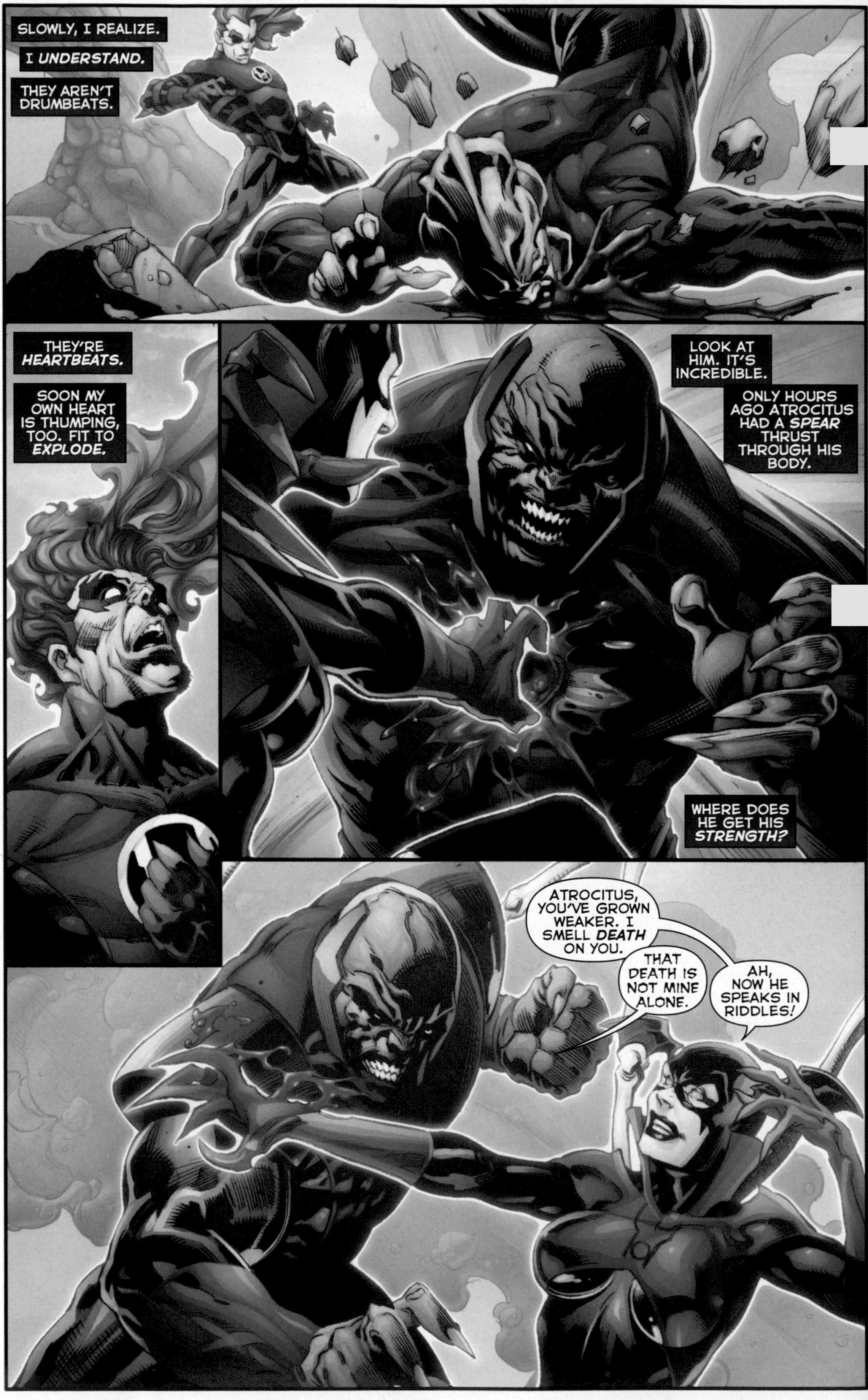
SLOWLY, I REALIZE.
I UNDERSTAND.
THEY AREN'T DRUMBEATS.
THEY'RE HEARTBEATS.
SOON MY OWN HEART IS THUMPING, TOO. FIT TO EXPLODE.
LOOK AT HIM. IT'S INCREDIBLE.
ONLY HOURS AGO ATROCITUS HAD A SPEAR THRUST THROUGH HIS BODY.
WHERE DOES HE GET HIS STRENGTH?
ATROCITUS, YOU'VE GROWN WEAKER. I SMELL DEATH ON YOU.
THAT DEATH IS NOT MINE ALONE.
AH, NOW HE SPEAKS IN RIDDLES!

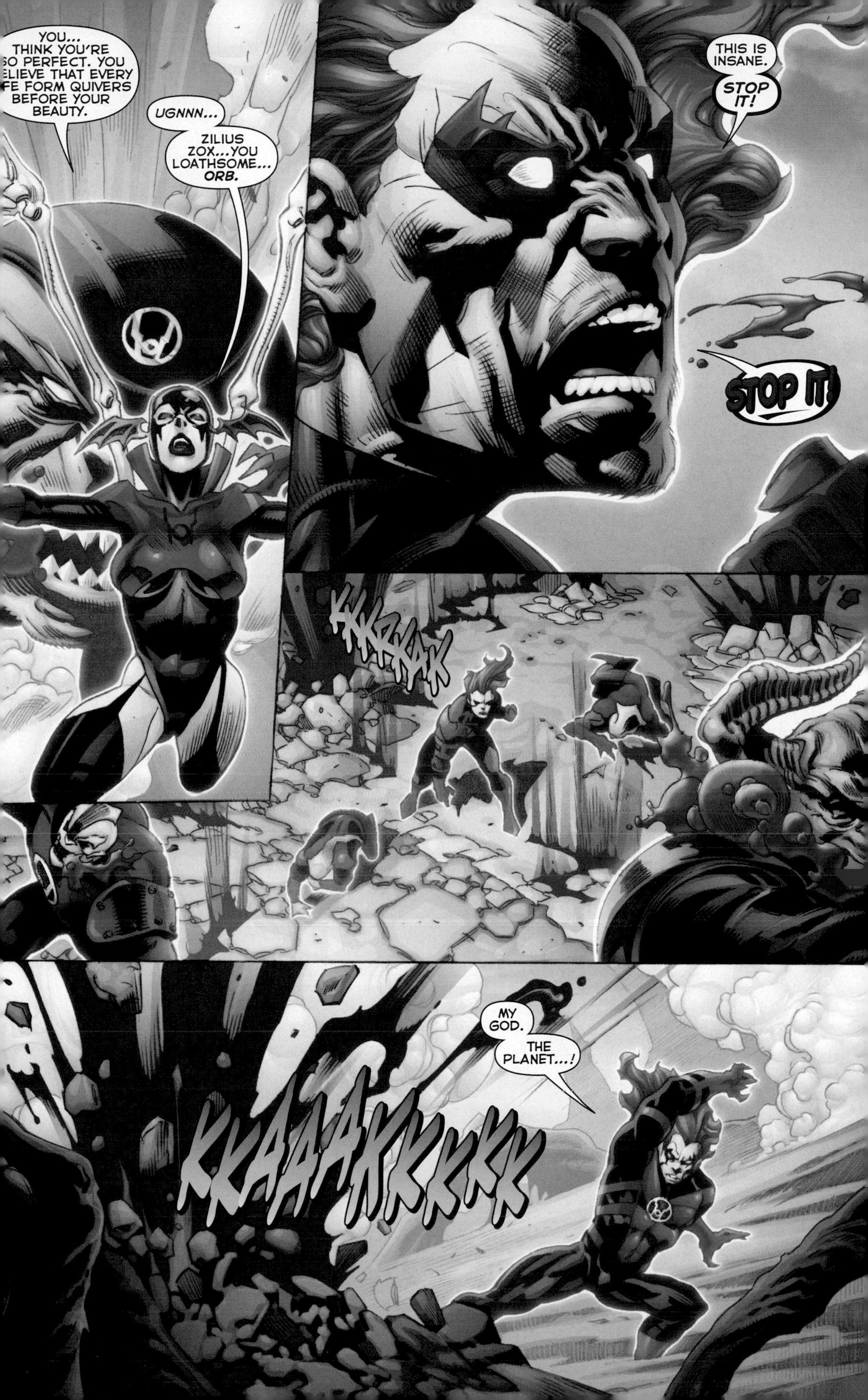
YOU... THINK YOU'RE SO PERFECT. YOU ELIEVE THAT EVERY FE FORM QUIVERS BEFORE YOUR BEAUTY.
UGNNN...
ZILIUS ZOX...YOU LOATHSOME... ORB.
THIS IS INSANE.
STOP IT!
STOP IT!
KKKRKAK
MY GOD.
THE PLANET...!
KKAAAKKKKK

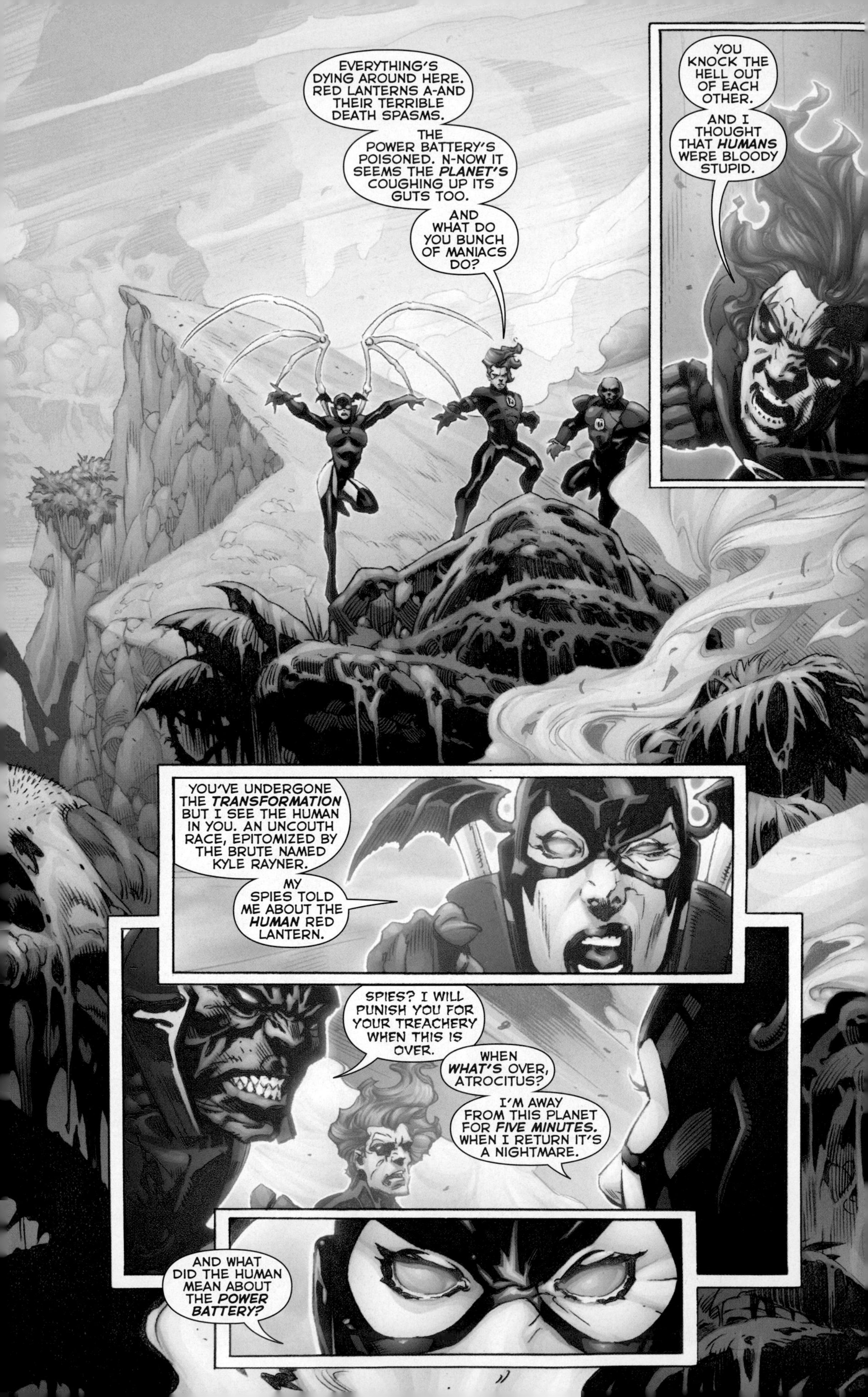
EVERYTHING'S DYING AROUND HERE. RED LANTERNS A-AND THEIR TERRIBLE DEATH SPASMS.
THE POWER BATTERY'S POISONED. N-NOW IT SEEMS THE *PLANET'S* COUGHING UP ITS GUTS TOO.
AND WHAT DO YOU BUNCH OF MANIACS DO?
YOU KNOCK THE HELL OUT OF EACH OTHER.
AND I THOUGHT THAT *HUMANS* WERE BLOODY STUPID.
YOU'VE UNDERGONE THE *TRANSFORMATION* BUT I SEE THE HUMAN IN YOU. AN UNCOUTH RACE, EPITOMIZED BY THE BRUTE NAMED KYLE RAYNER.
MY SPIES TOLD ME ABOUT THE *HUMAN* RED LANTERN.
SPIES? I WILL PUNISH YOU FOR YOUR TREACHERY WHEN THIS IS OVER.
WHEN *WHAT'S* OVER, ATROCITUS?
I'M AWAY FROM THIS PLANET FOR *FIVE MINUTES.* WHEN I RETURN IT'S A NIGHTMARE.
AND WHAT DID THE HUMAN MEAN ABOUT THE *POWER BATTERY?*

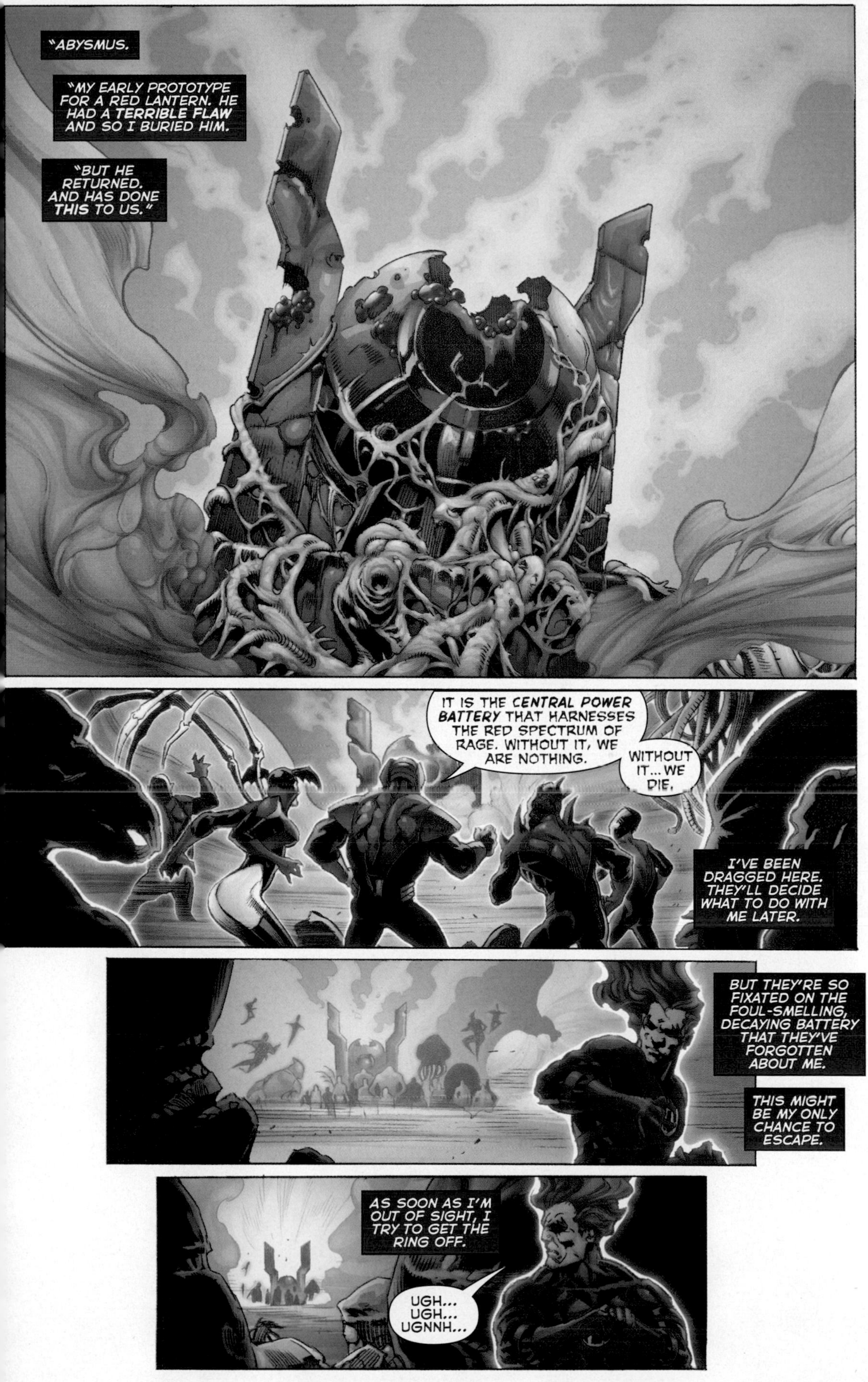
"ABYSMUS.
"MY EARLY PROTOTYPE FOR A RED LANTERN. HE HAD A TERRIBLE FLAW AND SO I BURIED HIM.
"BUT HE RETURNED. AND HAS DONE THIS TO US."
IT IS THE CENTRAL POWER BATTERY THAT HARNESSES THE RED SPECTRUM OF RAGE. WITHOUT IT, WE ARE NOTHING.
WITHOUT IT... WE DIE.
I'VE BEEN DRAGGED HERE. THEY'LL DECIDE WHAT TO DO WITH ME LATER.
BUT THEY'RE SO FIXATED ON THE FOUL-SMELLING, DECAYING BATTERY THAT THEY'VE FORGOTTEN ABOUT ME.
THIS MIGHT BE MY ONLY CHANCE TO ESCAPE.
AS SOON AS I'M OUT OF SIGHT, I TRY TO GET THE RING OFF.
UGH... UGH... UGNNH...

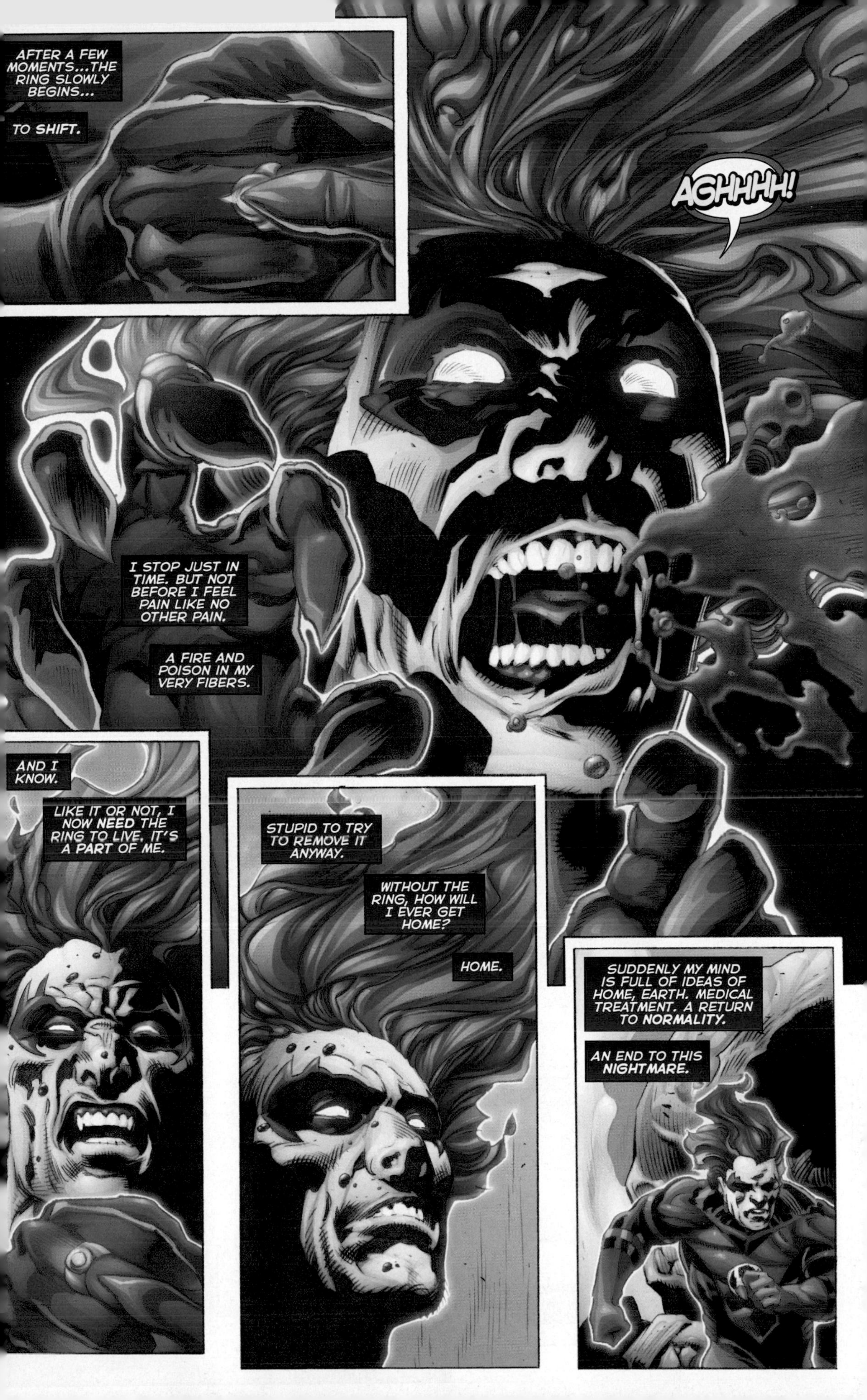
AFTER A FEW MOMENTS...THE RING SLOWLY BEGINS...
TO SHIFT.
AGHHHH!
I STOP JUST IN TIME. BUT NOT BEFORE I FEEL PAIN LIKE NO OTHER PAIN.
A FIRE AND POISON IN MY VERY FIBERS.
AND I KNOW.
LIKE IT OR NOT, I NOW NEED THE RING TO LIVE. IT'S A PART OF ME.
STUPID TO TRY TO REMOVE IT ANYWAY.
WITHOUT THE RING, HOW WILL I EVER GET HOME?
HOME.
SUDDENLY MY MIND IS FULL OF IDEAS OF HOME, EARTH. MEDICAL TREATMENT. A RETURN TO NORMALITY.
AN END TO THIS NIGHTMARE.

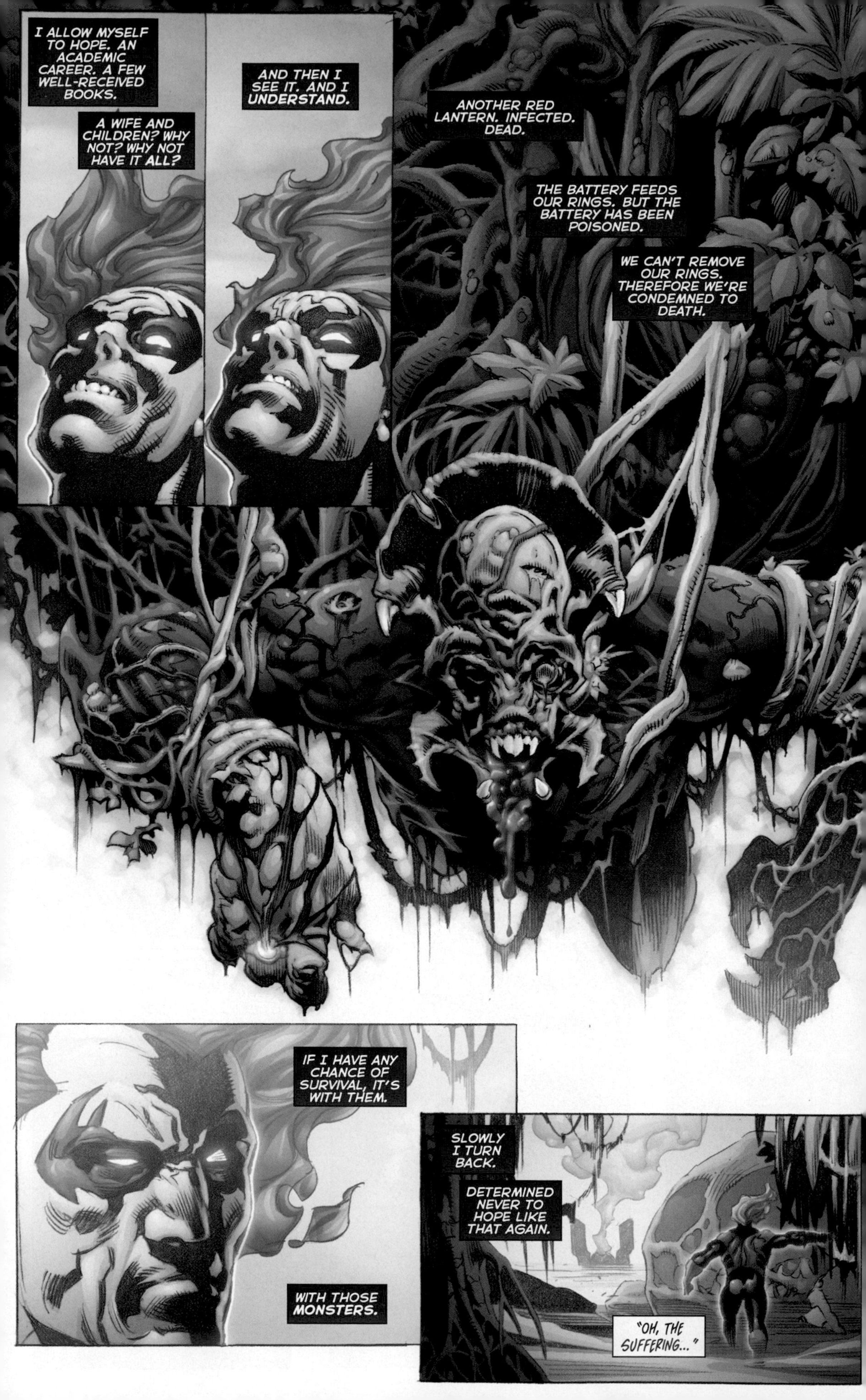

I ALLOW MYSELF TO HOPE. AN ACADEMIC CAREER. A FEW WELL-RECEIVED BOOKS.
A WIFE AND CHILDREN? WHY NOT? WHY NOT HAVE IT ALL?
AND THEN I SEE IT. AND I UNDERSTAND.
ANOTHER RED LANTERN. INFECTED. DEAD.
THE BATTERY FEEDS OUR RINGS. BUT THE BATTERY HAS BEEN POISONED.
WE CAN'T REMOVE OUR RINGS. THEREFORE WE'RE CONDEMNED TO DEATH.
IF I HAVE ANY CHANCE OF SURVIVAL, IT'S WITH THEM.
WITH THOSE MONSTERS.
SLOWLY I TURN BACK.
DETERMINED NEVER TO HOPE LIKE THAT AGAIN.
"OH, THE SUFFERING..."

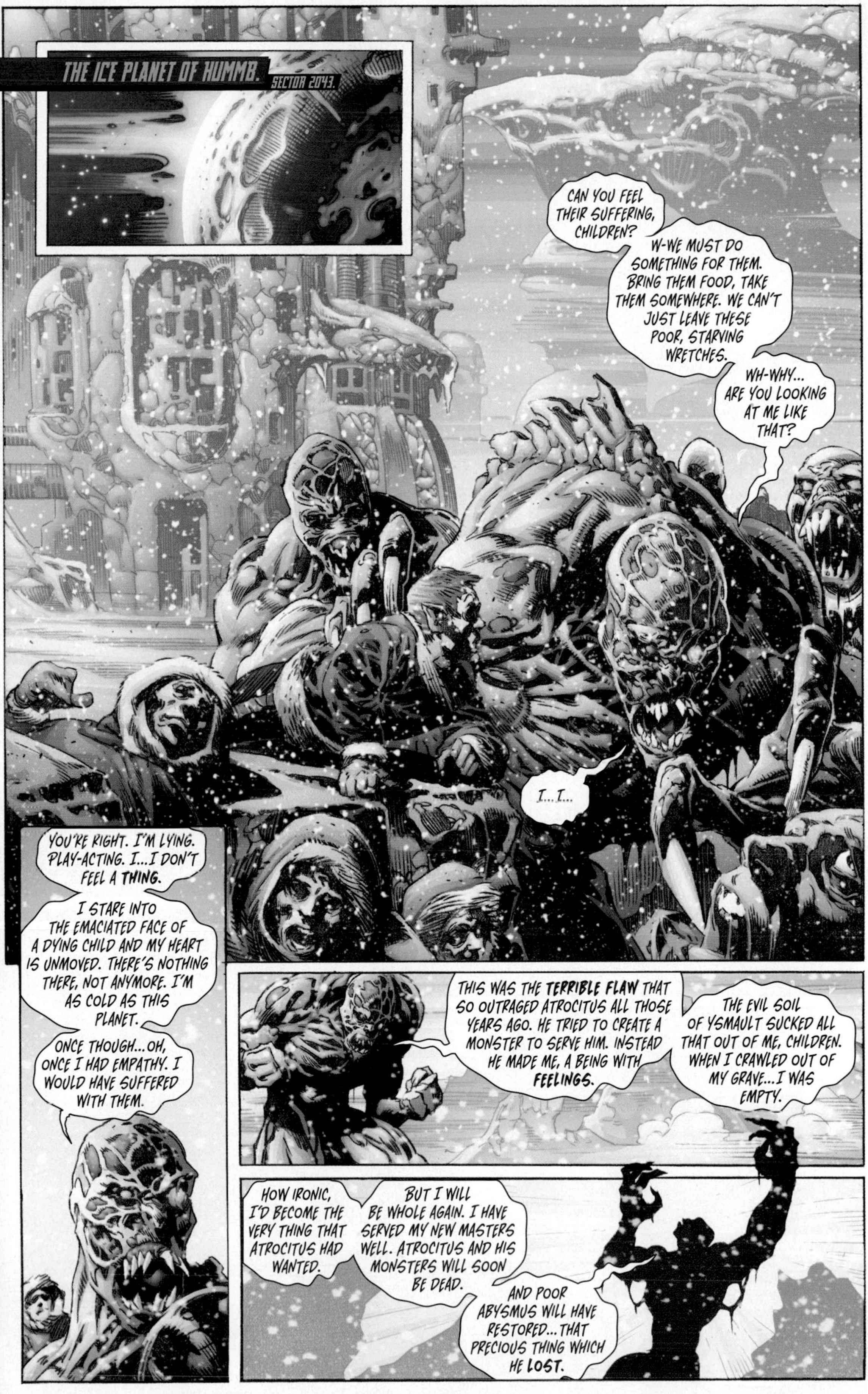
THE ICE PLANET OF HUMMB.
SECTOR 2043.
CAN YOU FEEL THEIR SUFFERING, CHILDREN?
W-WE MUST DO SOMETHING FOR THEM. BRING THEM FOOD, TAKE THEM SOMEWHERE. WE CAN'T JUST LEAVE THESE POOR, STARVING WRETCHES.
WH-WHY... ARE YOU LOOKING AT ME LIKE THAT?
I... I...
YOU'RE RIGHT. I'M LYING. PLAY-ACTING. I...I DON'T FEEL A THING.
I STARE INTO THE EMACIATED FACE OF A DYING CHILD AND MY HEART IS UNMOVED. THERE'S NOTHING THERE, NOT ANYMORE. I'M AS COLD AS THIS PLANET.
ONCE THOUGH...OH, ONCE I HAD EMPATHY. I WOULD HAVE SUFFERED WITH THEM.
THIS WAS THE TERRIBLE FLAW THAT SO OUTRAGED ATROCITUS ALL THOSE YEARS AGO. HE TRIED TO CREATE A MONSTER TO SERVE HIM. INSTEAD HE MADE ME, A BEING WITH FEELINGS.
THE EVIL SOIL OF YSMAULT SUCKED ALL THAT OUT OF ME, CHILDREN. WHEN I CRAWLED OUT OF MY GRAVE...I WAS EMPTY.
HOW IRONIC, I'D BECOME THE VERY THING THAT ATROCITUS HAD WANTED.
BUT I WILL BE WHOLE AGAIN. I HAVE SERVED MY NEW MASTERS WELL. ATROCITUS AND HIS MONSTERS WILL SOON BE DEAD.
AND POOR ABYSMUS WILL HAVE RESTORED...THAT PRECIOUS THING WHICH HE LOST.

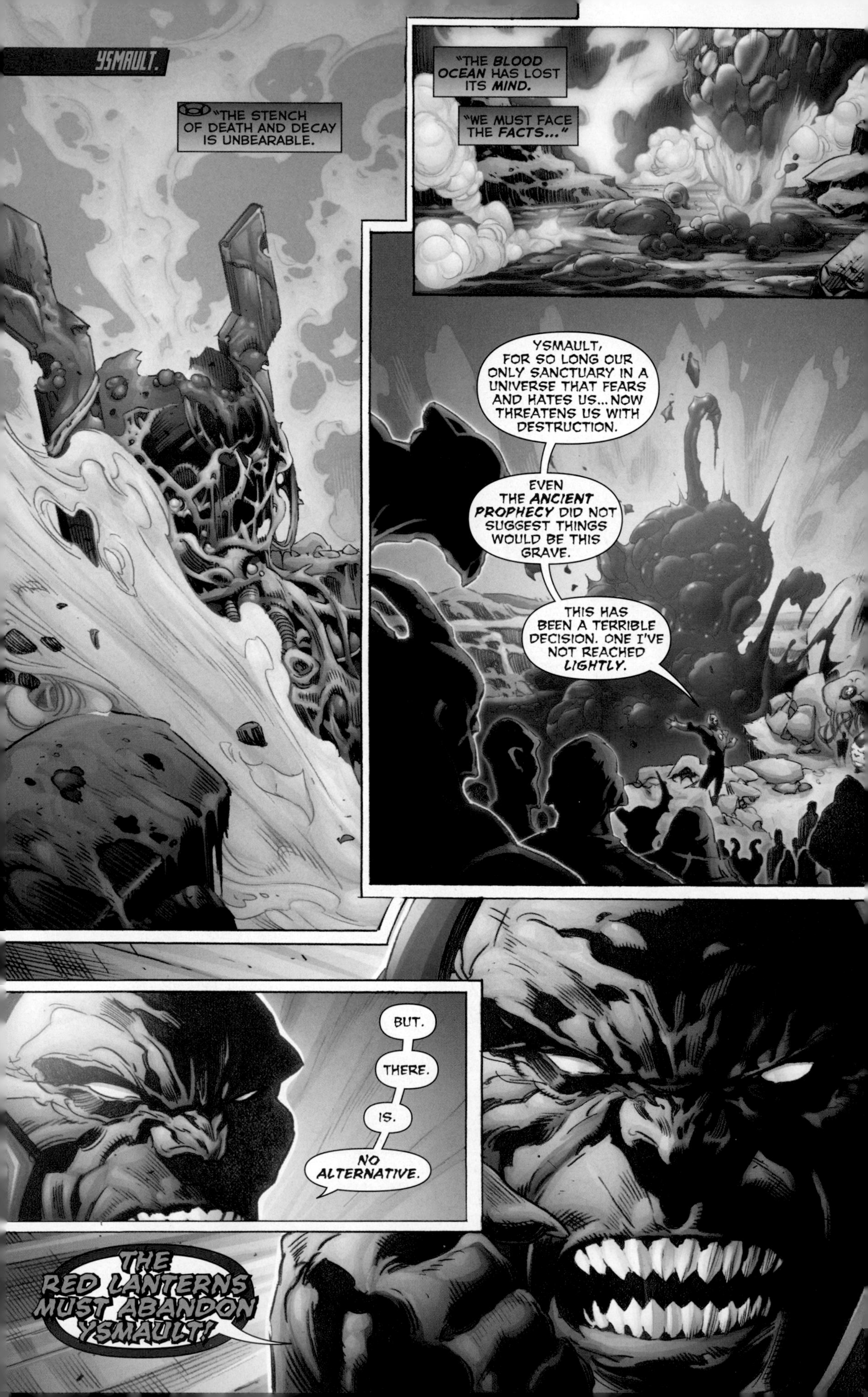
YSMAULT.
"THE STENCH OF DEATH AND DECAY IS UNBEARABLE.
"THE BLOOD OCEAN HAS LOST ITS MIND.
"WE MUST FACE THE FACTS..."
YSMAULT, FOR SO LONG OUR ONLY SANCTUARY IN A UNIVERSE THAT FEARS AND HATES US...NOW THREATENS US WITH DESTRUCTION.
EVEN THE ANCIENT PROPHECY DID NOT SUGGEST THINGS WOULD BE THIS GRAVE.
THIS HAS BEEN A TERRIBLE DECISION. ONE I'VE NOT REACHED LIGHTLY.
BUT.
THERE.
IS.
NO ALTERNATIVE.
THE RED LANTERNS MUST ABANDON YSMAULT!

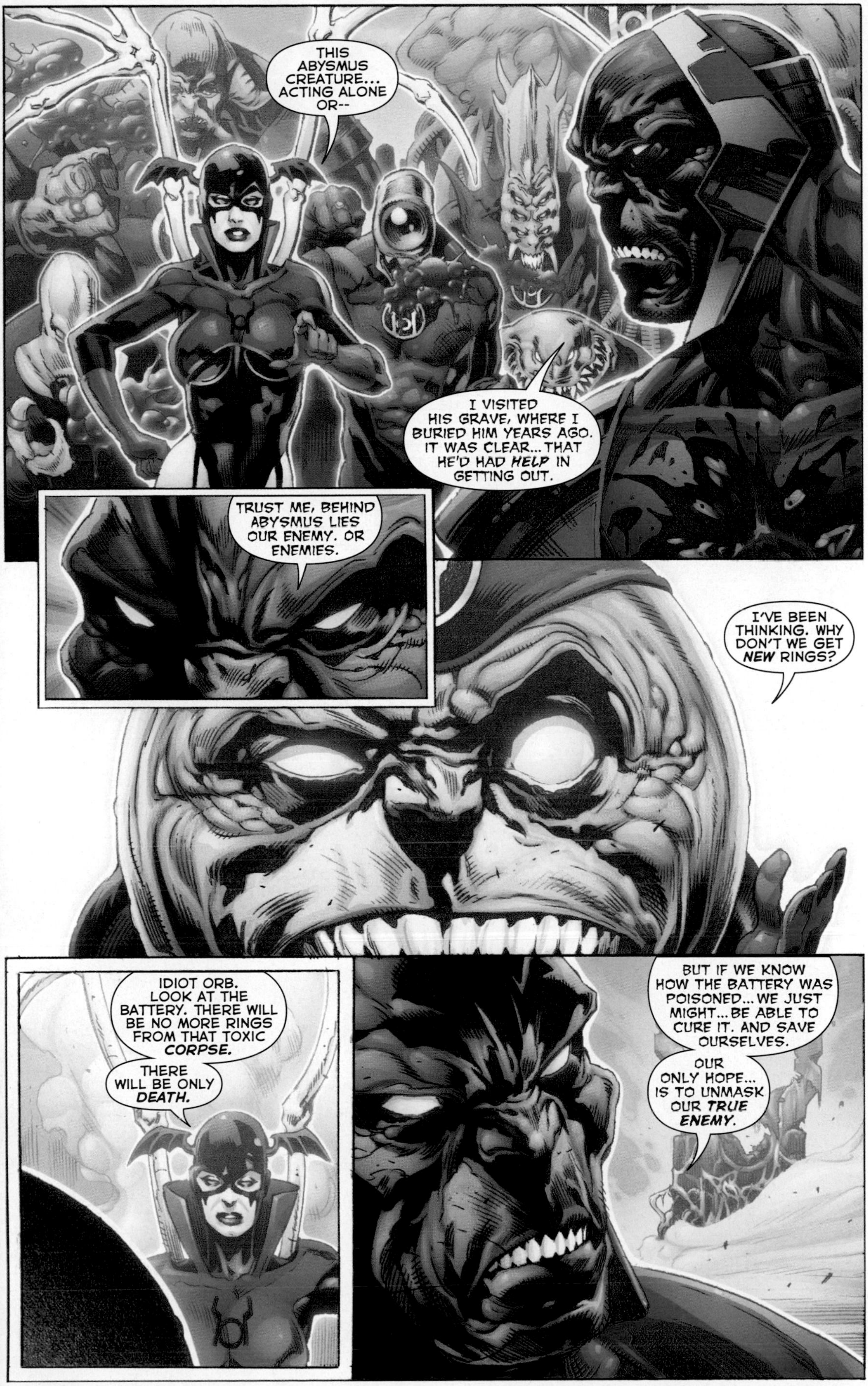
THIS ABYSMUS CREATURE... ACTING ALONE OR--
I VISITED HIS GRAVE, WHERE I BURIED HIM YEARS AGO. IT WAS CLEAR... THAT HE'D HAD *HELP* IN GETTING OUT.
TRUST ME, BEHIND ABYSMUS LIES OUR ENEMY. OR ENEMIES.
I'VE BEEN THINKING. WHY DON'T WE GET *NEW* RINGS?
IDIOT ORB. LOOK AT THE BATTERY. THERE WILL BE NO MORE RINGS FROM THAT TOXIC *CORPSE.*
THERE WILL BE ONLY *DEATH.*
BUT IF WE KNOW HOW THE BATTERY WAS POISONED... WE JUST MIGHT... BE ABLE TO CURE IT. AND SAVE OURSELVES.
OUR ONLY HOPE... IS TO UNMASK OUR *TRUE ENEMY.*

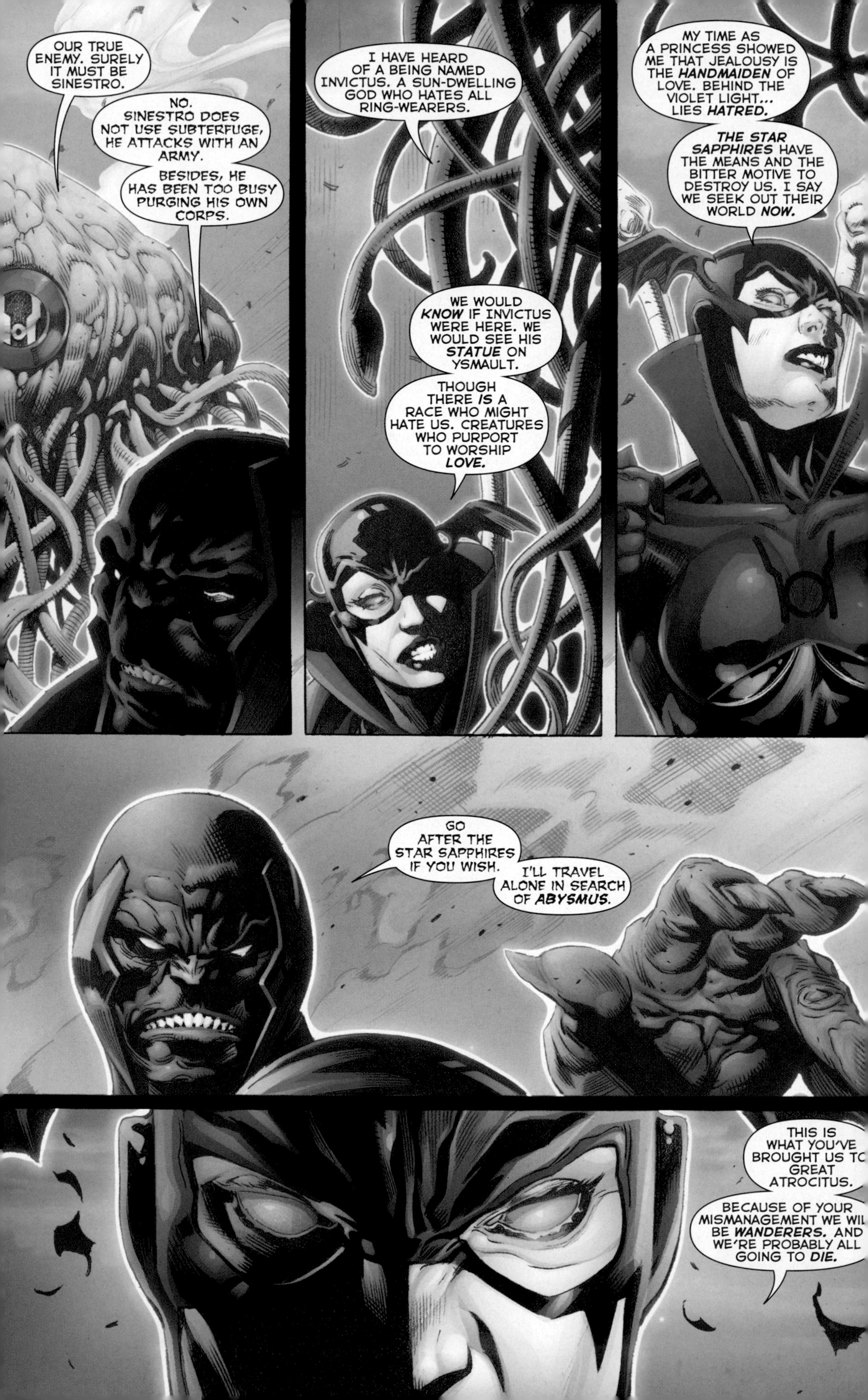
OUR TRUE ENEMY. SURELY IT MUST BE SINESTRO.
NO. SINESTRO DOES NOT USE SUBTERFUGE, HE ATTACKS WITH AN ARMY.
BESIDES, HE HAS BEEN TOO BUSY PURGING HIS OWN CORPS.
I HAVE HEARD OF A BEING NAMED INVICTUS. A SUN-DWELLING GOD WHO HATES ALL RING-WEARERS.
WE WOULD KNOW IF INVICTUS WERE HERE. WE WOULD SEE HIS STATUE ON YSMAULT.
THOUGH THERE IS A RACE WHO MIGHT HATE US. CREATURES WHO PURPORT TO WORSHIP LOVE.
MY TIME AS A PRINCESS SHOWED ME THAT JEALOUSY IS THE HANDMAIDEN OF LOVE. BEHIND THE VIOLET LIGHT... LIES HATRED.
THE STAR SAPPHIRES HAVE THE MEANS AND THE BITTER MOTIVE TO DESTROY US. I SAY WE SEEK OUT THEIR WORLD NOW.
GO AFTER THE STAR SAPPHIRES IF YOU WISH.
I'LL TRAVEL ALONE IN SEARCH OF ABYSMUS.
THIS IS WHAT YOU'VE BROUGHT US TO GREAT ATROCITUS.
BECAUSE OF YOUR MISMANAGEMENT WE WILL BE WANDERERS. AND WE'RE PROBABLY ALL GOING TO DIE.

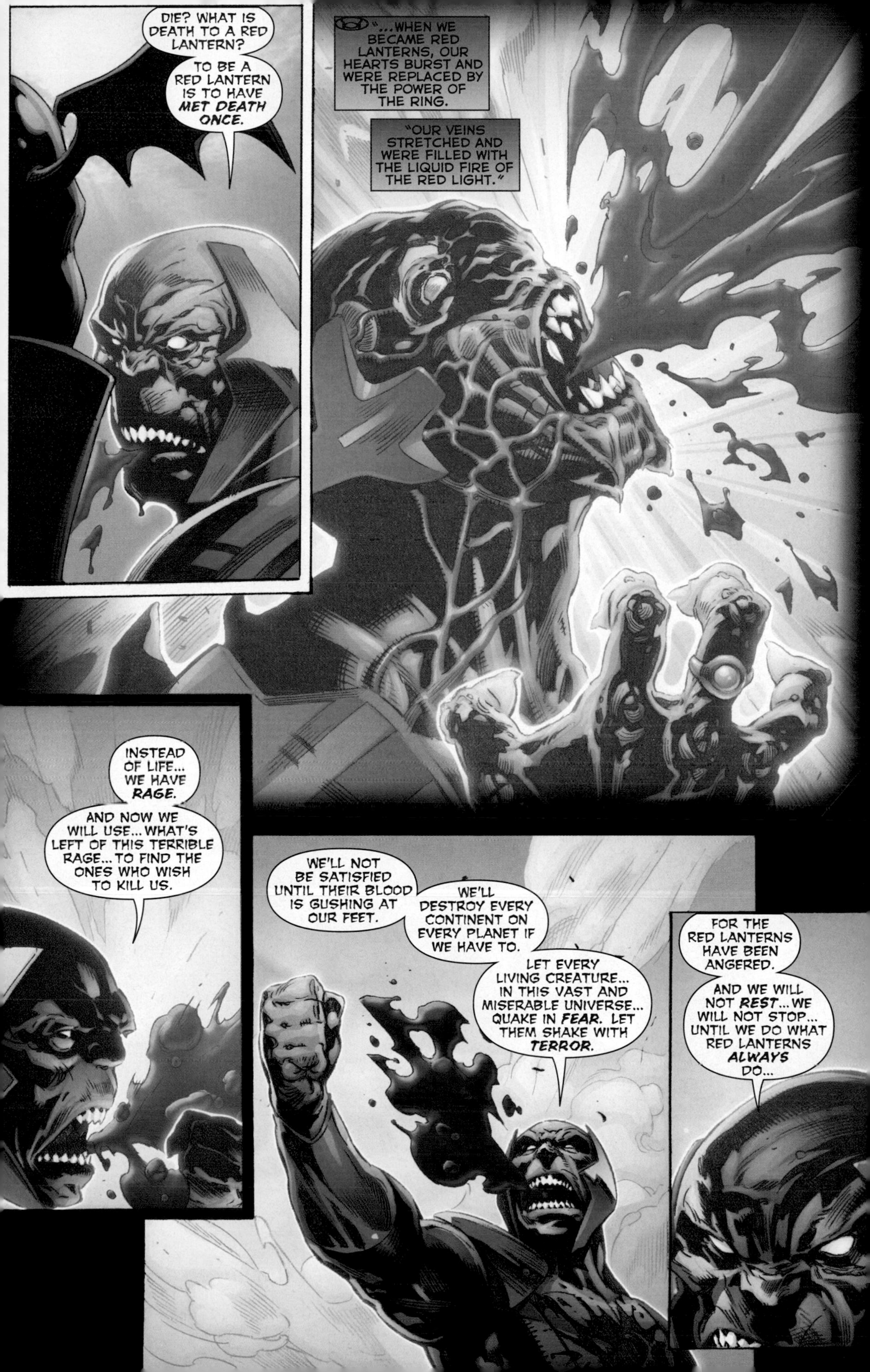
DIE? WHAT IS DEATH TO A RED LANTERN?
TO BE A RED LANTERN IS TO HAVE MET DEATH ONCE.
"...WHEN WE BECAME RED LANTERNS, OUR HEARTS BURST AND WERE REPLACED BY THE POWER OF THE RING.
"OUR VEINS STRETCHED AND WERE FILLED WITH THE LIQUID FIRE OF THE RED LIGHT."
INSTEAD OF LIFE... WE HAVE RAGE.
AND NOW WE WILL USE... WHAT'S LEFT OF THIS TERRIBLE RAGE... TO FIND THE ONES WHO WISH TO KILL US.
WE'LL NOT BE SATISFIED UNTIL THEIR BLOOD IS GUSHING AT OUR FEET.
WE'LL DESTROY EVERY CONTINENT ON EVERY PLANET IF WE HAVE TO.
LET EVERY LIVING CREATURE... IN THIS VAST AND MISERABLE UNIVERSE... QUAKE IN FEAR. LET THEM SHAKE WITH TERROR.
FOR THE RED LANTERNS HAVE BEEN ANGERED.
AND WE WILL NOT REST... WE WILL NOT STOP... UNTIL WE DO WHAT RED LANTERNS ALWAYS DO...

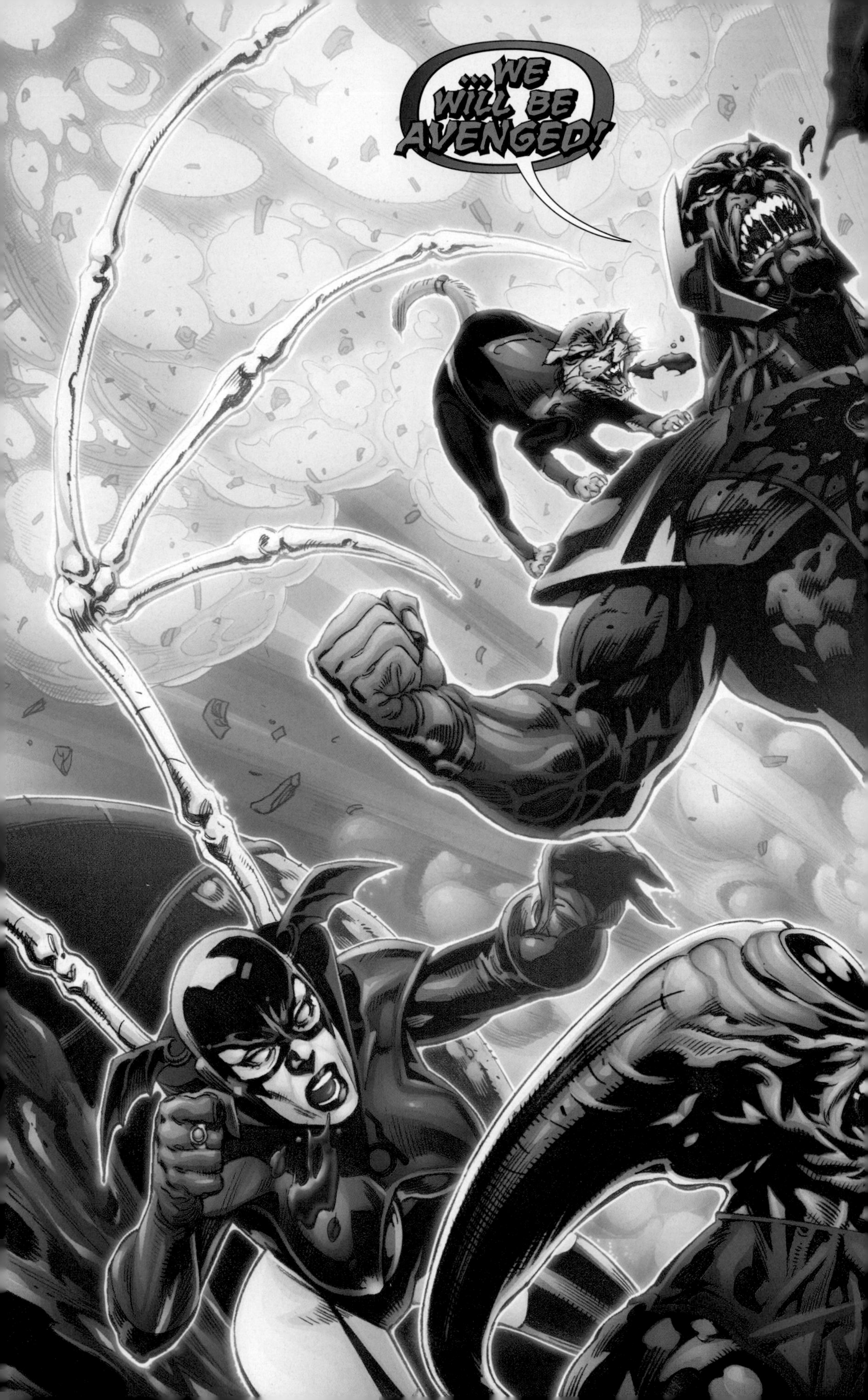
...WE WILL BE AVENGED!

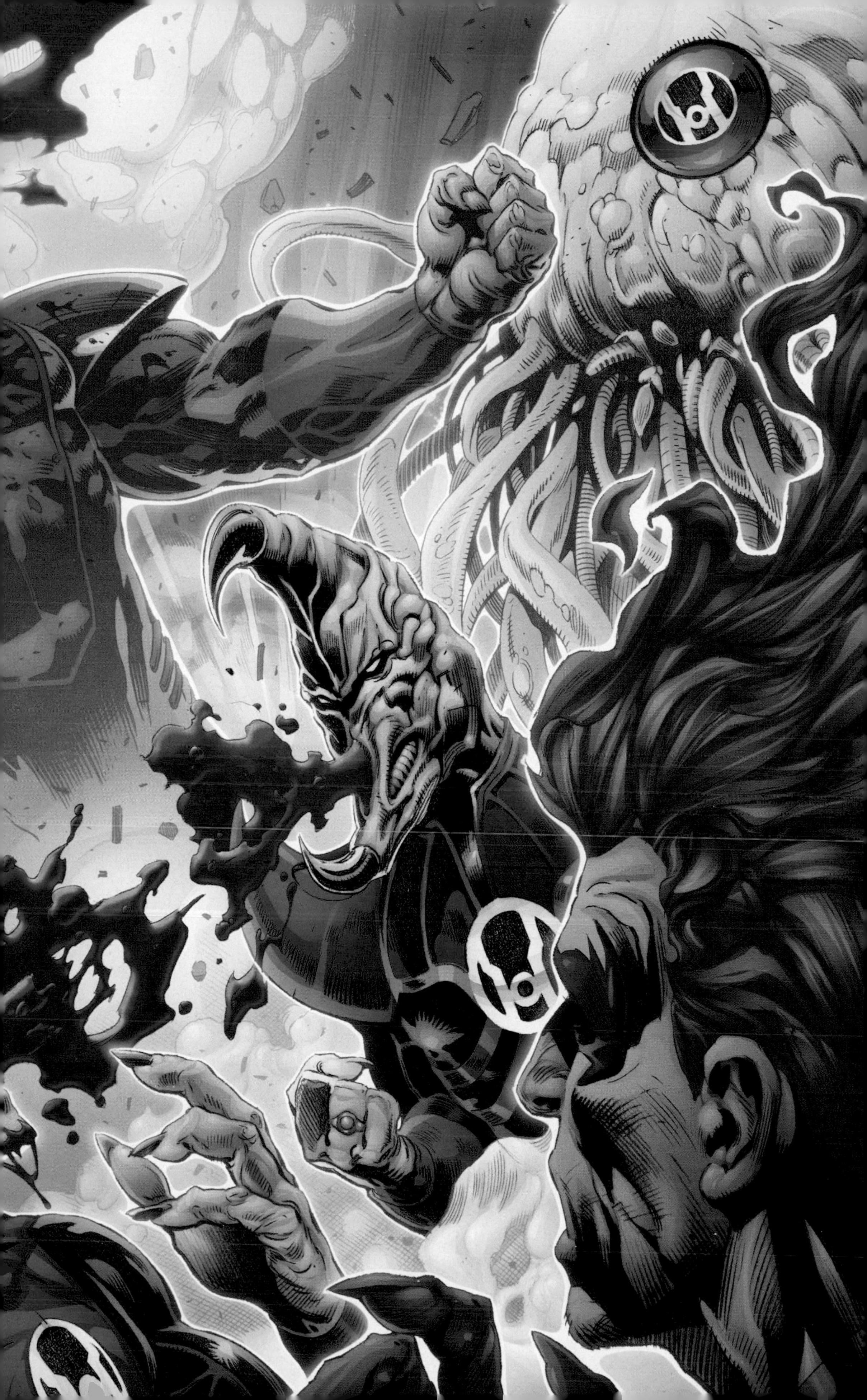

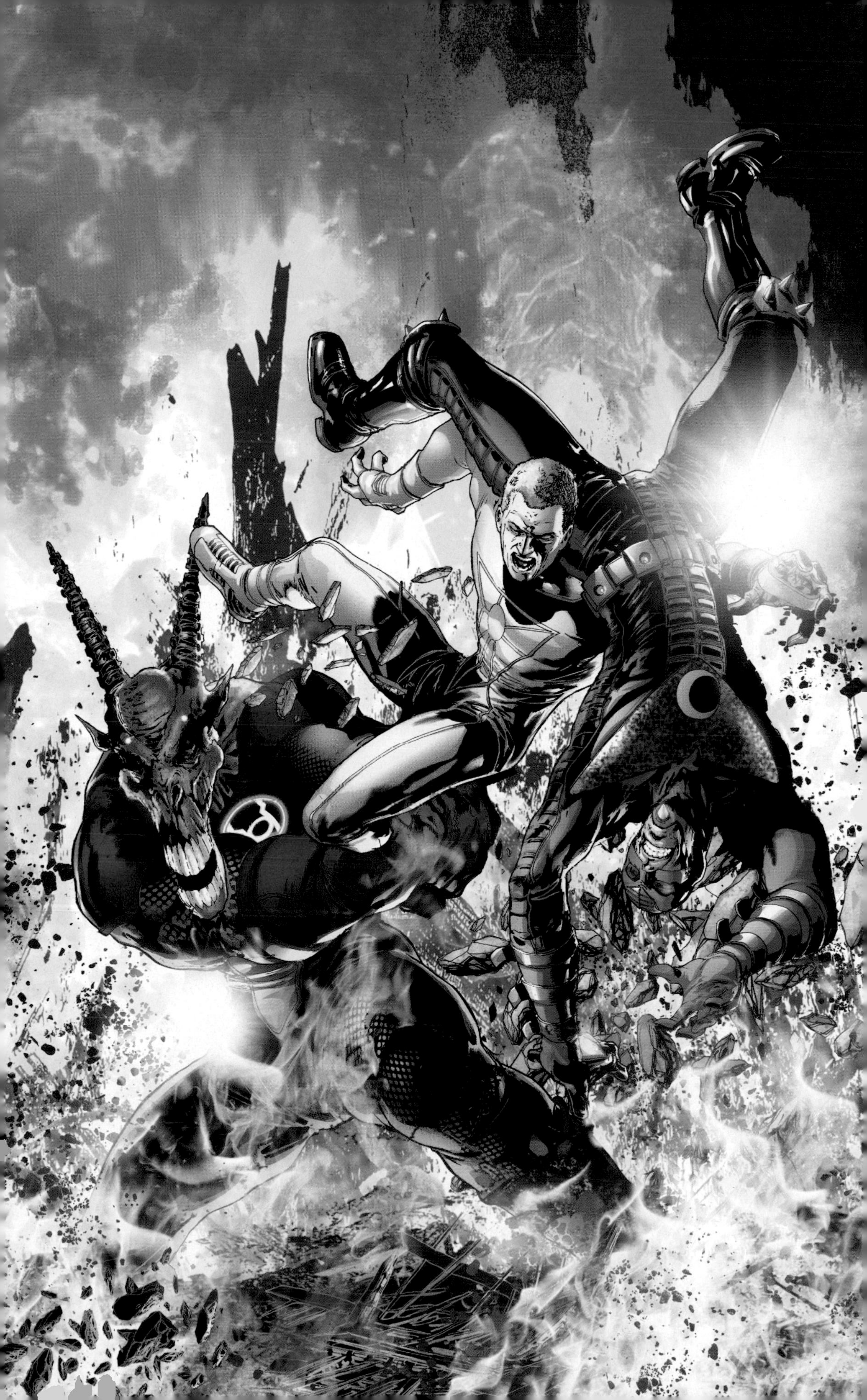

THE DA VINCI CODA

PETER MILLIGAN
writer

MIGUEL SEPULVEDA
artist

cover art by MIGUEL SEPULVEDA & ALEX SINCLAIR

STORMWATCH created by JIM LEE & BRANDON CHOI

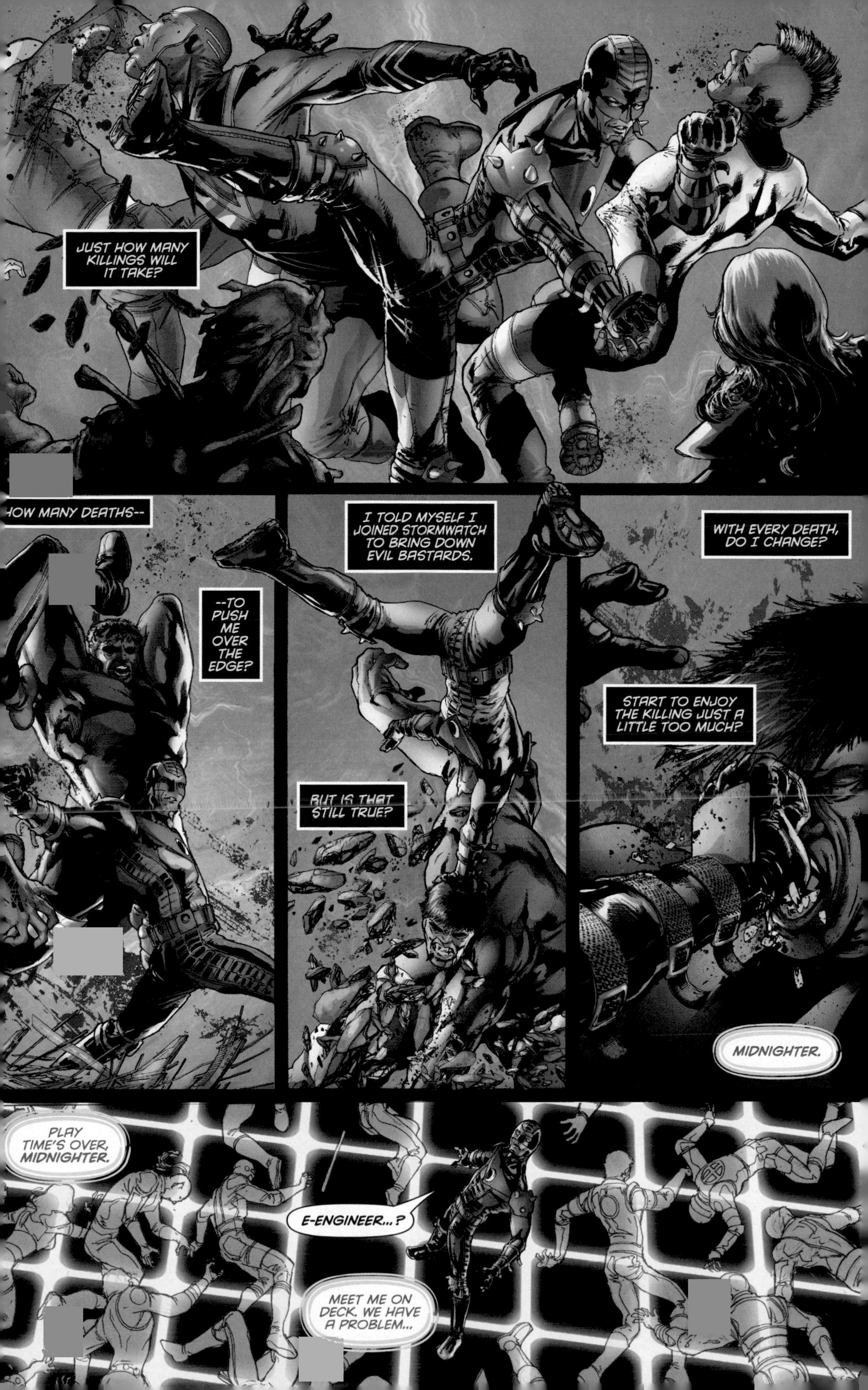

JUST HOW MANY KILLINGS WILL IT TAKE?
HOW MANY DEATHS--
--TO PUSH ME OVER THE EDGE?
I TOLD MYSELF I JOINED STORMWATCH TO BRING DOWN EVIL BASTARDS.
BUT IS THAT STILL TRUE?
WITH EVERY DEATH, DO I CHANGE?
START TO ENJOY THE KILLING JUST A LITTLE TOO MUCH?
MIDNIGHTER.
PLAY TIME'S OVER, MIDNIGHTER.
E-ENGINEER...?
MEET ME ON DECK. WE HAVE A PROBLEM...

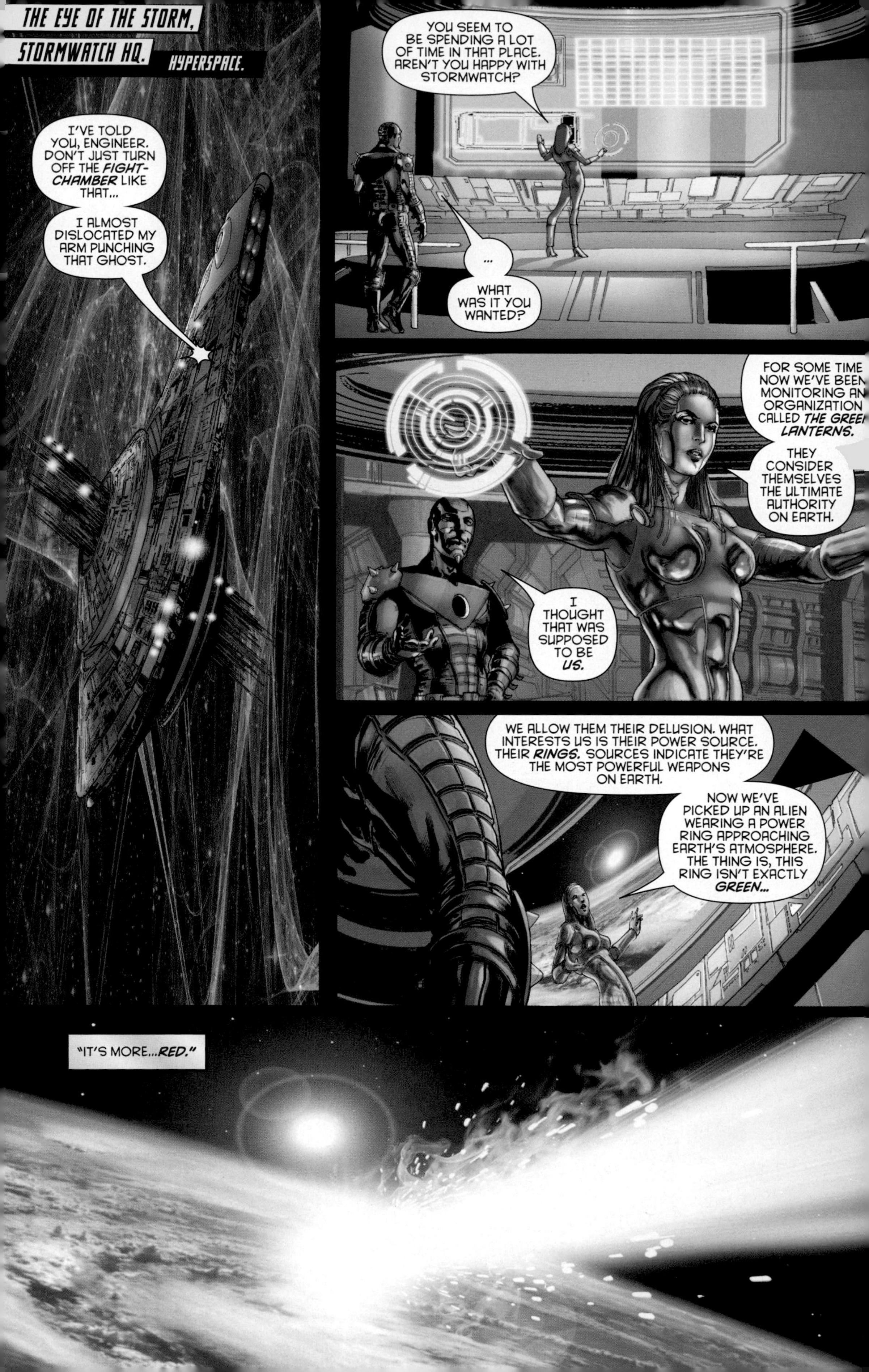

THE EYE OF THE STORM,
STORMWATCH HQ.
HYPERSPACE.
I'VE TOLD YOU, ENGINEER. DON'T JUST TURN OFF THE FIGHT-CHAMBER LIKE THAT...
I ALMOST DISLOCATED MY ARM PUNCHING THAT GHOST.
YOU SEEM TO BE SPENDING A LOT OF TIME IN THAT PLACE. AREN'T YOU HAPPY WITH STORMWATCH?
...
WHAT WAS IT YOU WANTED?
FOR SOME TIME NOW WE'VE BEEN MONITORING AN ORGANIZATION CALLED THE GREEN LANTERNS.
THEY CONSIDER THEMSELVES THE ULTIMATE AUTHORITY ON EARTH.
I THOUGHT THAT WAS SUPPOSED TO BE US.
WE ALLOW THEM THEIR DELUSION. WHAT INTERESTS US IS THEIR POWER SOURCE. THEIR RINGS. SOURCES INDICATE THEY'RE THE MOST POWERFUL WEAPONS ON EARTH.
NOW WE'VE PICKED UP AN ALIEN WEARING A POWER RING APPROACHING EARTH'S ATMOSPHERE. THE THING IS, THIS RING ISN'T EXACTLY GREEN...
"IT'S MORE...RED."

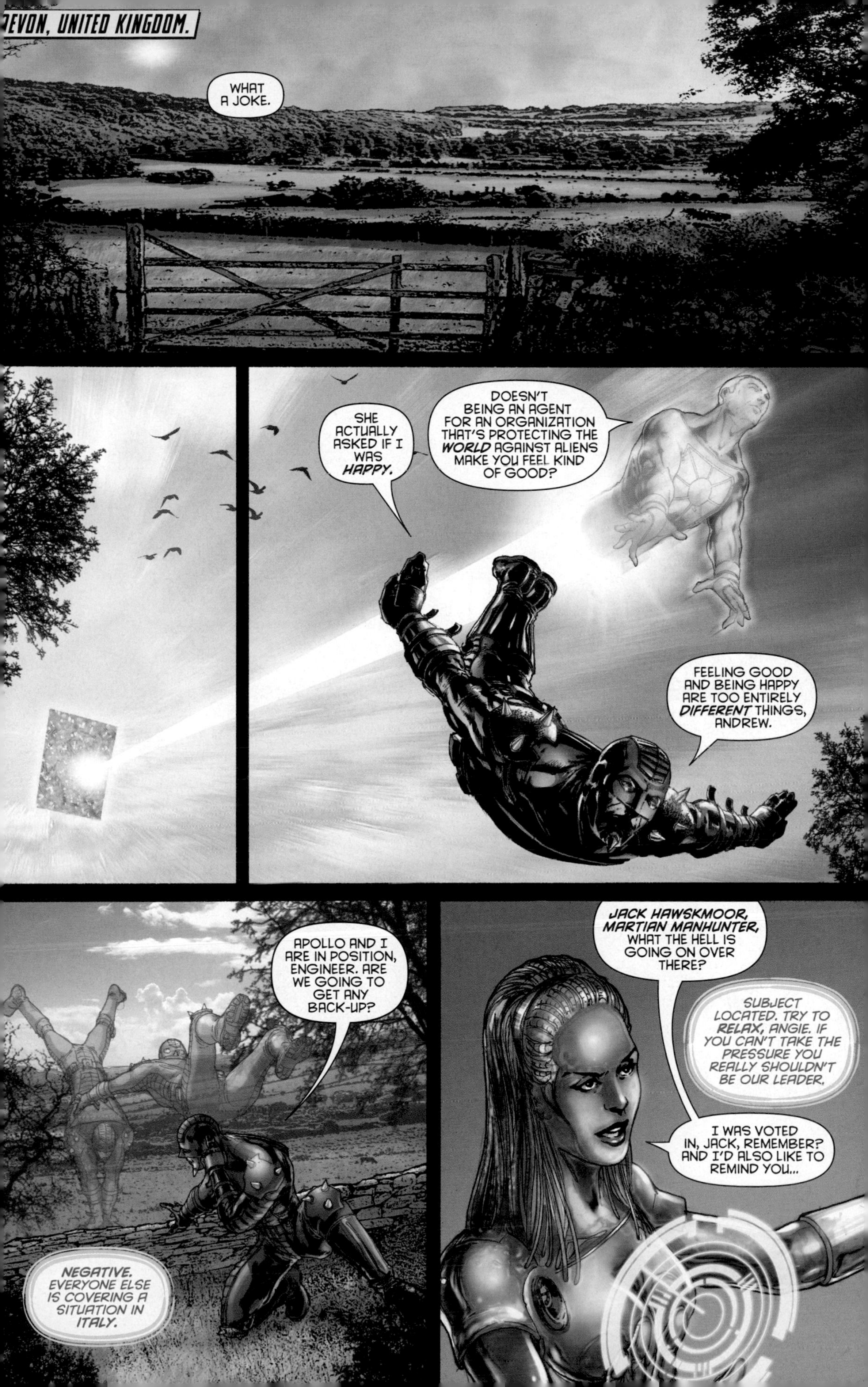
DEVON, UNITED KINGDOM.
WHAT A JOKE.
SHE ACTUALLY ASKED IF I WAS HAPPY.
DOESN'T BEING AN AGENT FOR AN ORGANIZATION THAT'S PROTECTING THE WORLD AGAINST ALIENS MAKE YOU FEEL KIND OF GOOD?
FEELING GOOD AND BEING HAPPY ARE TOO ENTIRELY DIFFERENT THINGS, ANDREW.
APOLLO AND I ARE IN POSITION, ENGINEER. ARE WE GOING TO GET ANY BACK-UP?
NEGATIVE. EVERYONE ELSE IS COVERING A SITUATION IN ITALY.
JACK HAWSKMOOR, MARTIAN MANHUNTER, WHAT THE HELL IS GOING ON OVER THERE?
SUBJECT LOCATED. TRY TO RELAX, ANGIE. IF YOU CAN'T TAKE THE PRESSURE YOU REALLY SHOULDN'T BE OUR LEADER.
I WAS VOTED IN, JACK, REMEMBER? AND I'D ALSO LIKE TO REMIND YOU...

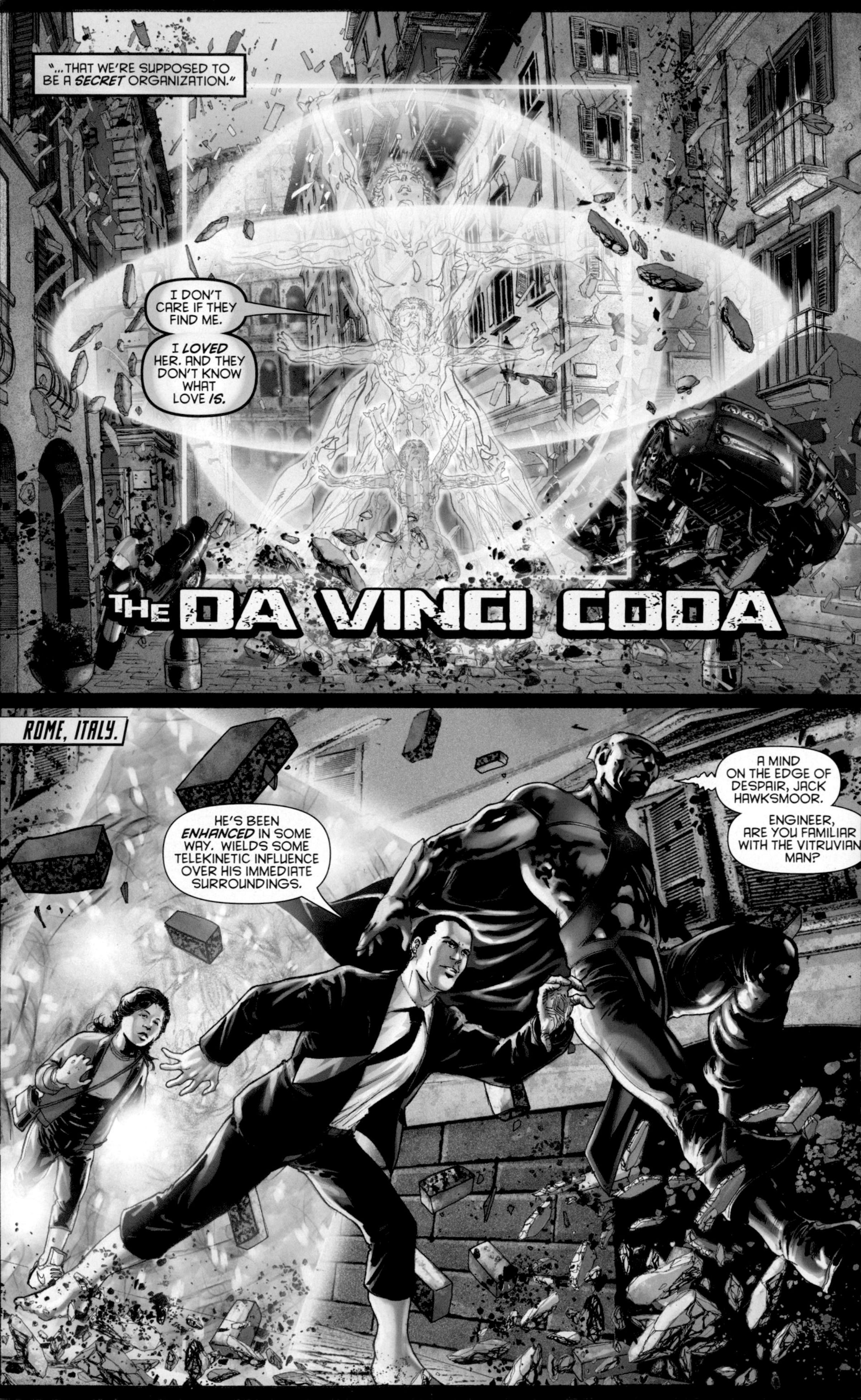
"...THAT WE'RE SUPPOSED TO BE A SECRET ORGANIZATION."
I DON'T CARE IF THEY FIND ME.
I LOVED HER. AND THEY DON'T KNOW WHAT LOVE IS.
THE DA VINCI CODA
ROME, ITALY.
HE'S BEEN ENHANCED IN SOME WAY. WIELDS SOME TELEKINETIC INFLUENCE OVER HIS IMMEDIATE SURROUNDINGS.
A MIND ON THE EDGE OF DESPAIR, JACK HAWKSMOOR.
ENGINEER, ARE YOU FAMILIAR WITH THE VITRUVIAN MAN?

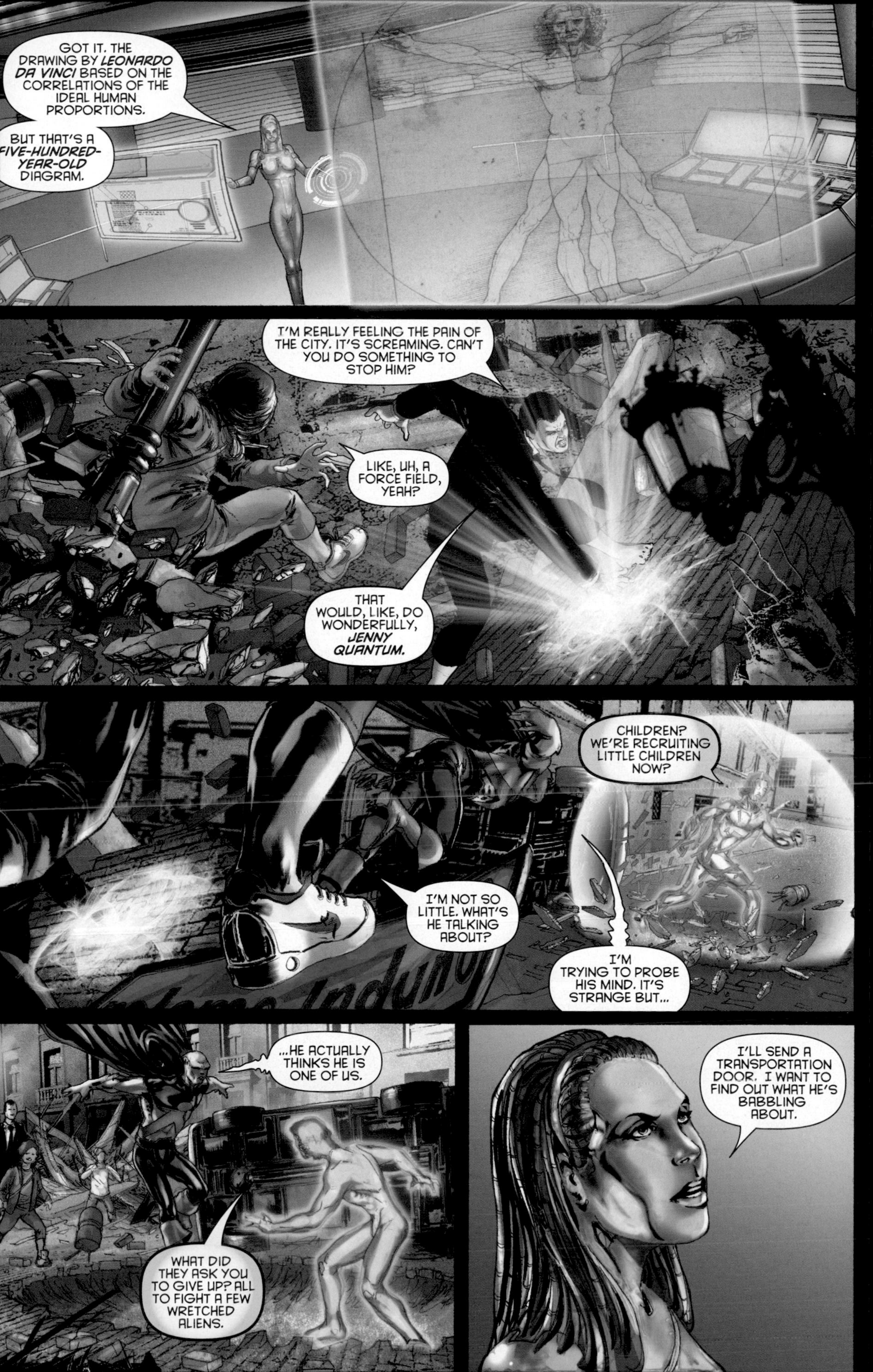
GOT IT. THE DRAWING BY LEONARDO DA VINCI BASED ON THE CORRELATIONS OF THE IDEAL HUMAN PROPORTIONS.
BUT THAT'S A FIVE-HUNDRED-YEAR-OLD DIAGRAM.
I'M REALLY FEELING THE PAIN OF THE CITY. IT'S SCREAMING. CAN'T YOU DO SOMETHING TO STOP HIM?
LIKE, UH, A FORCE FIELD, YEAH?
THAT WOULD, LIKE, DO WONDERFULLY, JENNY QUANTUM.
CHILDREN? WE'RE RECRUITING LITTLE CHILDREN NOW?
I'M NOT SO LITTLE. WHAT'S HE TALKING ABOUT?
I'M TRYING TO PROBE HIS MIND. IT'S STRANGE BUT...
...HE ACTUALLY THINKS HE IS ONE OF US.
WHAT DID THEY ASK YOU TO GIVE UP? ALL TO FIGHT A FEW WRETCHED ALIENS.
I'LL SEND A TRANSPORTATION DOOR. I WANT TO FIND OUT WHAT HE'S BABBLING ABOUT.

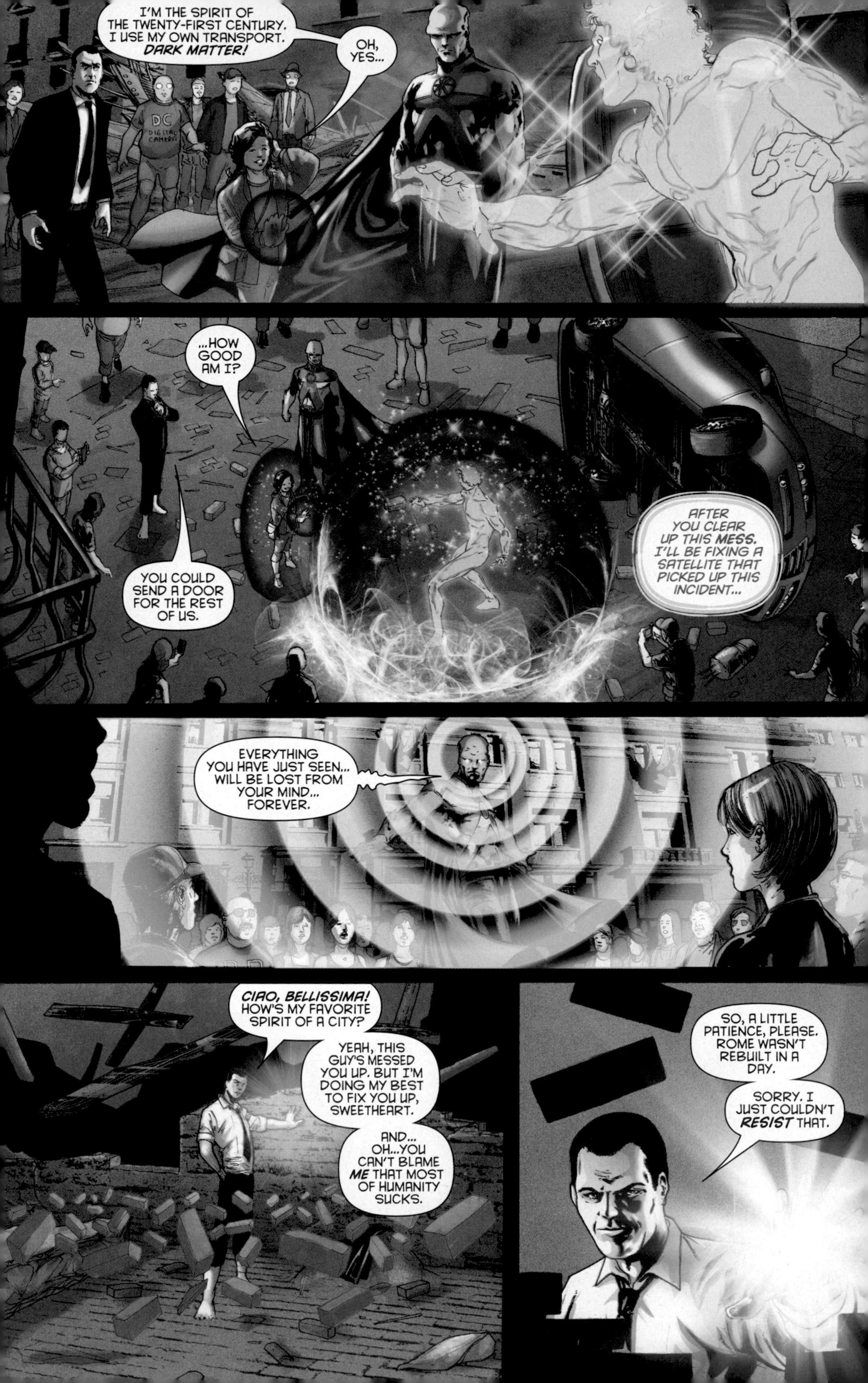
I'M THE SPIRIT OF THE TWENTY-FIRST CENTURY. I USE MY OWN TRANSPORT. DARK MATTER!
OH, YES...
DC DIGITAL CAMERA
...HOW GOOD AM I?
YOU COULD SEND A DOOR FOR THE REST OF US.
AFTER YOU CLEAR UP THIS MESS. I'LL BE FIXING A SATELLITE THAT PICKED UP THIS INCIDENT...
EVERYTHING YOU HAVE JUST SEEN... WILL BE LOST FROM YOUR MIND... FOREVER.
CIAO, BELLISSIMA! HOW'S MY FAVORITE SPIRIT OF A CITY?
YEAH, THIS GUY'S MESSED YOU UP. BUT I'M DOING MY BEST TO FIX YOU UP, SWEETHEART.
AND... OH...YOU CAN'T BLAME ME THAT MOST OF HUMANITY SUCKS.
SO, A LITTLE PATIENCE, PLEASE. ROME WASN'T REBUILT IN A DAY.
SORRY. I JUST COULDN'T RESIST THAT.

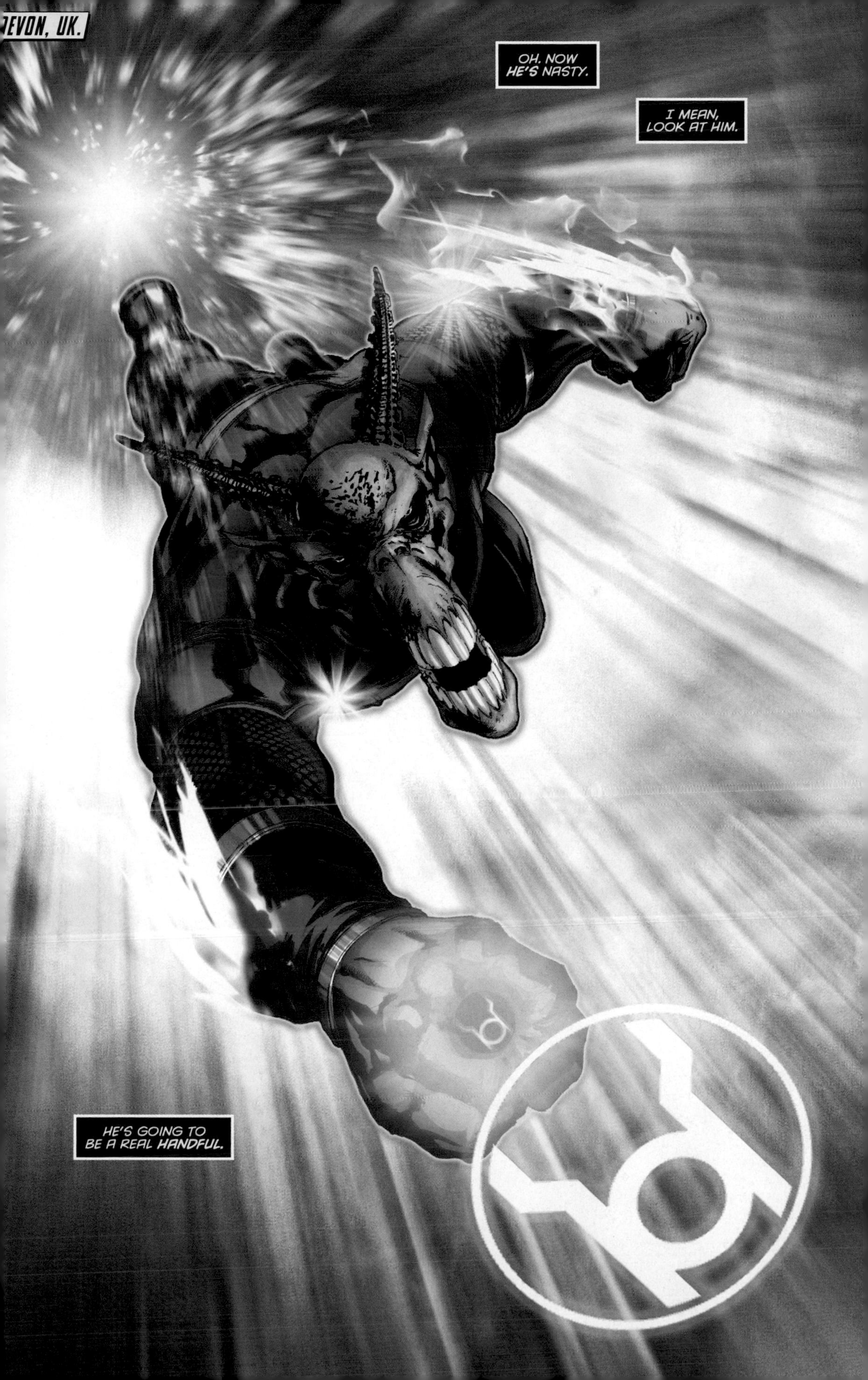
EVON, UK.
OH. NOW HE'S NASTY.
I MEAN, LOOK AT HIM.
HE'S GOING TO BE A REAL HANDFUL.

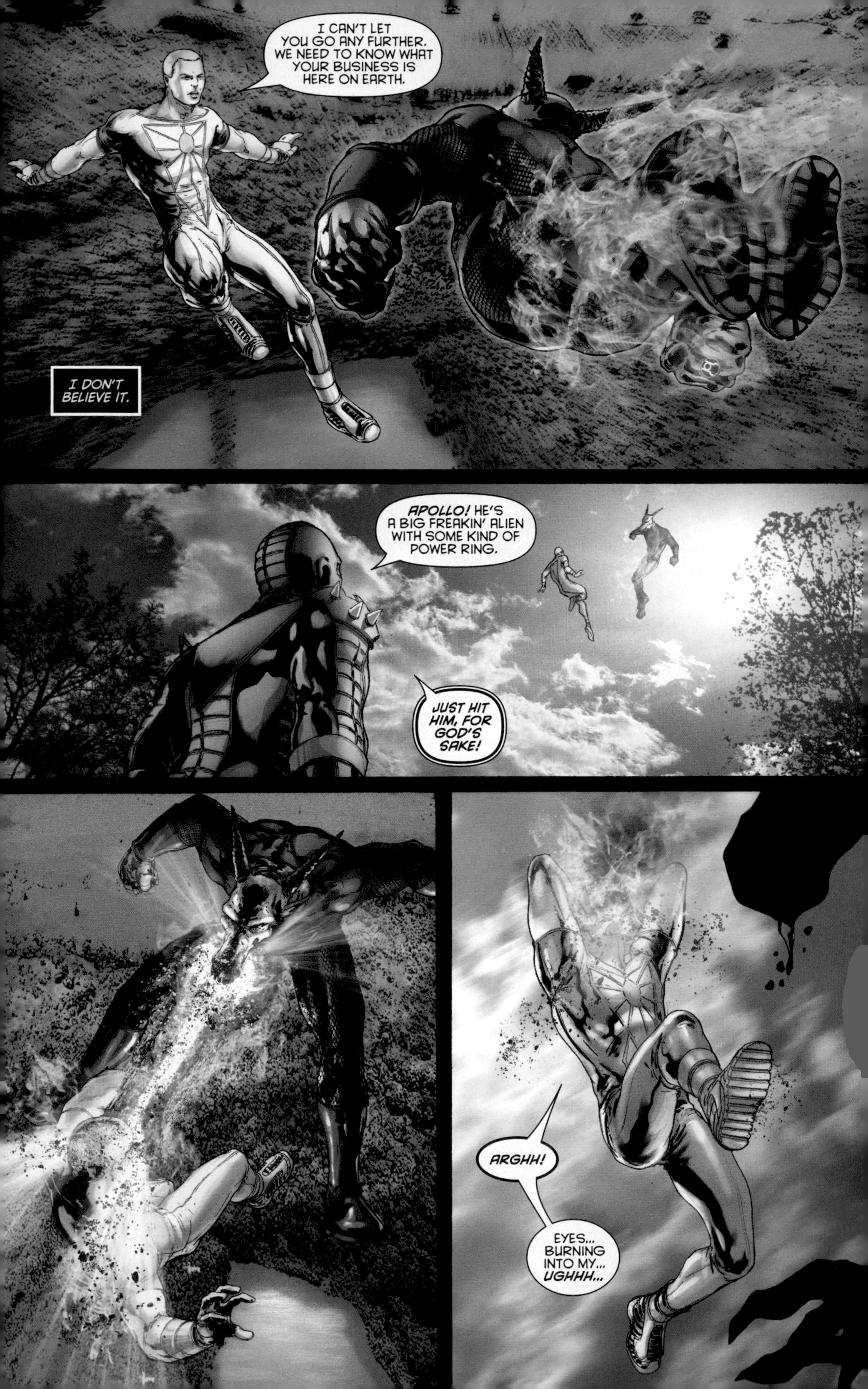
I CAN'T LET YOU GO ANY FURTHER. WE NEED TO KNOW WHAT YOUR BUSINESS IS HERE ON EARTH.
I DON'T BELIEVE IT.
APOLLO! HE'S A BIG FREAKIN' ALIEN WITH SOME KIND OF POWER RING.
JUST HIT HIM, FOR GOD'S SAKE!
ARGHH!
EYES... BURNING INTO MY... UGHHH...

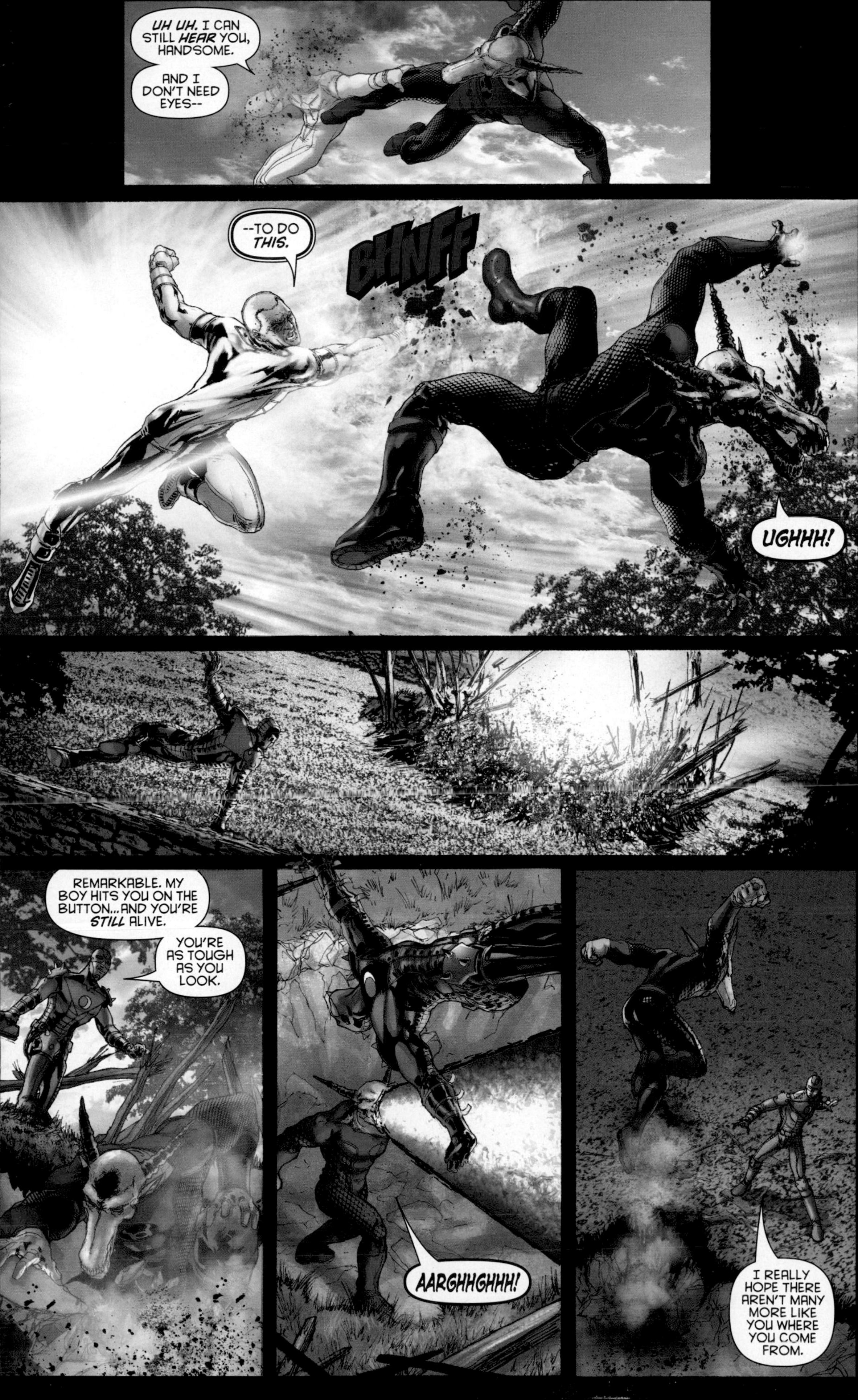
UH UH. I CAN STILL HEAR YOU, HANDSOME.
AND I DON'T NEED EYES--
--TO DO THIS.
BHNFF
UGHHH!
REMARKABLE. MY BOY HITS YOU ON THE BUTTON...AND YOU'RE STILL ALIVE.
YOU'RE AS TOUGH AS YOU LOOK.
AARGHHGHHH!
I REALLY HOPE THERE AREN'T MANY MORE LIKE YOU WHERE YOU COME FROM.

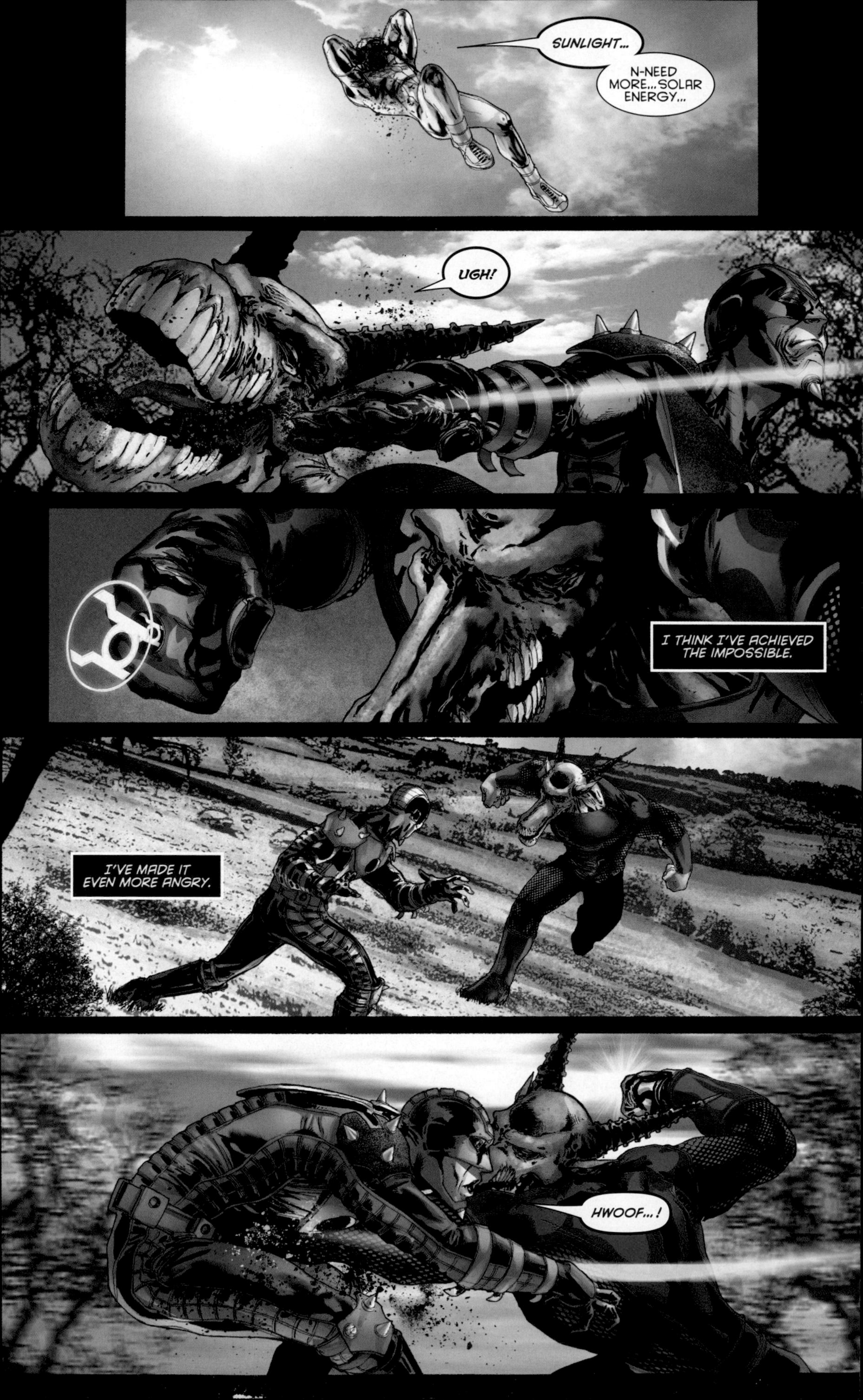
SUNLIGHT...
N-NEED MORE...SOLAR ENERGY...
UGH!
I THINK I'VE ACHIEVED THE IMPOSSIBLE.
I'VE MADE IT EVEN MORE ANGRY.
HWOOF...!

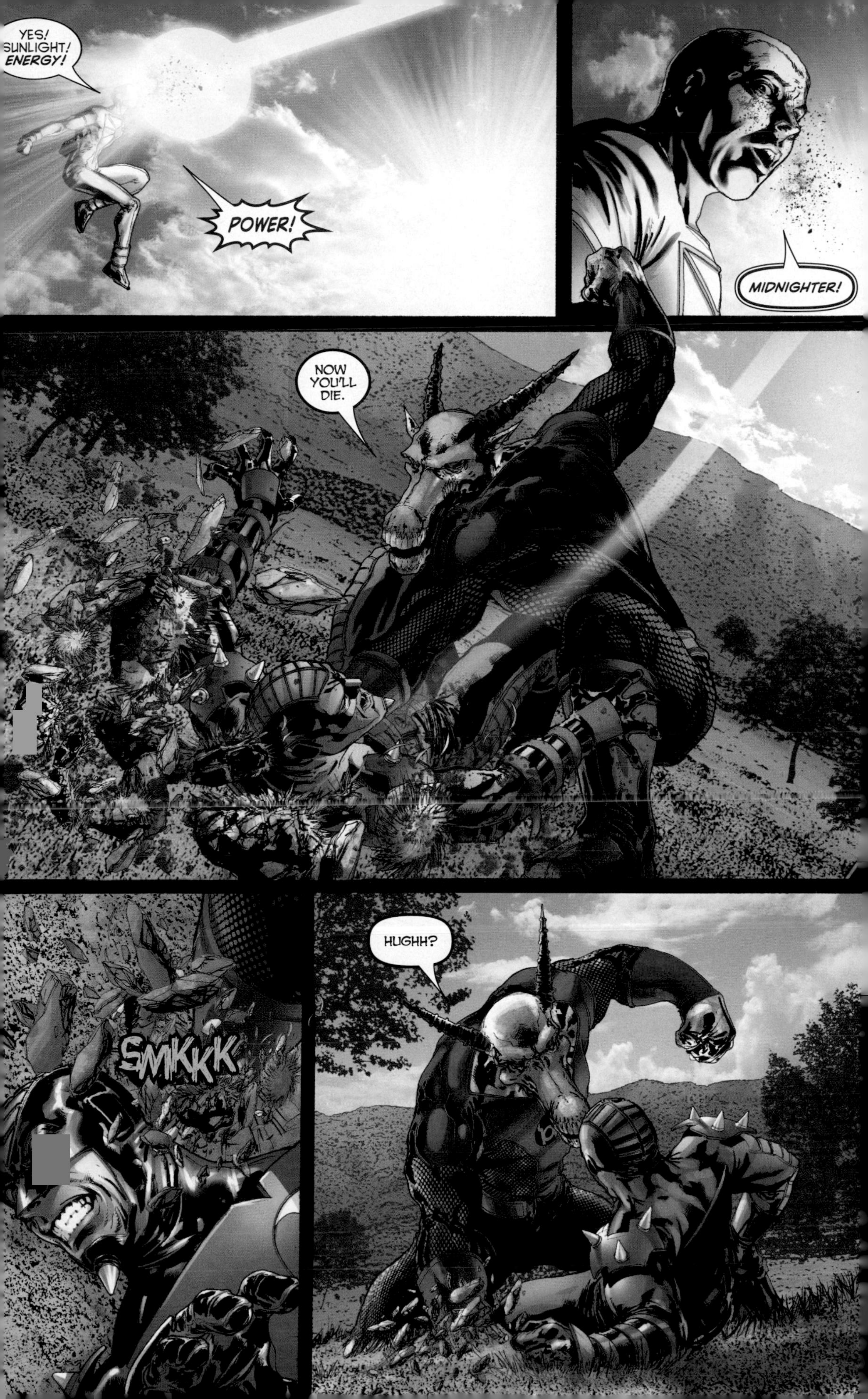
YES! SUNLIGHT! ENERGY!
POWER!
MIDNIGHTER!
NOW YOU'LL DIE.
SMKKK
HUGHH?

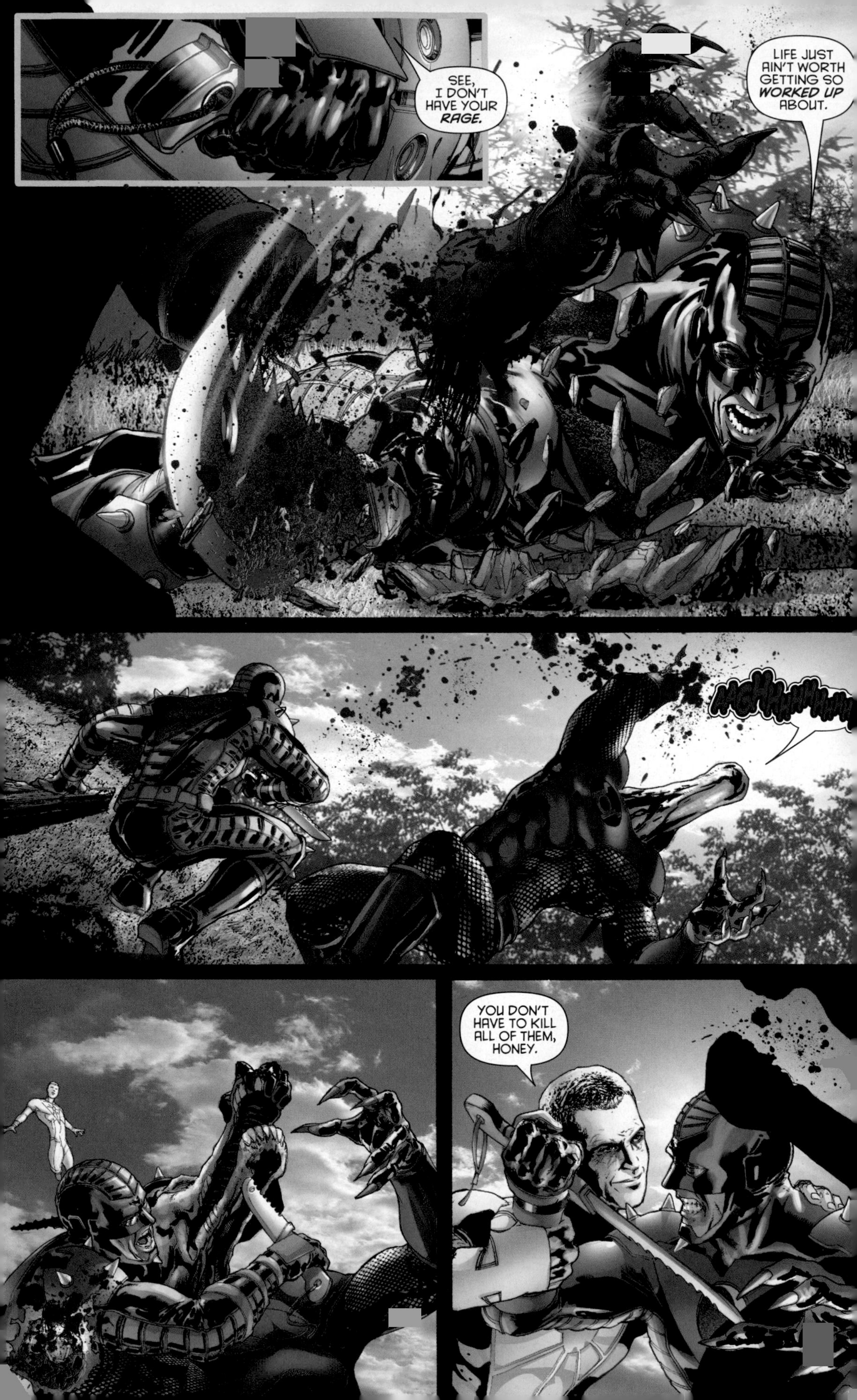
SEE, I DON'T HAVE YOUR RAGE.
LIFE JUST AIN'T WORTH GETTING SO WORKED UP ABOUT.
AAGHHHHHHH
YOU DON'T HAVE TO KILL ALL OF THEM, HONEY.

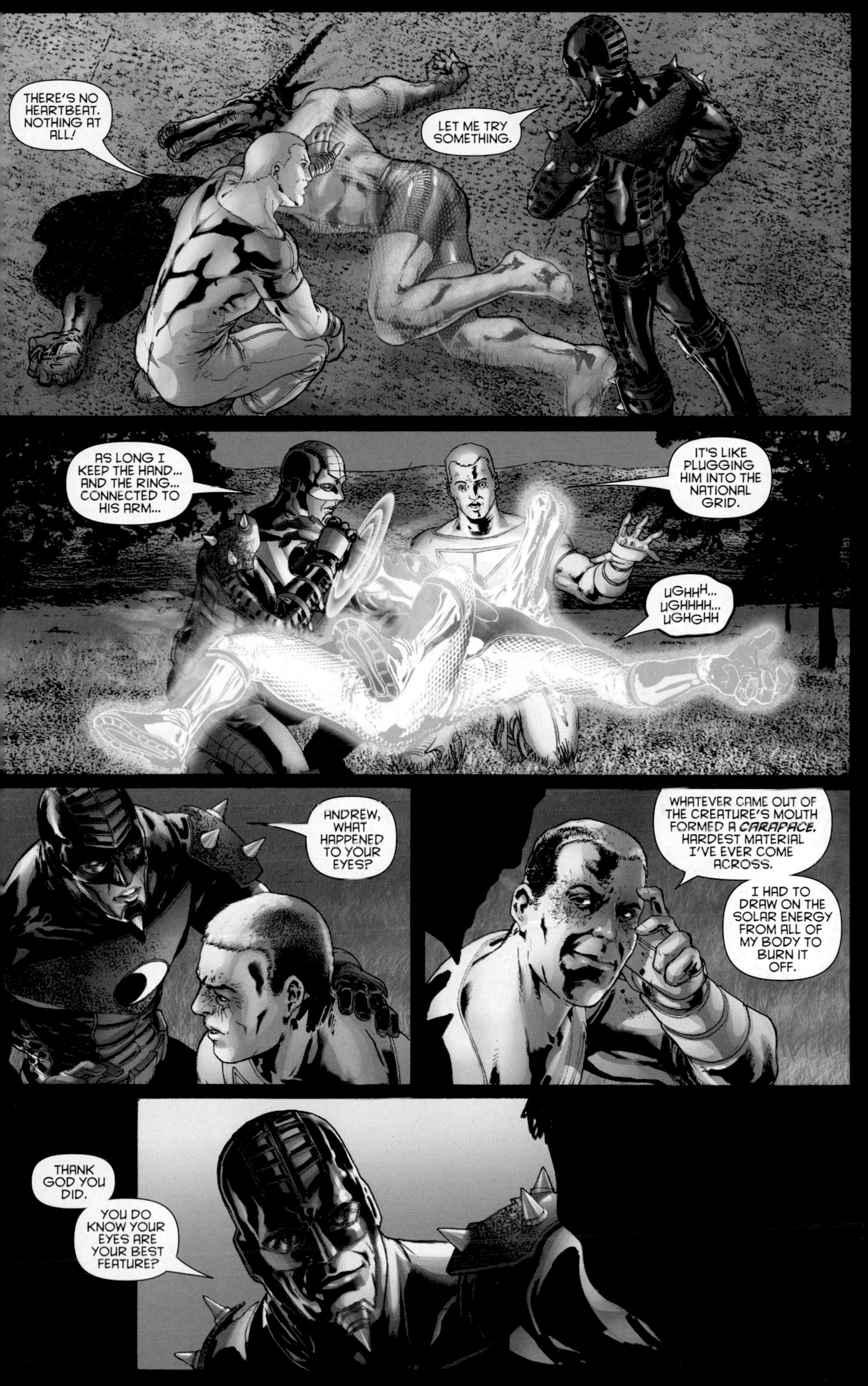
THERE'S NO HEARTBEAT. NOTHING AT ALL!
LET ME TRY SOMETHING.
AS LONG I KEEP THE HAND... AND THE RING... CONNECTED TO HIS ARM...
IT'S LIKE PLUGGING HIM INTO THE NATIONAL GRID.
UGHHH... UGHHHH... UGHGHH
ANDREW, WHAT HAPPENED TO YOUR EYES?
WHATEVER CAME OUT OF THE CREATURE'S MOUTH FORMED A *CARAPACE*. HARDEST MATERIAL I'VE EVER COME ACROSS.
I HAD TO DRAW ON THE SOLAR ENERGY FROM ALL OF MY BODY TO BURN IT OFF.
THANK GOD YOU DID.
YOU DO KNOW YOUR EYES ARE YOUR BEST FEATURE?

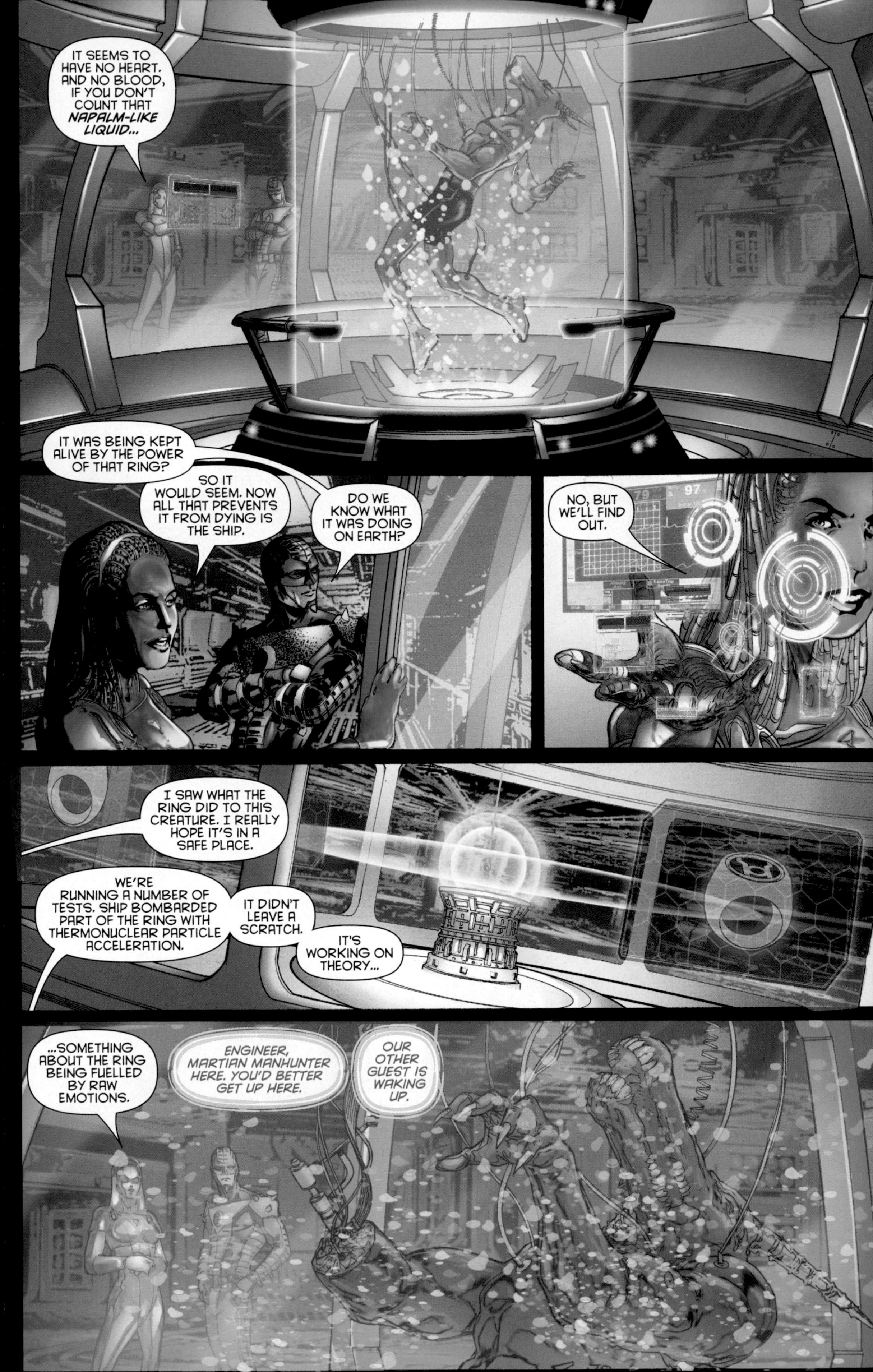
IT SEEMS TO HAVE NO HEART. AND NO BLOOD, IF YOU DON'T COUNT THAT *NAPALM-LIKE LIQUID*...
IT WAS BEING KEPT ALIVE BY THE POWER OF THAT RING?
SO IT WOULD SEEM. NOW ALL THAT PREVENTS IT FROM DYING IS THE SHIP.
DO WE KNOW WHAT IT WAS DOING ON EARTH?
NO, BUT WE'LL FIND OUT.
I SAW WHAT THE RING DID TO THIS CREATURE. I REALLY HOPE IT'S IN A SAFE PLACE.
WE'RE RUNNING A NUMBER OF TESTS. SHIP BOMBARDED PART OF THE RING WITH THERMONUCLEAR PARTICLE ACCELERATION.
IT DIDN'T LEAVE A SCRATCH.
IT'S WORKING ON THEORY...
...SOMETHING ABOUT THE RING BEING FUELLED BY RAW EMOTIONS.
ENGINEER, MARTIAN MANHUNTER HERE. YOU'D BETTER GET UP HERE.
OUR OTHER GUEST IS WAKING UP.

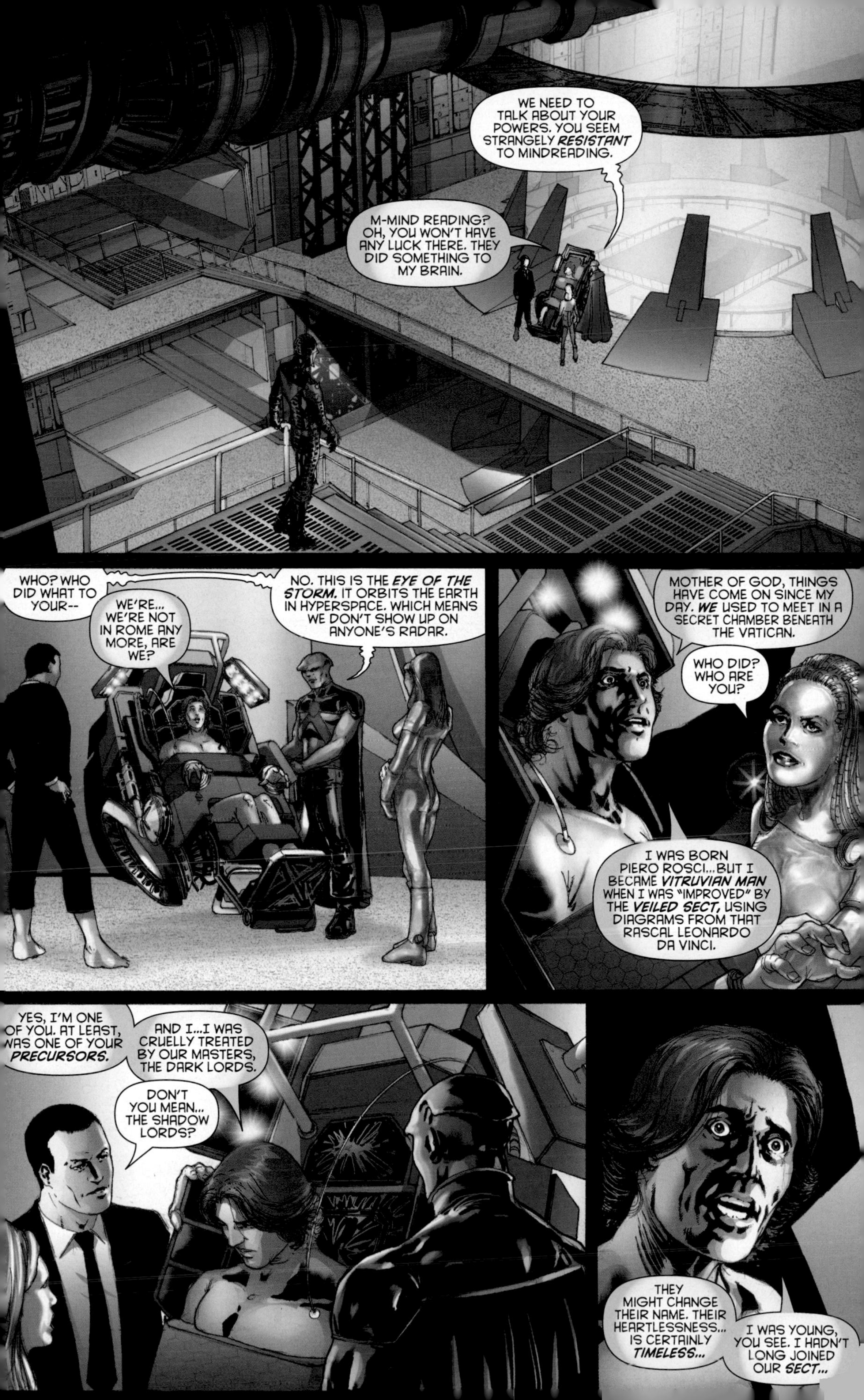
WE NEED TO TALK ABOUT YOUR POWERS. YOU SEEM STRANGELY RESISTANT TO MINDREADING.
M-MIND READING? OH, YOU WON'T HAVE ANY LUCK THERE. THEY DID SOMETHING TO MY BRAIN.
WHO? WHO DID WHAT TO YOUR--
WE'RE... WE'RE NOT IN ROME ANY MORE, ARE WE?
NO. THIS IS THE EYE OF THE STORM. IT ORBITS THE EARTH IN HYPERSPACE. WHICH MEANS WE DON'T SHOW UP ON ANYONE'S RADAR.
MOTHER OF GOD, THINGS HAVE COME ON SINCE MY DAY. WE USED TO MEET IN A SECRET CHAMBER BENEATH THE VATICAN.
WHO DID? WHO ARE YOU?
I WAS BORN PIERO ROSCI...BUT I BECAME VITRUVIAN MAN WHEN I WAS "IMPROVED" BY THE VEILED SECT, USING DIAGRAMS FROM THAT RASCAL LEONARDO DA VINCI.
YES, I'M ONE OF YOU. AT LEAST, WAS ONE OF YOUR PRECURSORS.
AND I...I WAS CRUELLY TREATED BY OUR MASTERS, THE DARK LORDS.
DON'T YOU MEAN... THE SHADOW LORDS?
THEY MIGHT CHANGE THEIR NAME. THEIR HEARTLESSNESS... IS CERTAINLY TIMELESS...
I WAS YOUNG, YOU SEE. I HADN'T LONG JOINED OUR SECT...

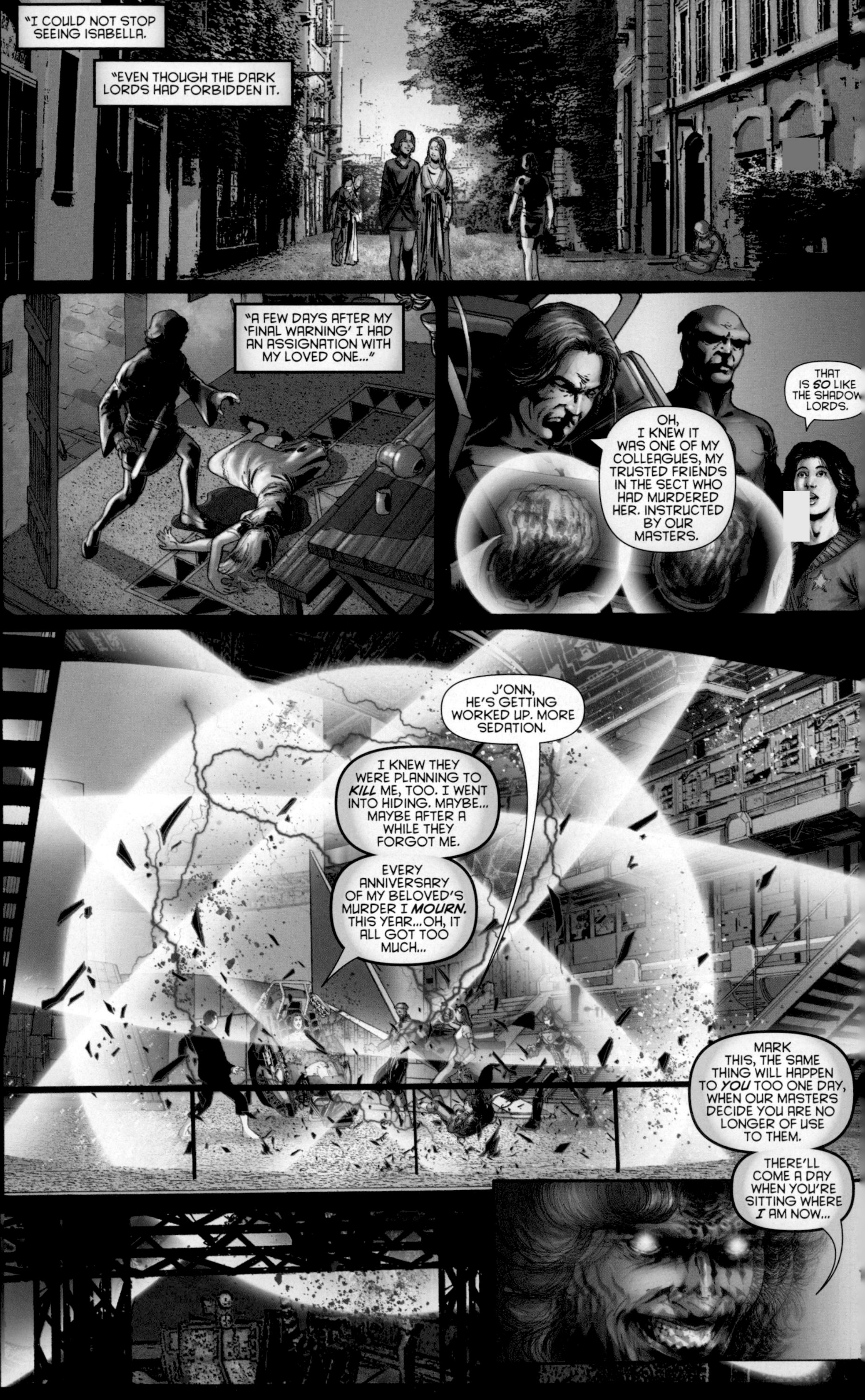
"I COULD NOT STOP SEEING ISABELLA.
"EVEN THOUGH THE DARK LORDS HAD FORBIDDEN IT.
"A FEW DAYS AFTER MY 'FINAL WARNING' I HAD AN ASSIGNATION WITH MY LOVED ONE..."
OH, I KNEW IT WAS ONE OF MY COLLEAGUES, MY TRUSTED FRIENDS IN THE SECT WHO HAD MURDERED HER. INSTRUCTED BY OUR MASTERS.
THAT IS SO LIKE THE SHADOW LORDS.
I KNEW THEY WERE PLANNING TO KILL ME, TOO. I WENT INTO HIDING. MAYBE... MAYBE AFTER A WHILE THEY FORGOT ME.
EVERY ANNIVERSARY OF MY BELOVED'S MURDER I MOURN. THIS YEAR...OH, IT ALL GOT TOO MUCH...
J'ONN, HE'S GETTING WORKED UP. MORE SEDATION.
MARK THIS, THE SAME THING WILL HAPPEN TO YOU TOO ONE DAY, WHEN OUR MASTERS DECIDE YOU ARE NO LONGER OF USE TO THEM.
THERE'LL COME A DAY WHEN YOU'RE SITTING WHERE I AM NOW...

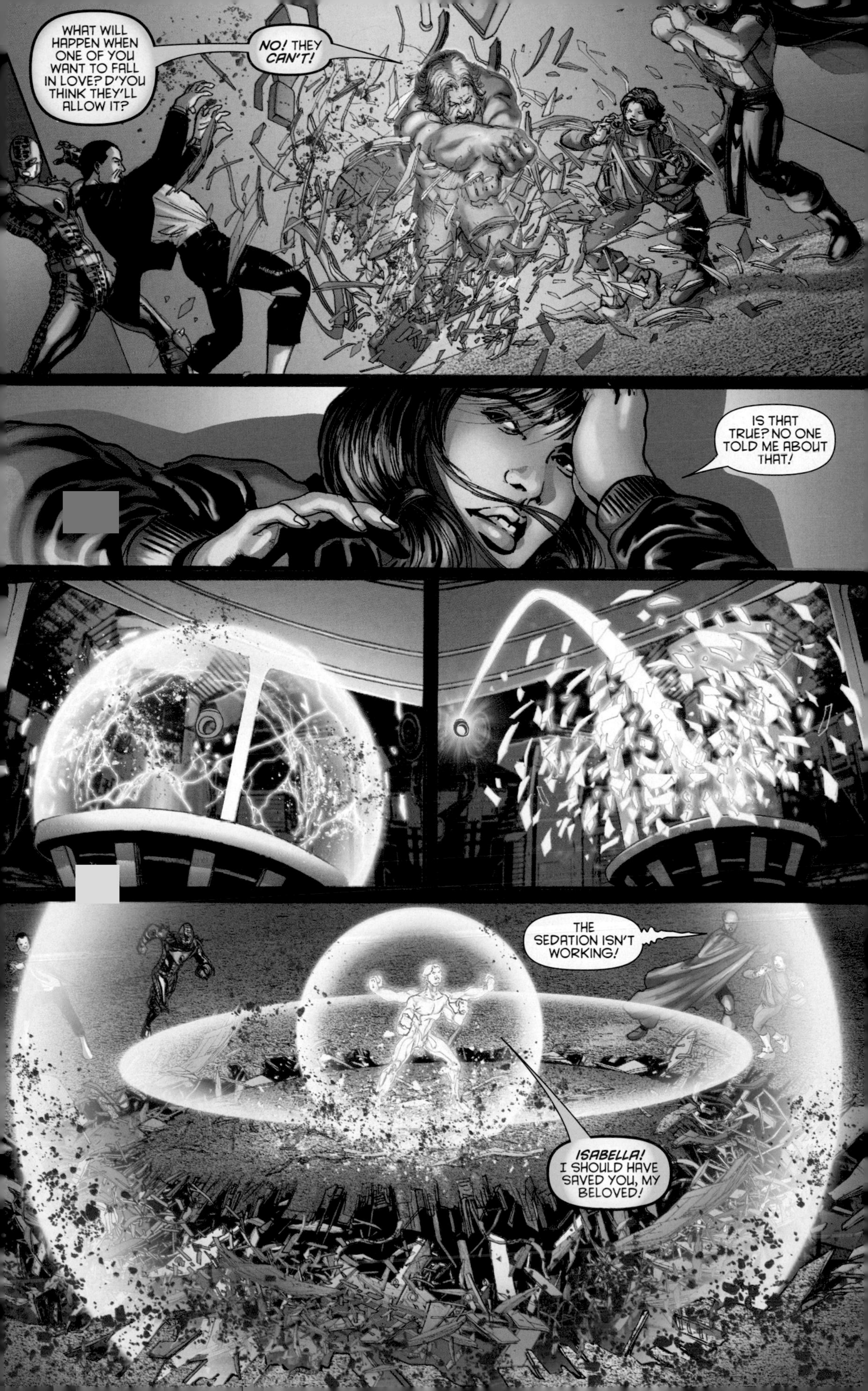

WHAT WILL HAPPEN WHEN ONE OF YOU WANT TO FALL IN LOVE? D'YOU THINK THEY'LL ALLOW IT?
NO! THEY *CAN'T!*
IS THAT TRUE? NO ONE TOLD ME ABOUT THAT!
THE SEDATION ISN'T WORKING!
ISABELLA! I SHOULD HAVE SAVED YOU, MY BELOVED!

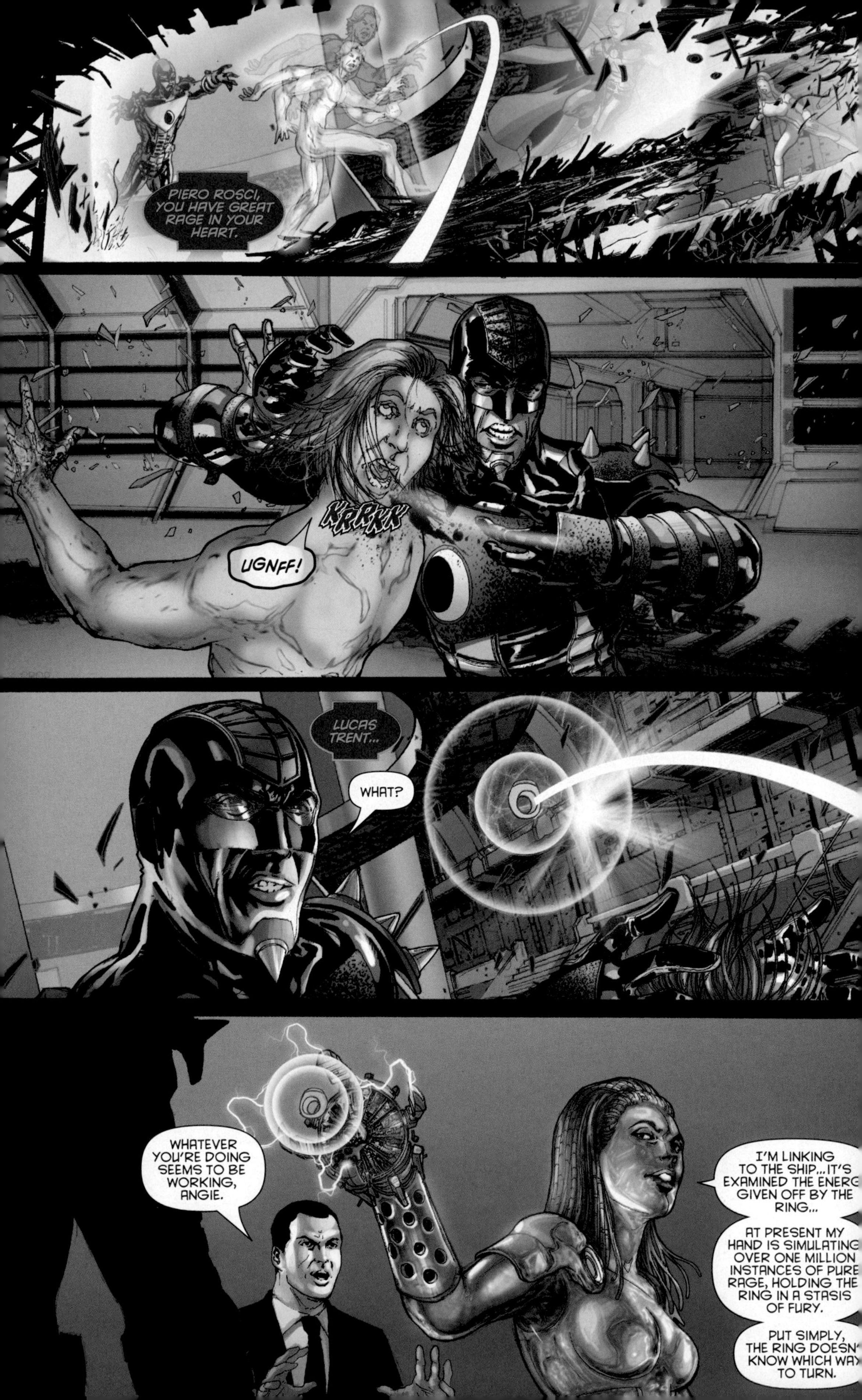
PIERO ROSCI, YOU HAVE GREAT RAGE IN YOUR HEART.
KRRKK
UGNFF!
LUCAS TRENT...
WHAT?
WHATEVER YOU'RE DOING SEEMS TO BE WORKING, ANGIE.
I'M LINKING TO THE SHIP...IT'S EXAMINED THE ENERG GIVEN OFF BY THE RING...
AT PRESENT MY HAND IS SIMULATING OVER ONE MILLION INSTANCES OF PURE RAGE, HOLDING THE RING IN A STASIS OF FURY.
PUT SIMPLY, THE RING DOESN' KNOW WHICH WAY TO TURN.

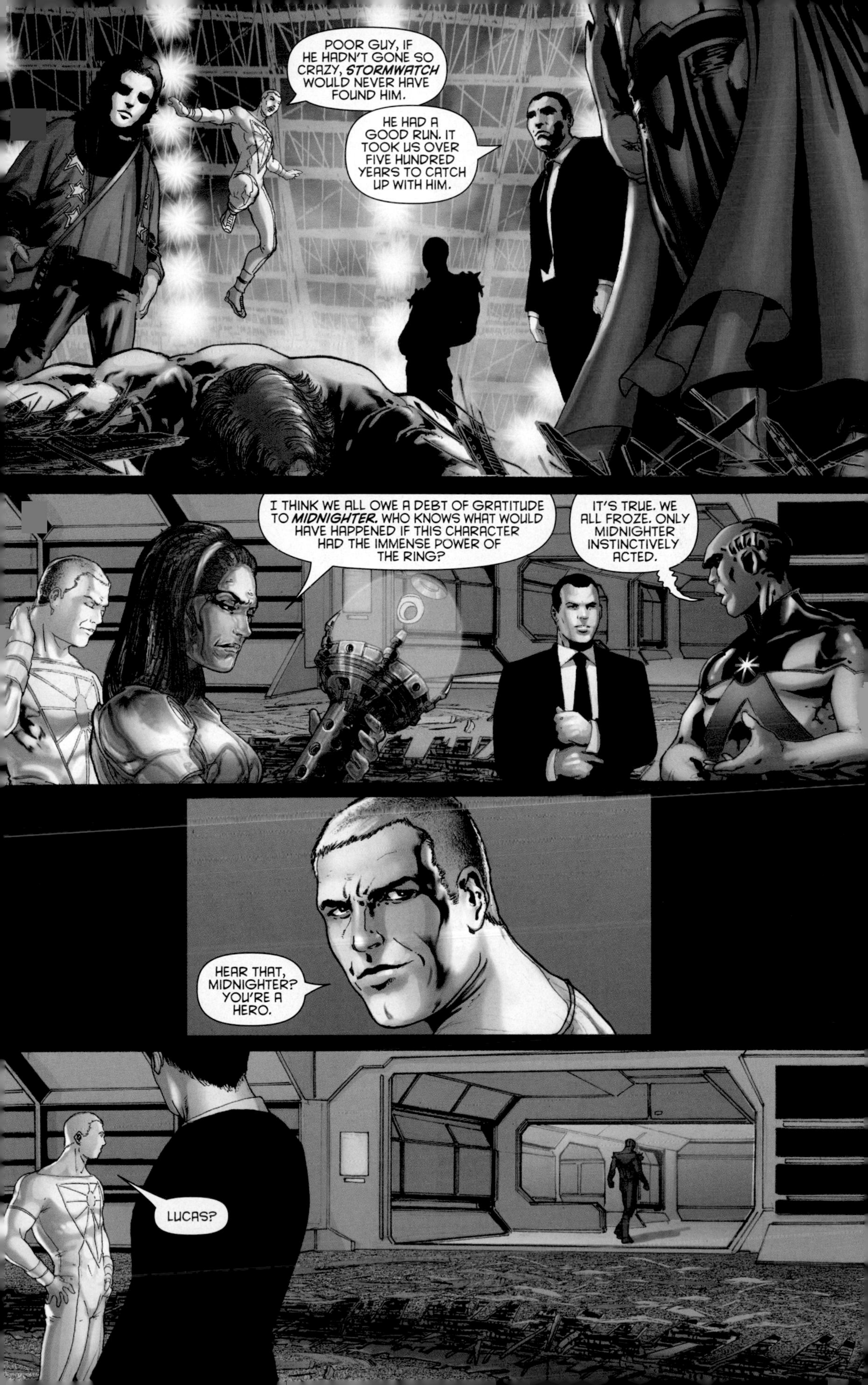
POOR GUY, IF HE HADN'T GONE SO CRAZY, STORMWATCH WOULD NEVER HAVE FOUND HIM.
HE HAD A GOOD RUN. IT TOOK US OVER FIVE HUNDRED YEARS TO CATCH UP WITH HIM.
I THINK WE ALL OWE A DEBT OF GRATITUDE TO MIDNIGHTER. WHO KNOWS WHAT WOULD HAVE HAPPENED IF THIS CHARACTER HAD THE IMMENSE POWER OF THE RING?
IT'S TRUE. WE ALL FROZE. ONLY MIDNIGHTER INSTINCTIVELY ACTED.
HEAR THAT, MIDNIGHTER? YOU'RE A HERO.
LUCAS?

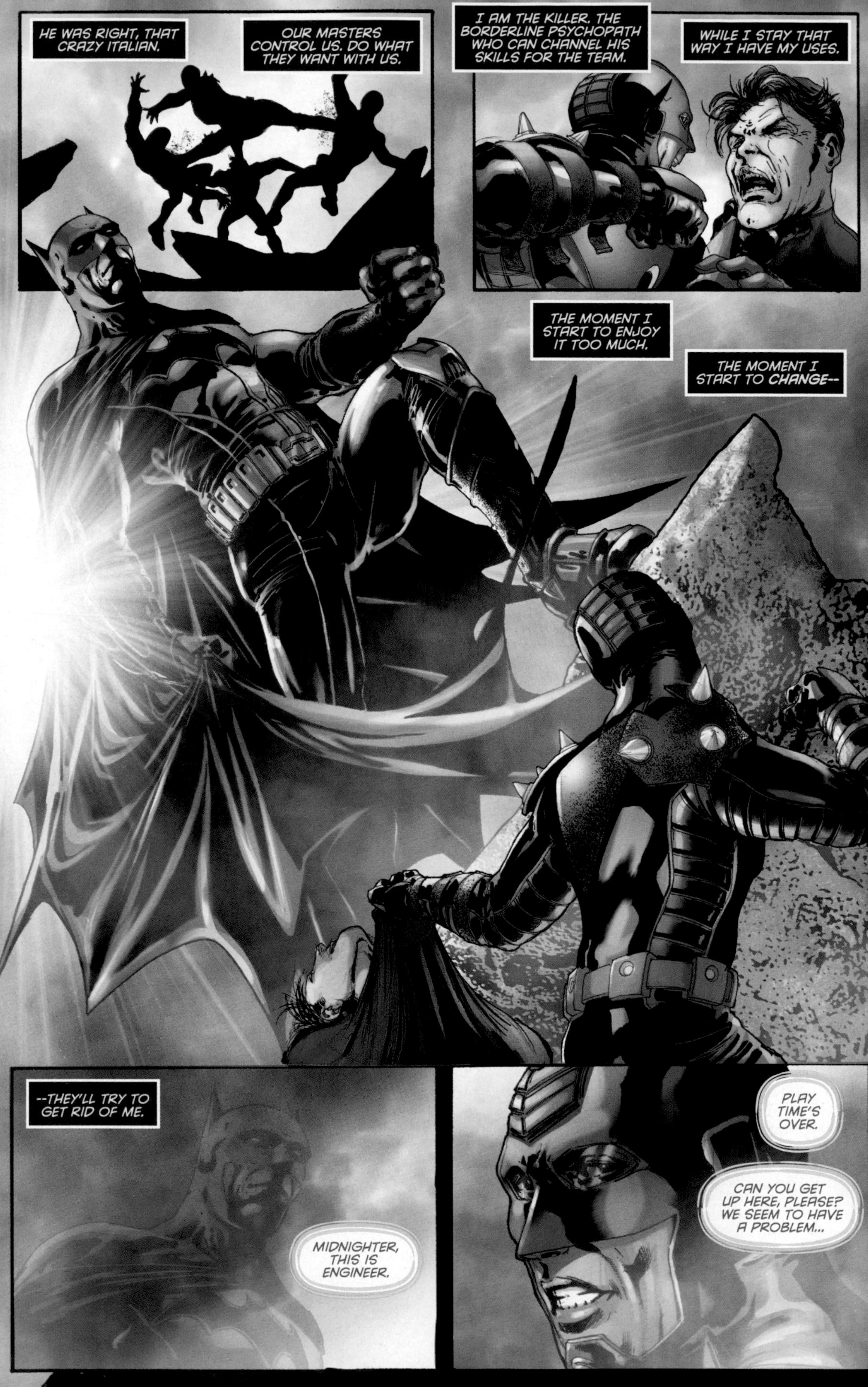
HE WAS RIGHT, THAT CRAZY ITALIAN.
OUR MASTERS CONTROL US. DO WHAT THEY WANT WITH US.
I AM THE KILLER. THE BORDERLINE PSYCHOPATH WHO CAN CHANNEL HIS SKILLS FOR THE TEAM.
WHILE I STAY THAT WAY I HAVE MY USES.
THE MOMENT I START TO ENJOY IT TOO MUCH.
THE MOMENT I START TO CHANGE--
--THEY'LL TRY TO GET RID OF ME.
MIDNIGHTER, THIS IS ENGINEER.
PLAY TIME'S OVER.
CAN YOU GET UP HERE, PLEASE? WE SEEM TO HAVE A PROBLEM...

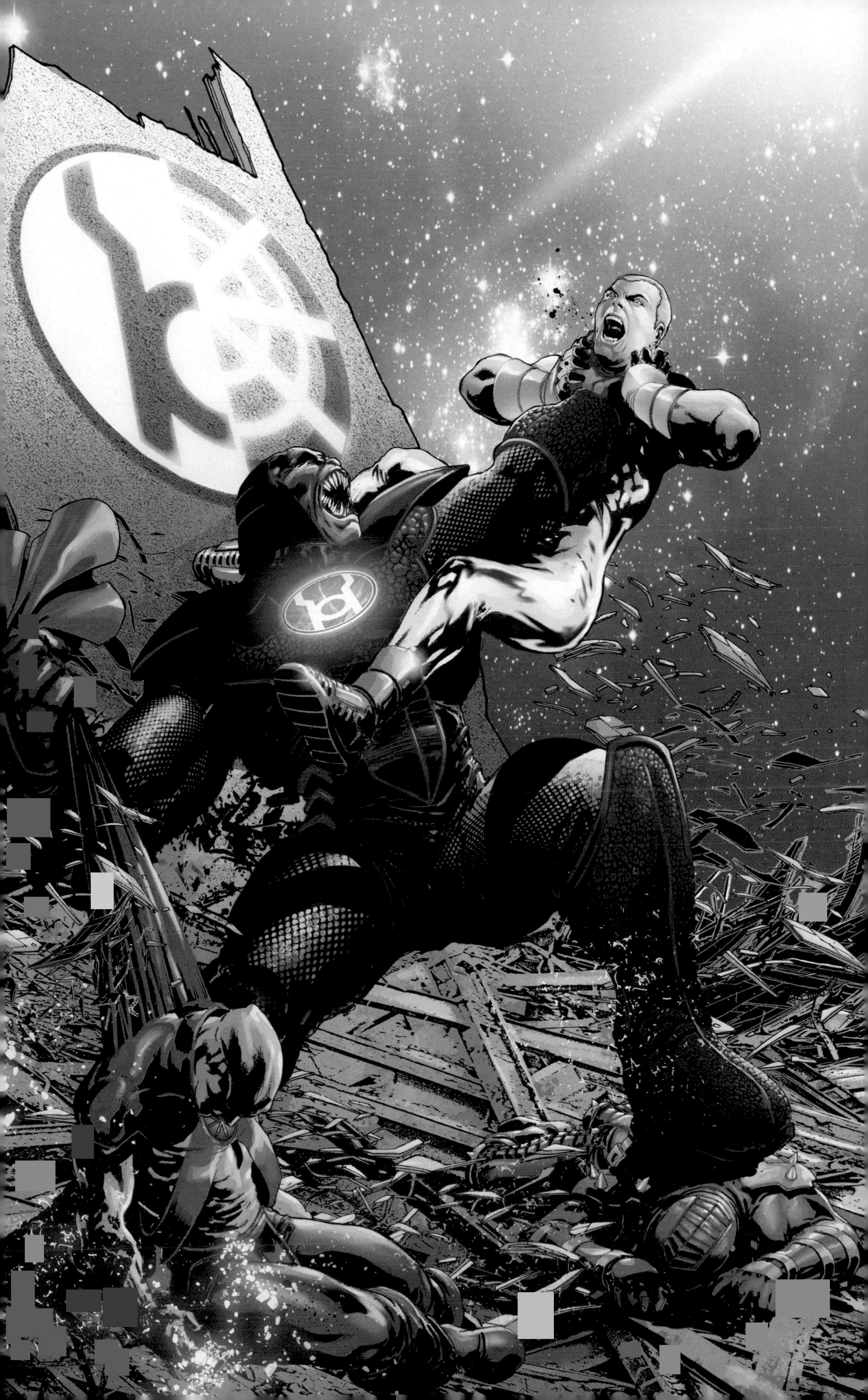

TWO LANTERNS

PETER MILLIGAN
writer

MIGUEL SEPULVEDA
artist

cover art by MIGUEL SEPULVEDA & RAIN BEREDO

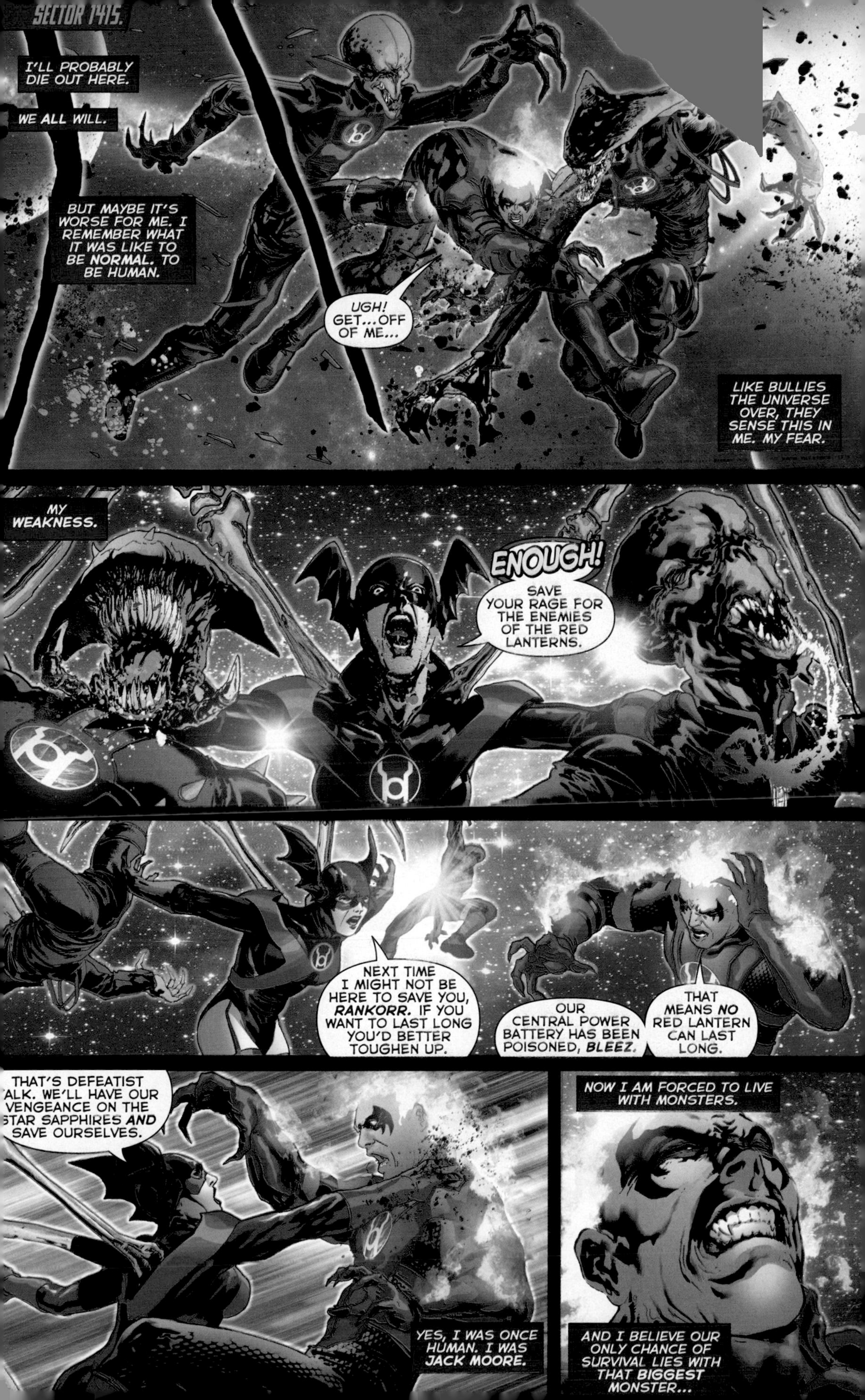

SECTOR 1415.
I'LL PROBABLY DIE OUT HERE.
WE ALL WILL.
BUT MAYBE IT'S WORSE FOR ME. I REMEMBER WHAT IT WAS LIKE TO BE NORMAL. TO BE HUMAN.
UGH! GET...OFF OF ME...
LIKE BULLIES THE UNIVERSE OVER, THEY SENSE THIS IN ME. MY FEAR.
MY WEAKNESS.
ENOUGH!
SAVE YOUR RAGE FOR THE ENEMIES OF THE RED LANTERNS.
NEXT TIME I MIGHT NOT BE HERE TO SAVE YOU, RANKORR. IF YOU WANT TO LAST LONG YOU'D BETTER TOUGHEN UP.
OUR CENTRAL POWER BATTERY HAS BEEN POISONED, BLEEZ.
THAT MEANS NO RED LANTERN CAN LAST LONG.
THAT'S DEFEATIST TALK. WE'LL HAVE OUR VENGEANCE ON THE STAR SAPPHIRES AND SAVE OURSELVES.
YES, I WAS ONCE HUMAN. I WAS JACK MOORE.
NOW I AM FORCED TO LIVE WITH MONSTERS.
AND I BELIEVE OUR ONLY CHANCE OF SURVIVAL LIES WITH THAT BIGGEST MONSTER...

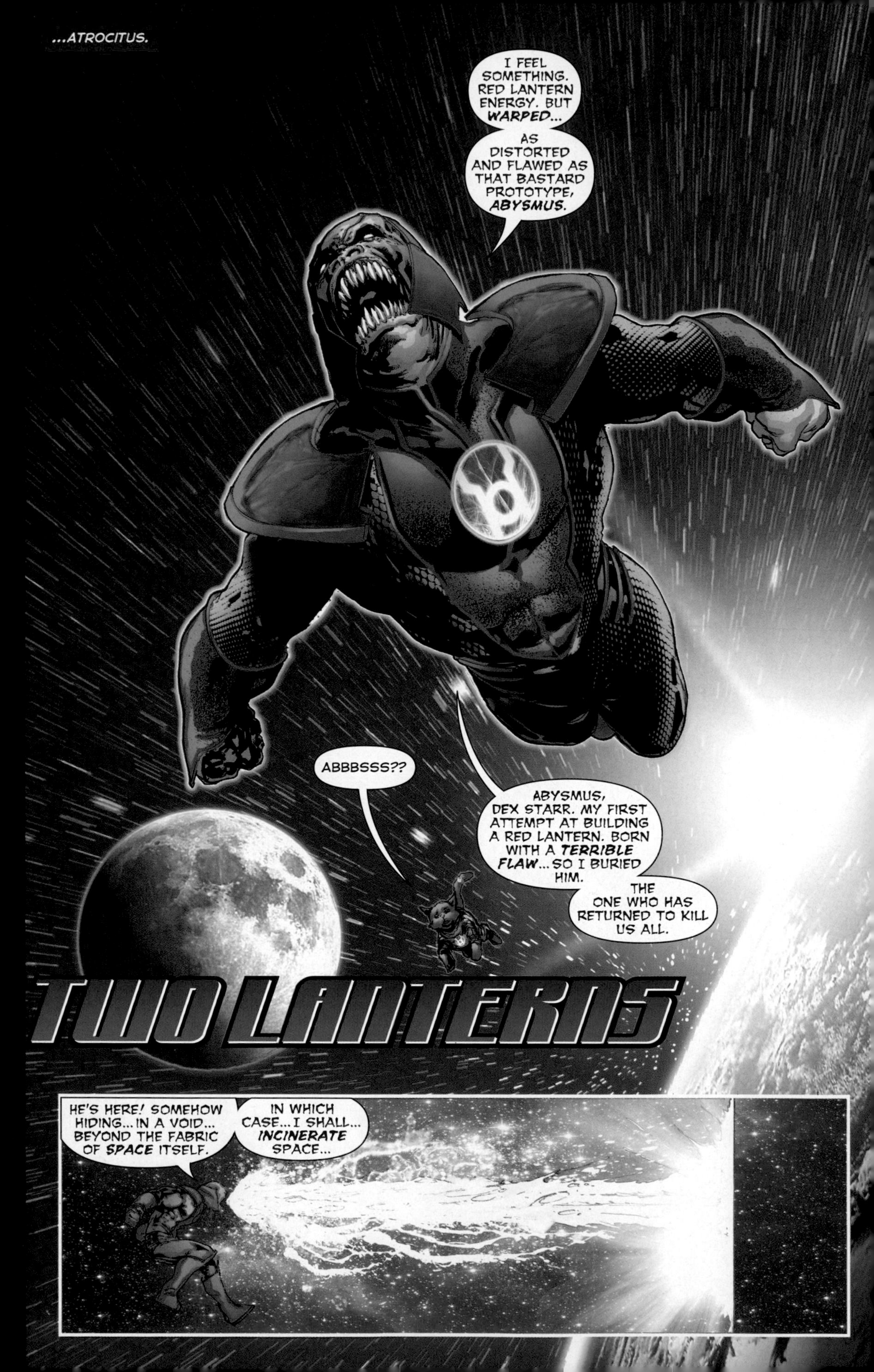
...ATROCITUS.
I FEEL SOMETHING. RED LANTERN ENERGY. BUT WARPED...
AS DISTORTED AND FLAWED AS THAT BASTARD PROTOTYPE, ABYSMUS.
ABBBSSS??
ABYSMUS, DEX STARR. MY FIRST ATTEMPT AT BUILDING A RED LANTERN. BORN WITH A TERRIBLE FLAW...SO I BURIED HIM.
THE ONE WHO HAS RETURNED TO KILL US ALL.
TWO LANTERNS
HE'S HERE! SOMEHOW HIDING...IN A VOID... BEYOND THE FABRIC OF SPACE ITSELF.
IN WHICH CASE...I SHALL... INCINERATE SPACE...

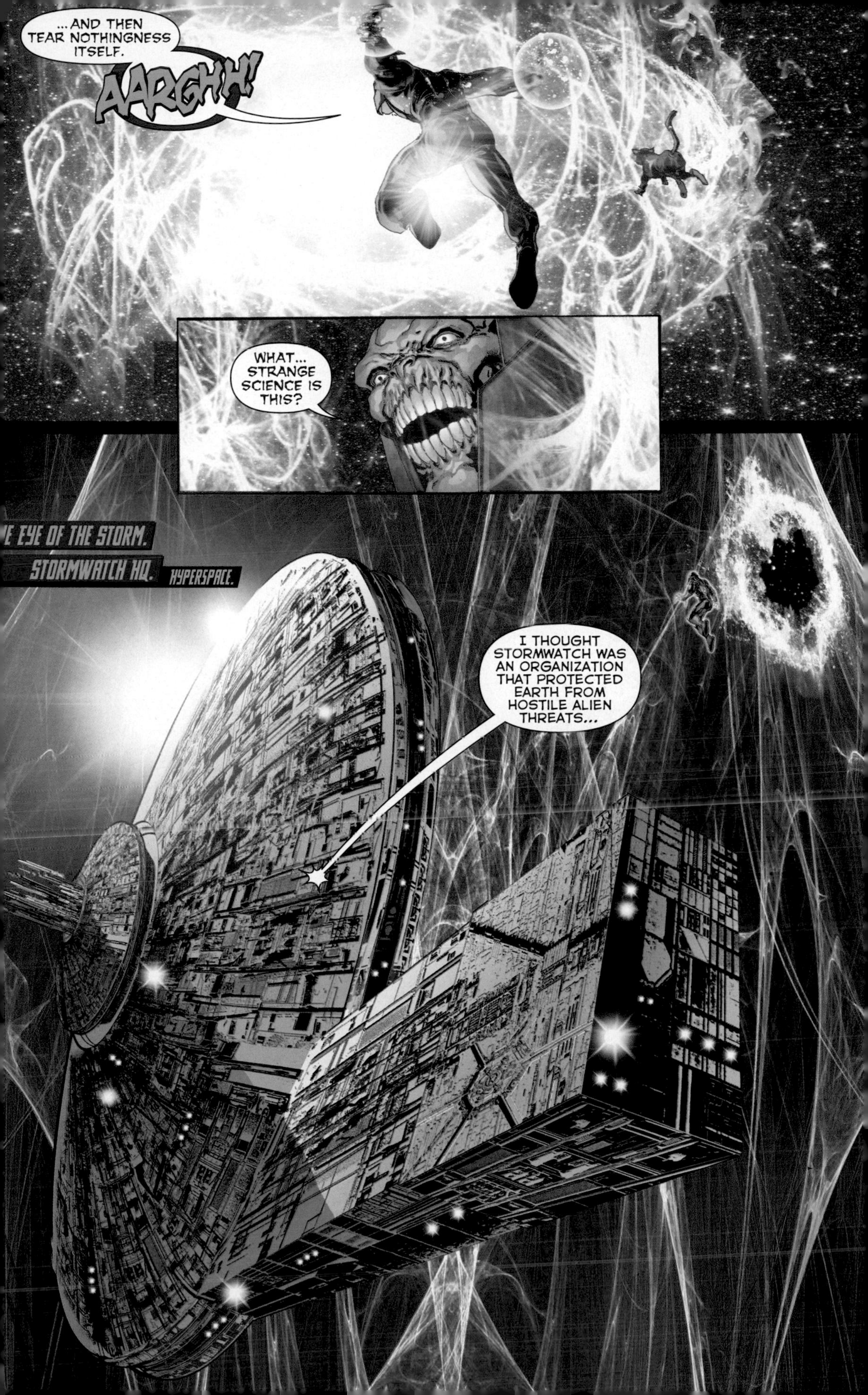

...AND THEN TEAR NOTHINGNESS ITSELF.
AARGHH!
WHAT... STRANGE SCIENCE IS THIS?
E EYE OF THE STORM.
STORMWATCH HQ.
HYPERSPACE.
I THOUGHT STORMWATCH WAS AN ORGANIZATION THAT PROTECTED EARTH FROM HOSTILE ALIEN THREATS...

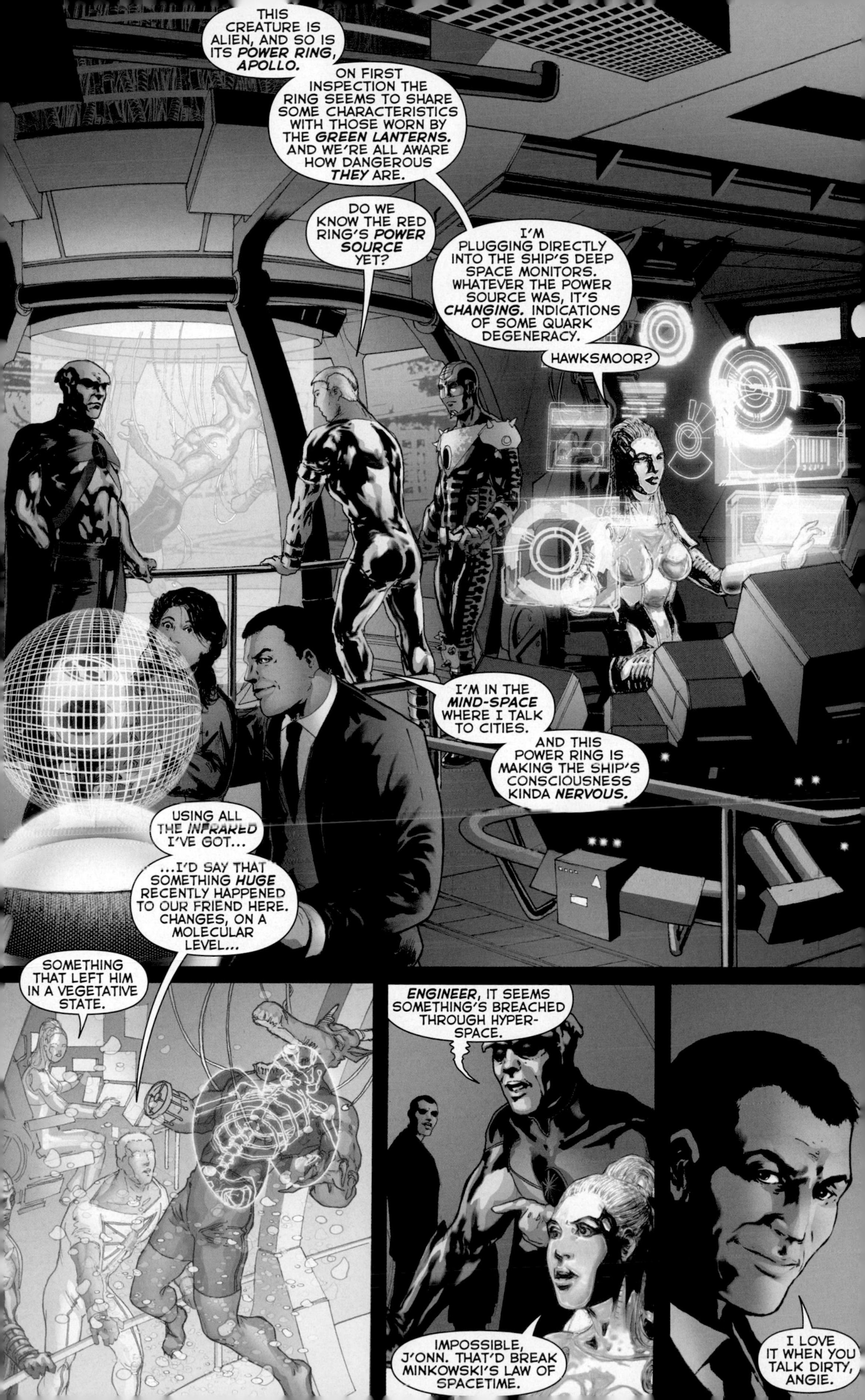
THIS CREATURE IS ALIEN, AND SO IS ITS POWER RING, APOLLO.
ON FIRST INSPECTION THE RING SEEMS TO SHARE SOME CHARACTERISTICS WITH THOSE WORN BY THE GREEN LANTERNS. AND WE'RE ALL AWARE HOW DANGEROUS THEY ARE.
DO WE KNOW THE RED RING'S POWER SOURCE YET?
I'M PLUGGING DIRECTLY INTO THE SHIP'S DEEP SPACE MONITORS. WHATEVER THE POWER SOURCE WAS, IT'S CHANGING. INDICATIONS OF SOME QUARK DEGENERACY.
HAWKSMOOR?
I'M IN THE MIND-SPACE WHERE I TALK TO CITIES.
AND THIS POWER RING IS MAKING THE SHIP'S CONSCIOUSNESS KINDA NERVOUS.
USING ALL THE INFRARED I'VE GOT...
...I'D SAY THAT SOMETHING HUGE RECENTLY HAPPENED TO OUR FRIEND HERE. CHANGES, ON A MOLECULAR LEVEL...
SOMETHING THAT LEFT HIM IN A VEGETATIVE STATE.
ENGINEER, IT SEEMS SOMETHING'S BREACHED THROUGH HYPER-SPACE.
IMPOSSIBLE, J'ONN. THAT'D BREAK MINKOWSKI'S LAW OF SPACETIME.
I LOVE IT WHEN YOU TALK DIRTY, ANGIE.

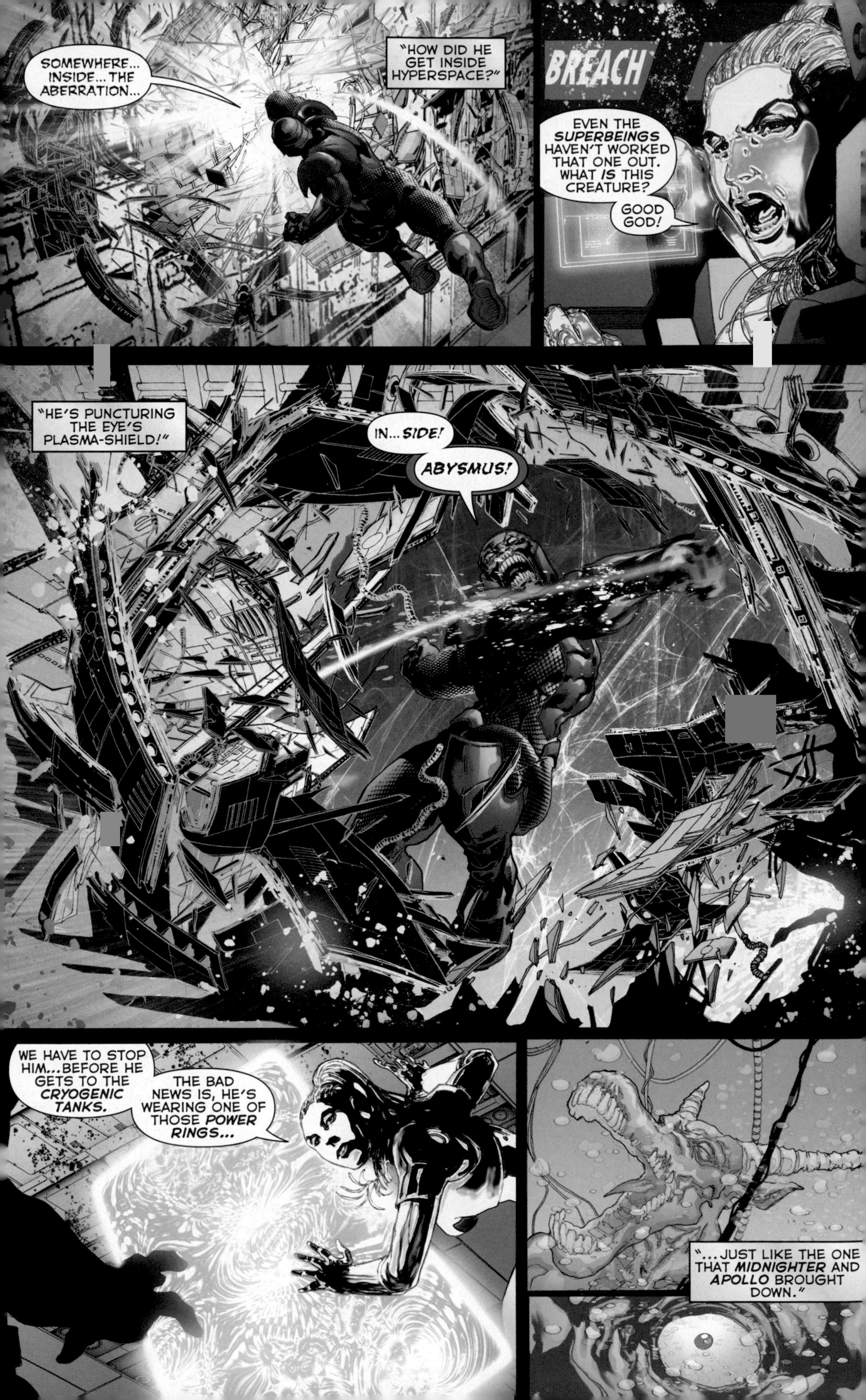
SOMEWHERE... INSIDE... THE ABERRATION...
"HOW DID HE GET INSIDE HYPERSPACE?"
BREACH
EVEN THE SUPERBEINGS HAVEN'T WORKED THAT ONE OUT. WHAT IS THIS CREATURE?
GOOD GOD!
"HE'S PUNCTURING THE EYE'S PLASMA-SHIELD!"
IN... SIDE!
ABYSMUS!
WE HAVE TO STOP HIM...BEFORE HE GETS TO THE CRYOGENIC TANKS.
THE BAD NEWS IS, HE'S WEARING ONE OF THOSE POWER RINGS...
"...JUST LIKE THE ONE THAT MIDNIGHTER AND APOLLO BROUGHT DOWN."

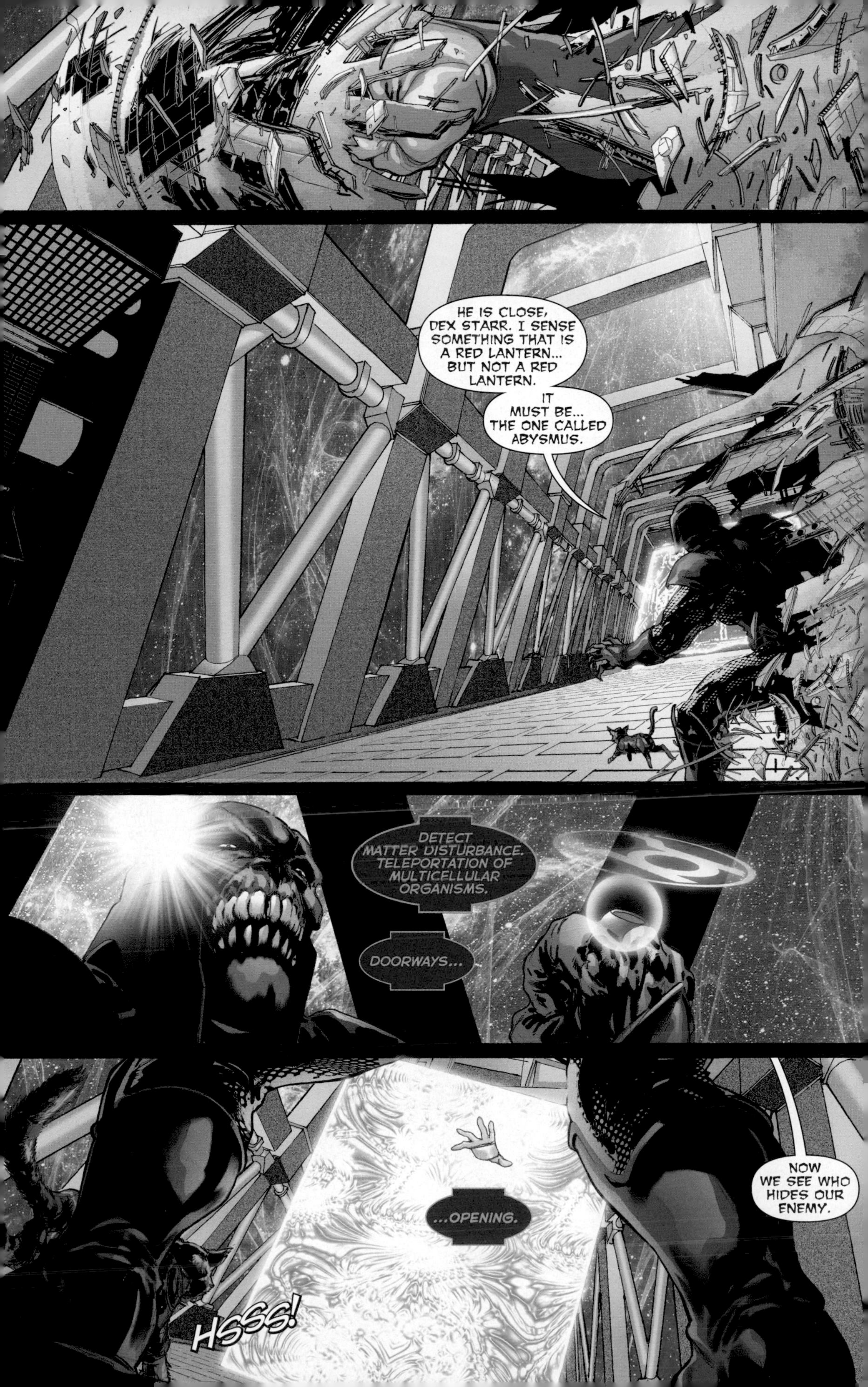
HE IS CLOSE, DEX STARR. I SENSE SOMETHING THAT IS A RED LANTERN... BUT NOT A RED LANTERN.
IT MUST BE... THE ONE CALLED ABYSMUS.
DETECT MATTER DISTURBANCE. TELEPORTATION OF MULTICELLULAR ORGANISMS.
DOORWAYS...
...OPENING.
NOW WE SEE WHO HIDES OUR ENEMY.
HSSS!

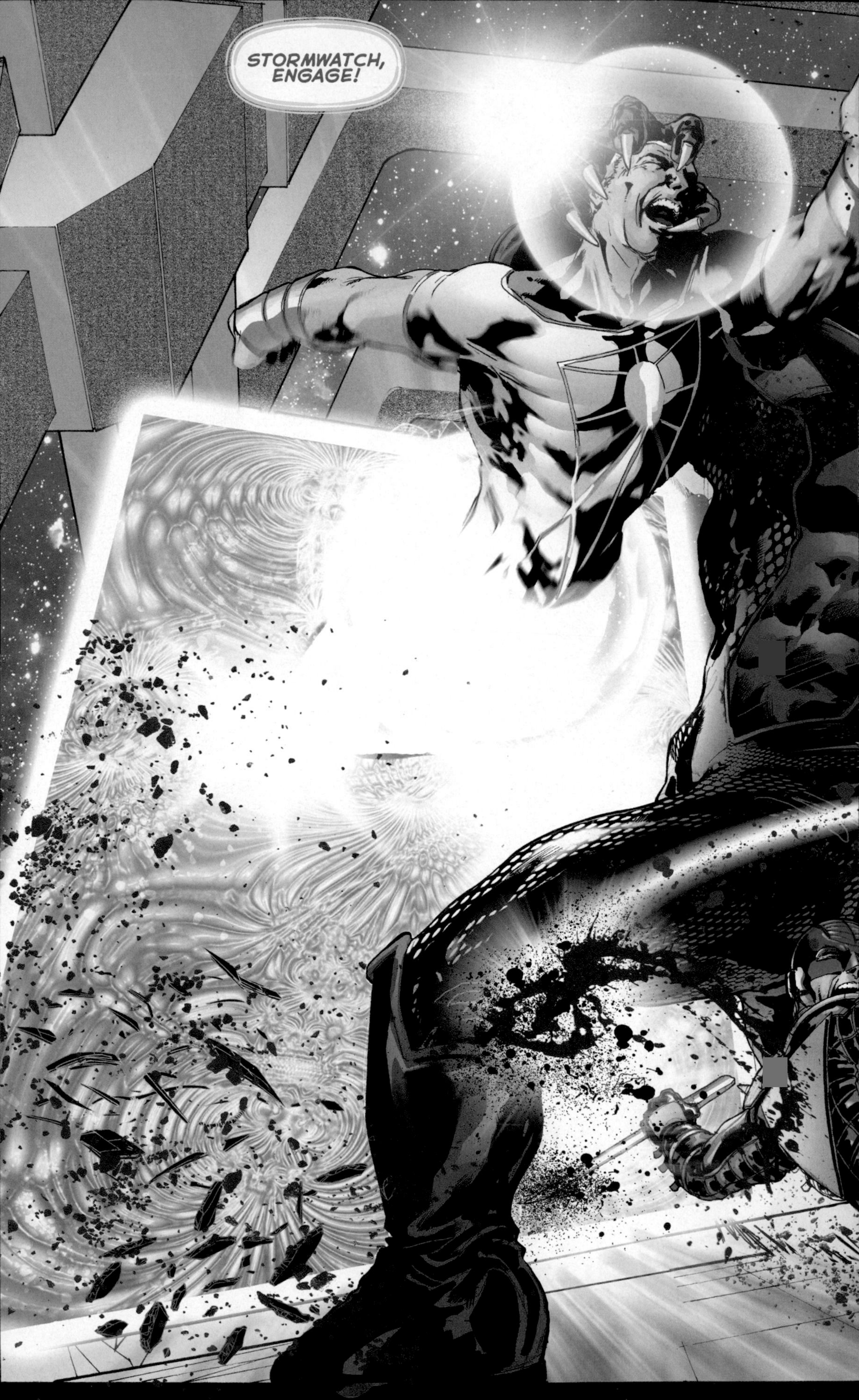
STORMWATCH, ENGAGE!

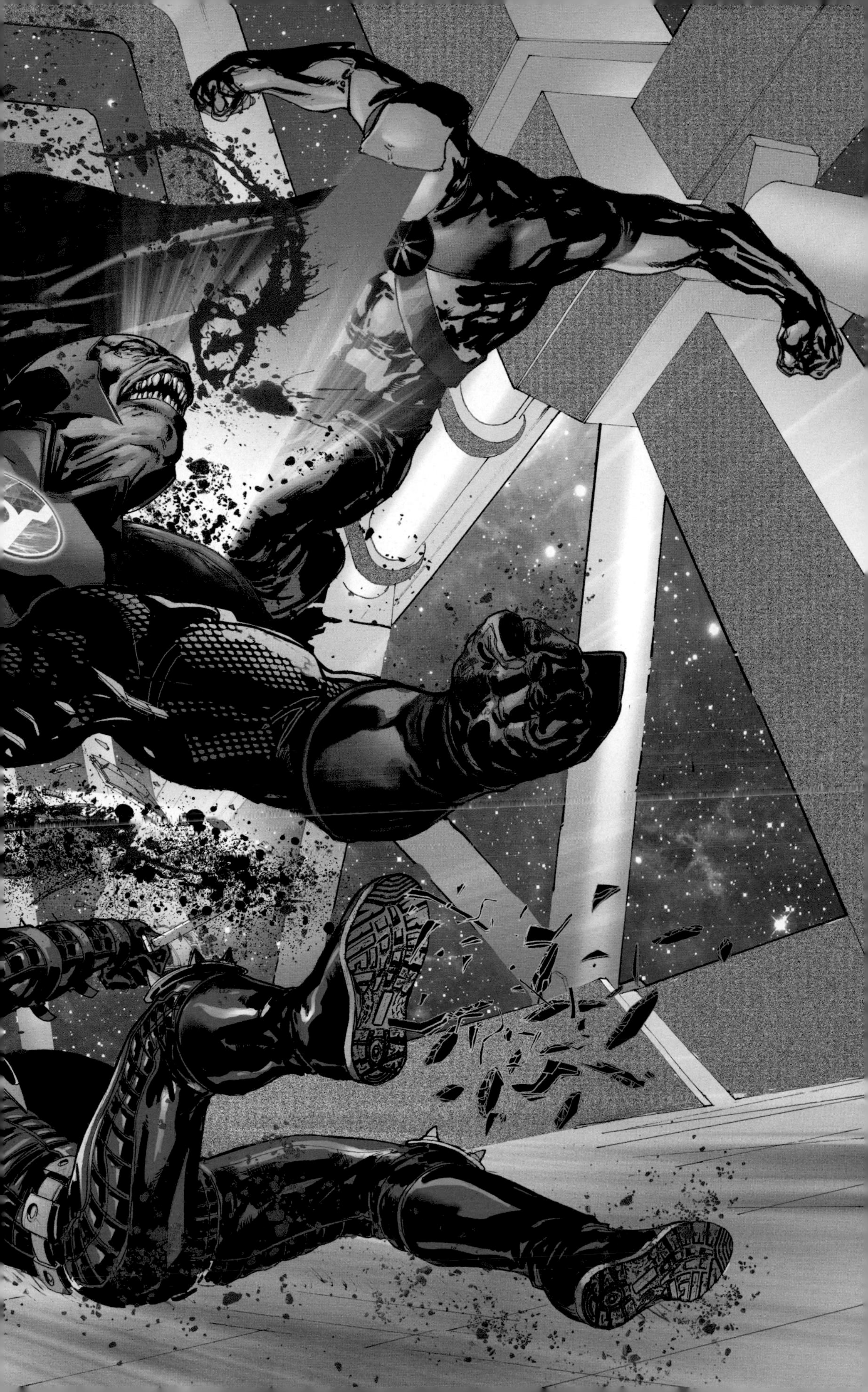

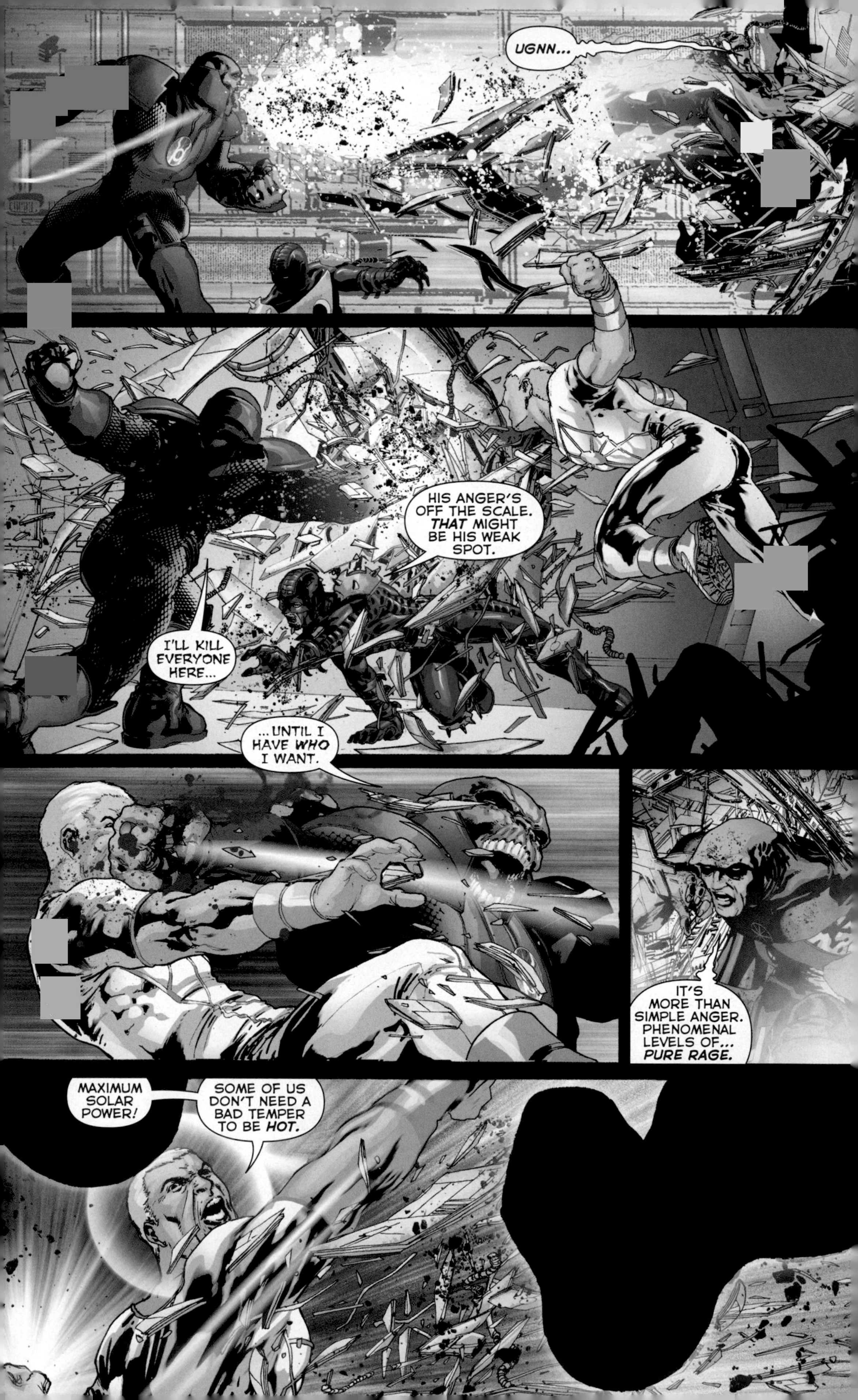
UGNN...
HIS ANGER'S OFF THE SCALE. *THAT* MIGHT BE HIS WEAK SPOT.
I'LL KILL EVERYONE HERE...
...UNTIL I HAVE *WHO* I WANT.
IT'S MORE THAN SIMPLE ANGER. PHENOMENAL LEVELS OF... *PURE RAGE.*
MAXIMUM SOLAR POWER!
SOME OF US DON'T NEED A BAD TEMPER TO BE *HOT.*

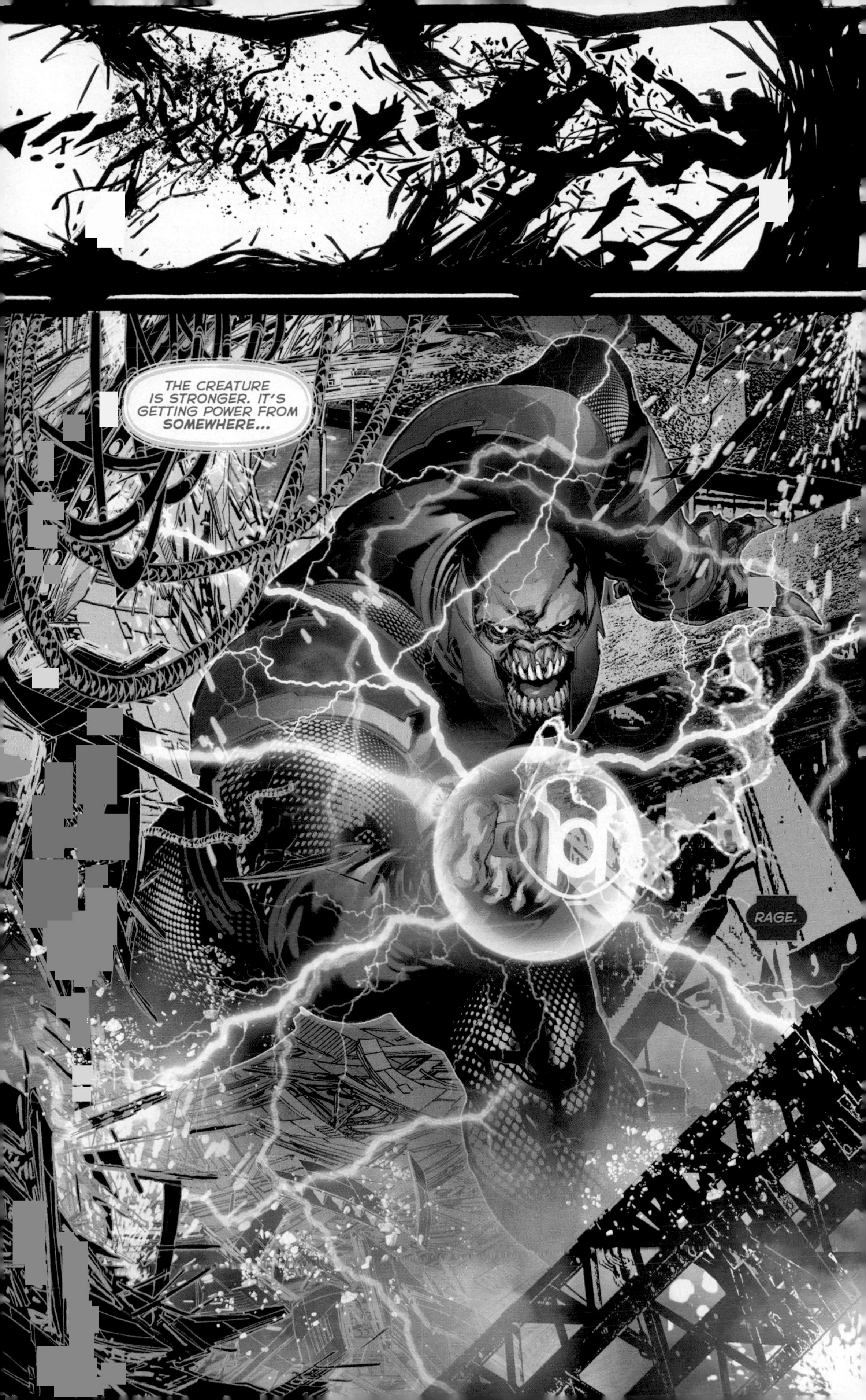
THE CREATURE IS STRONGER. IT'S GETTING POWER FROM SOMEWHERE...
RAGE.

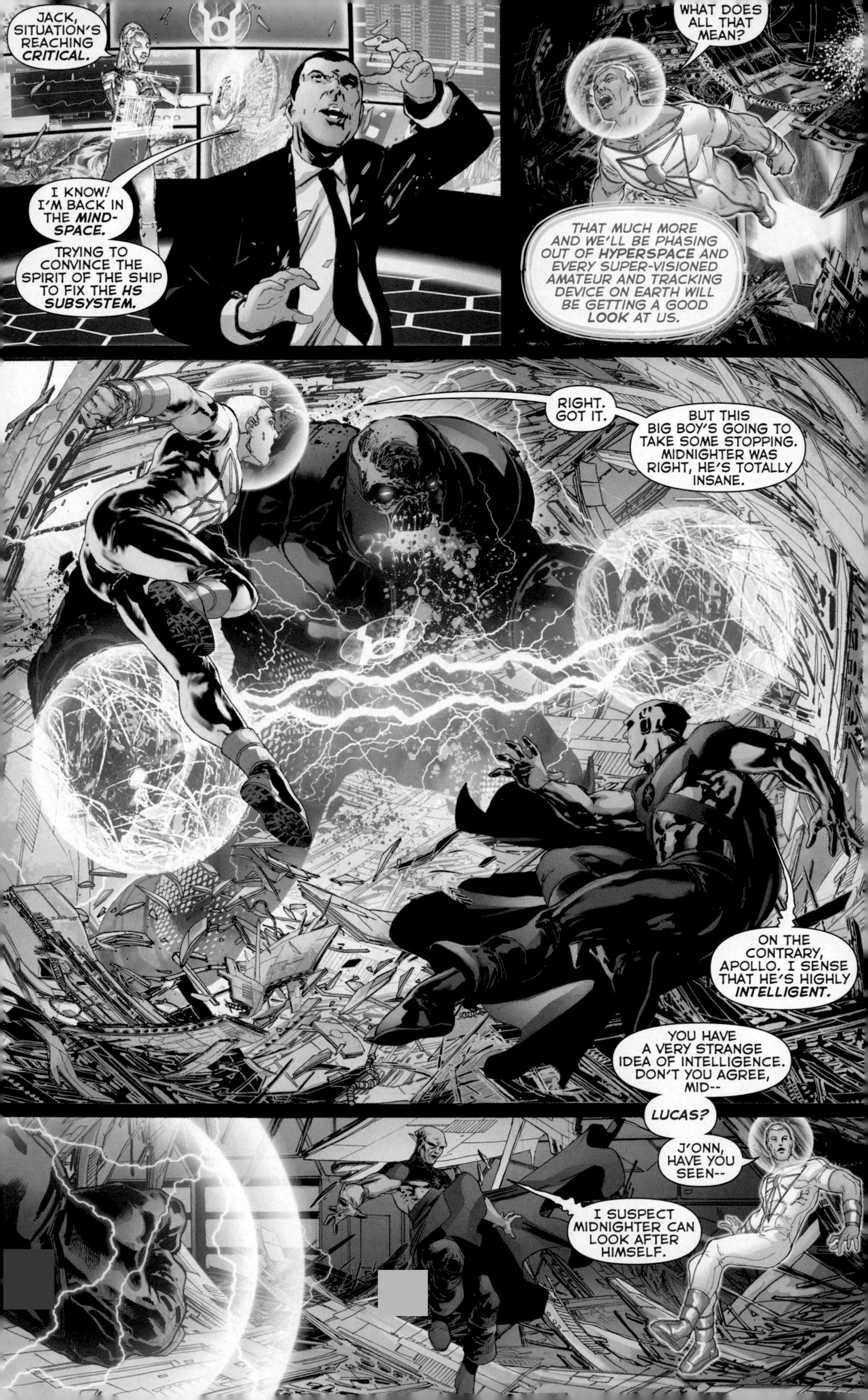
JACK, SITUATION'S REACHING *CRITICAL.*
I KNOW! I'M BACK IN THE *MIND-SPACE.*
TRYING TO CONVINCE THE SPIRIT OF THE SHIP TO FIX THE *HS SUBSYSTEM.*
WHAT DOES ALL THAT MEAN?
THAT MUCH MORE AND WE'LL BE PHASING OUT OF **HYPERSPACE** AND EVERY SUPER-VISIONED AMATEUR AND TRACKING DEVICE ON EARTH WILL BE GETTING A GOOD **LOOK** AT US.
RIGHT. GOT IT.
BUT THIS BIG BOY'S GOING TO TAKE SOME STOPPING. MIDNIGHTER WAS RIGHT, HE'S TOTALLY INSANE.
ON THE CONTRARY, APOLLO. I SENSE THAT HE'S HIGHLY *INTELLIGENT.*
YOU HAVE A VERY STRANGE IDEA OF INTELLIGENCE. DON'T YOU AGREE, MID--
LUCAS?
J'ONN, HAVE YOU SEEN--
I SUSPECT MIDNIGHTER CAN LOOK AFTER HIMSELF.

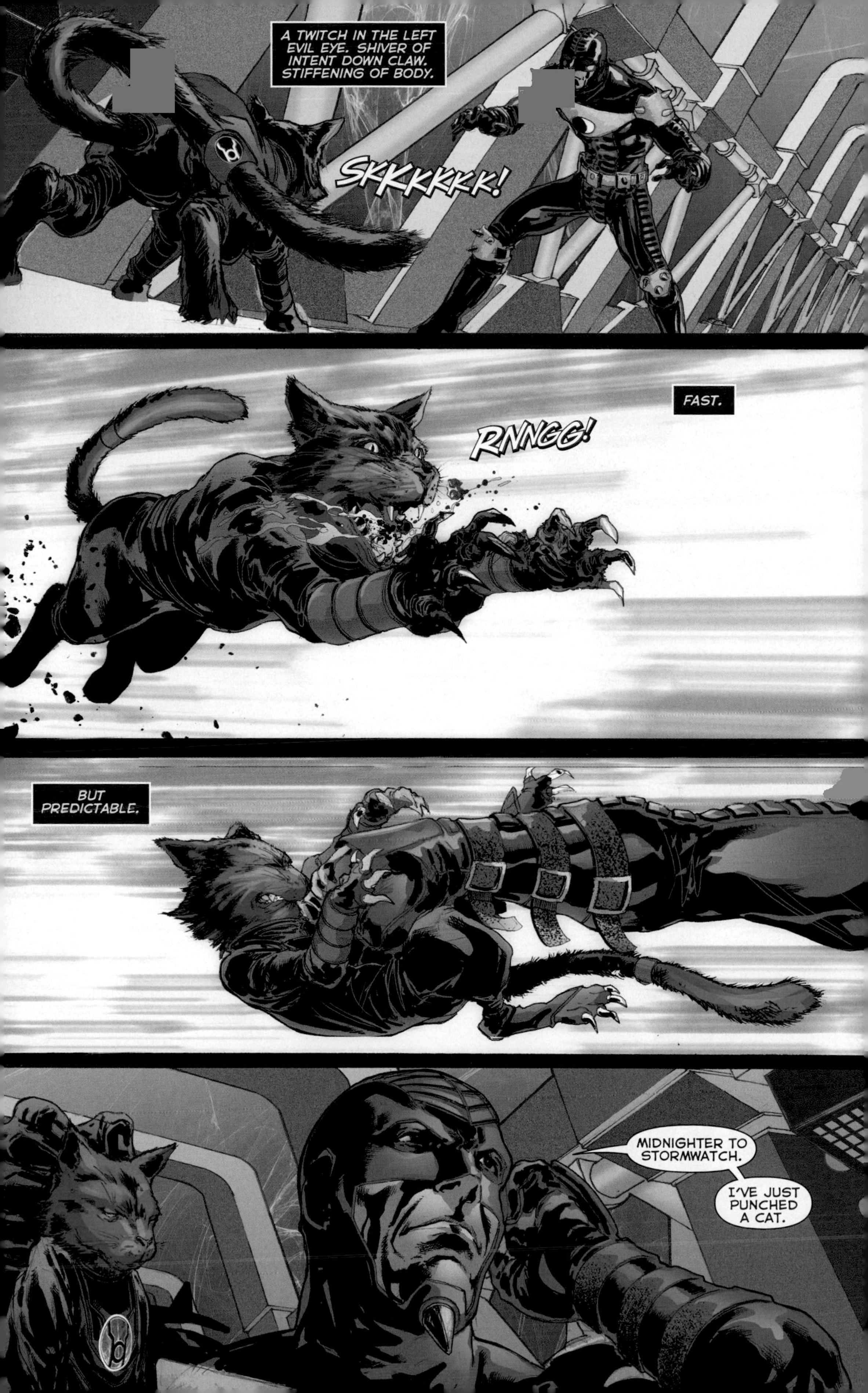
A TWITCH IN THE LEFT EVIL EYE. SHIVER OF INTENT DOWN CLAW. STIFFENING OF BODY.
SKKKKKK!
FAST.
RNNGG!
BUT PREDICTABLE.
MIDNIGHTER TO STORMWATCH.
I'VE JUST PUNCHED A CAT.

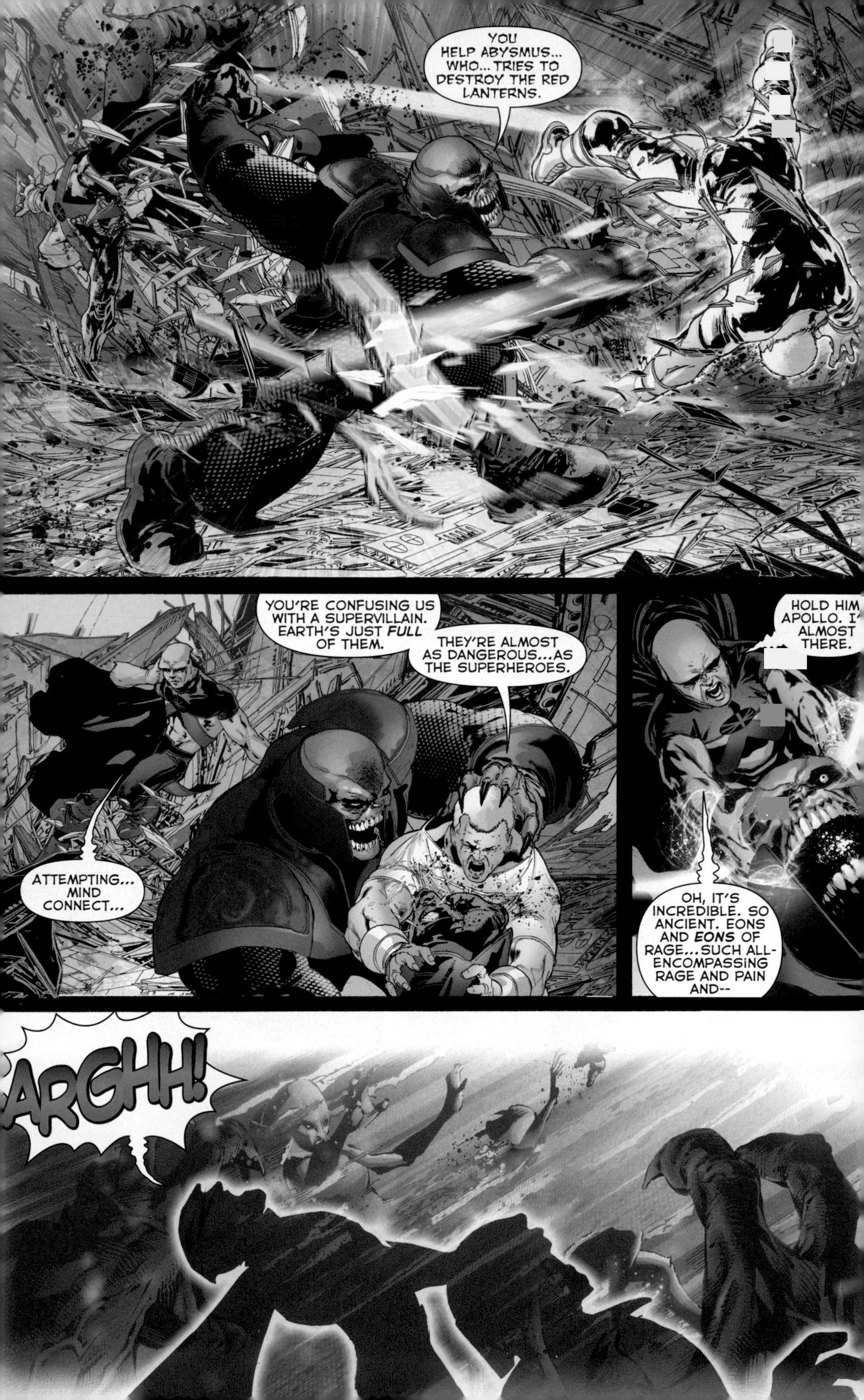
YOU HELP ABYSMUS... WHO... TRIES TO DESTROY THE RED LANTERNS.
YOU'RE CONFUSING US WITH A SUPERVILLAIN. EARTH'S JUST *FULL* OF THEM.
THEY'RE ALMOST AS DANGEROUS...AS THE SUPERHEROES.
ATTEMPTING... MIND CONNECT...
HOLD HIM APOLLO. I' ALMOST THERE.
OH, IT'S INCREDIBLE. SO ANCIENT. EONS AND *EONS* OF RAGE...SUCH ALL-ENCOMPASSING RAGE AND PAIN AND--
ARGHH!

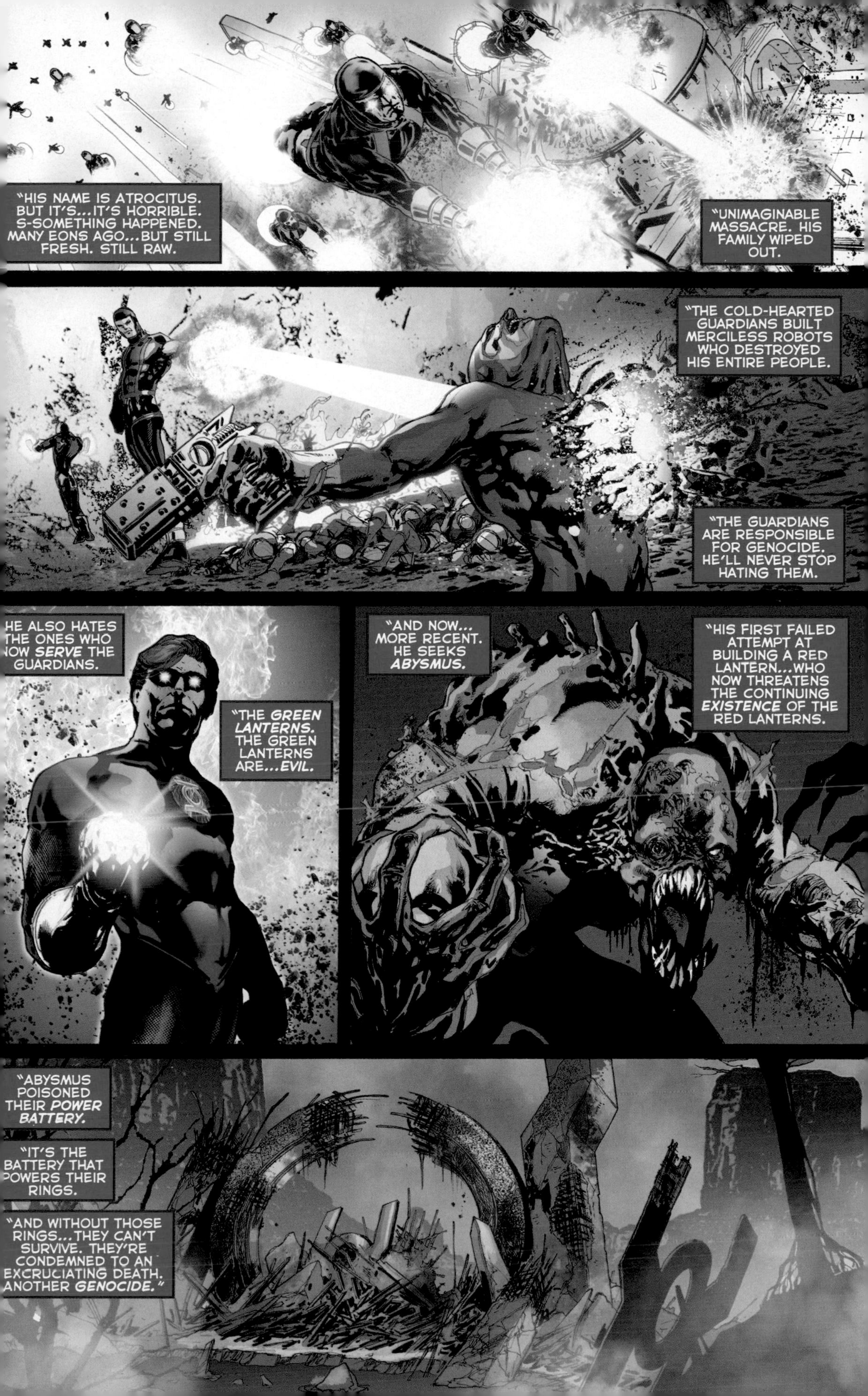
"HIS NAME IS ATROCITUS. BUT IT'S...IT'S HORRIBLE. S-SOMETHING HAPPENED. MANY EONS AGO...BUT STILL FRESH. STILL RAW.
"UNIMAGINABLE MASSACRE. HIS FAMILY WIPED OUT.
"THE COLD-HEARTED GUARDIANS BUILT MERCILESS ROBOTS WHO DESTROYED HIS ENTIRE PEOPLE.
"THE GUARDIANS ARE RESPONSIBLE FOR GENOCIDE. HE'LL NEVER STOP HATING THEM.
HE ALSO HATES THE ONES WHO NOW *SERVE* THE GUARDIANS.
"THE *GREEN LANTERNS.* THE GREEN LANTERNS ARE...*EVIL.*
"AND NOW... MORE RECENT. HE SEEKS *ABYSMUS.*
"HIS FIRST FAILED ATTEMPT AT BUILDING A RED LANTERN...WHO NOW THREATENS THE CONTINUING *EXISTENCE* OF THE RED LANTERNS.
"ABYSMUS POISONED THEIR *POWER BATTERY.*
"IT'S THE BATTERY THAT POWERS THEIR RINGS.
"AND WITHOUT THOSE RINGS...THEY CAN'T SURVIVE. THEY'RE CONDEMNED TO AN EXCRUCIATING DEATH. ANOTHER *GENOCIDE.*"

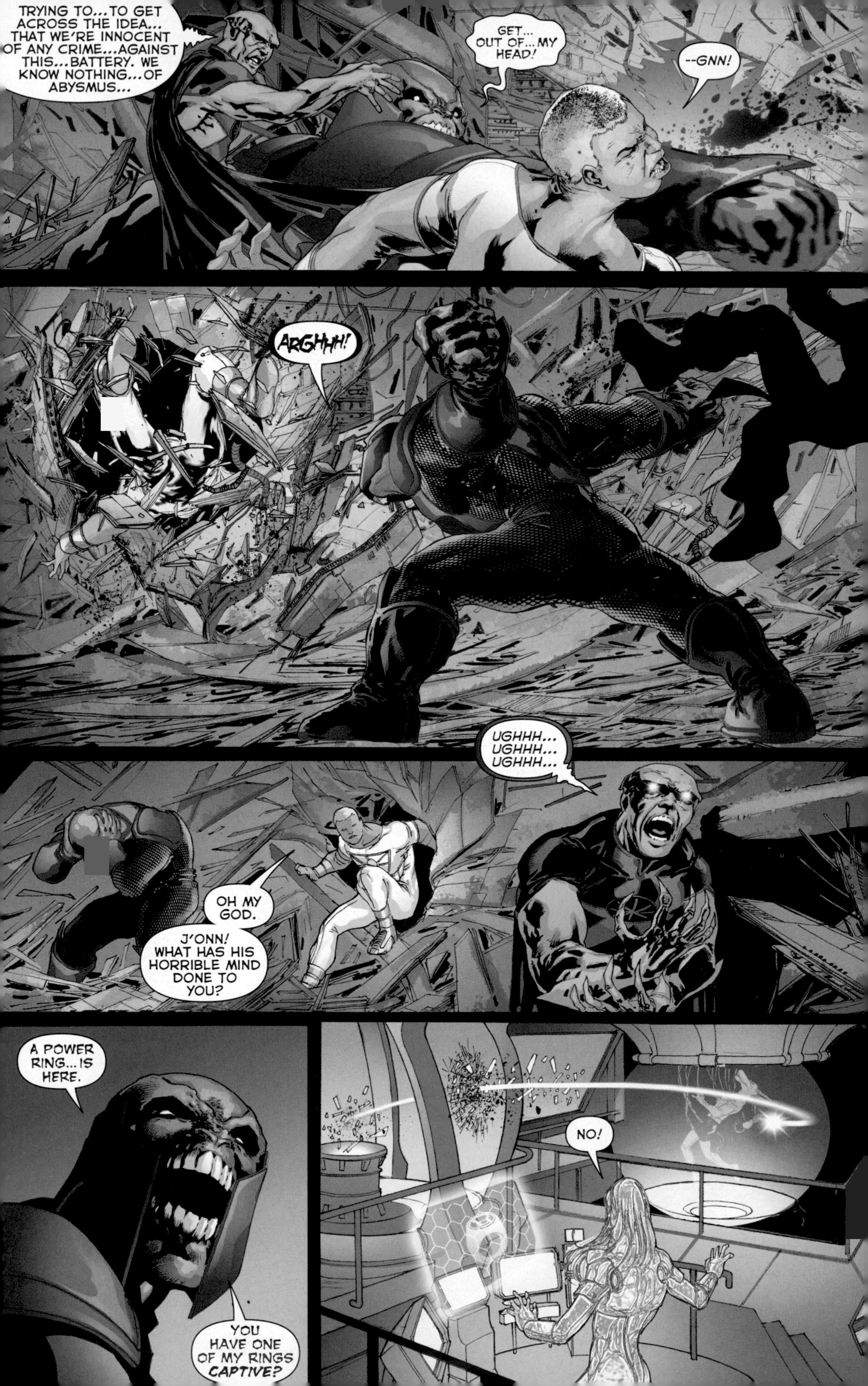
TRYING TO...TO GET ACROSS THE IDEA... THAT WE'RE INNOCENT OF ANY CRIME...AGAINST THIS...BATTERY. WE KNOW NOTHING...OF ABYSMUS...
GET... OUT OF...MY HEAD!
--GNN!
ARGHHH!
UGHHH... UGHHH... UGHHH...
OH MY GOD.
J'ONN! WHAT HAS HIS HORRIBLE MIND DONE TO YOU?
A POWER RING...IS HERE.
YOU HAVE ONE OF MY RINGS CAPTIVE?
NO!

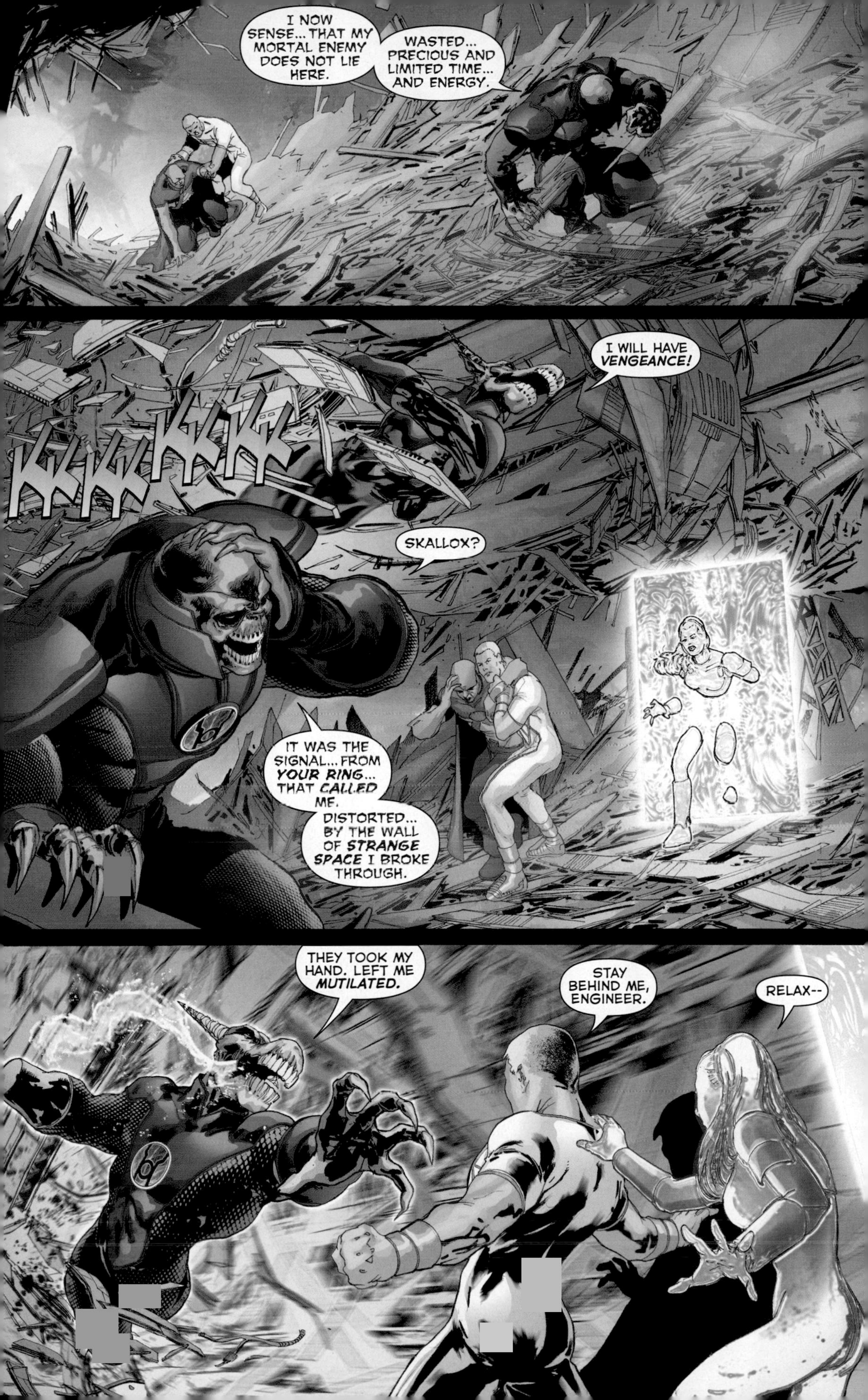
I NOW SENSE... THAT MY MORTAL ENEMY DOES NOT LIE HERE.
WASTED... PRECIOUS AND LIMITED TIME... AND ENERGY.
I WILL HAVE *VENGEANCE!*
KKKKKKKK
SKALLOX?
IT WAS THE SIGNAL... FROM *YOUR RING*... THAT *CALLED* ME.
DISTORTED... BY THE WALL OF *STRANGE SPACE* I BROKE THROUGH.
THEY TOOK MY HAND. LEFT ME *MUTILATED.*
STAY BEHIND ME, ENGINEER.
RELAX--

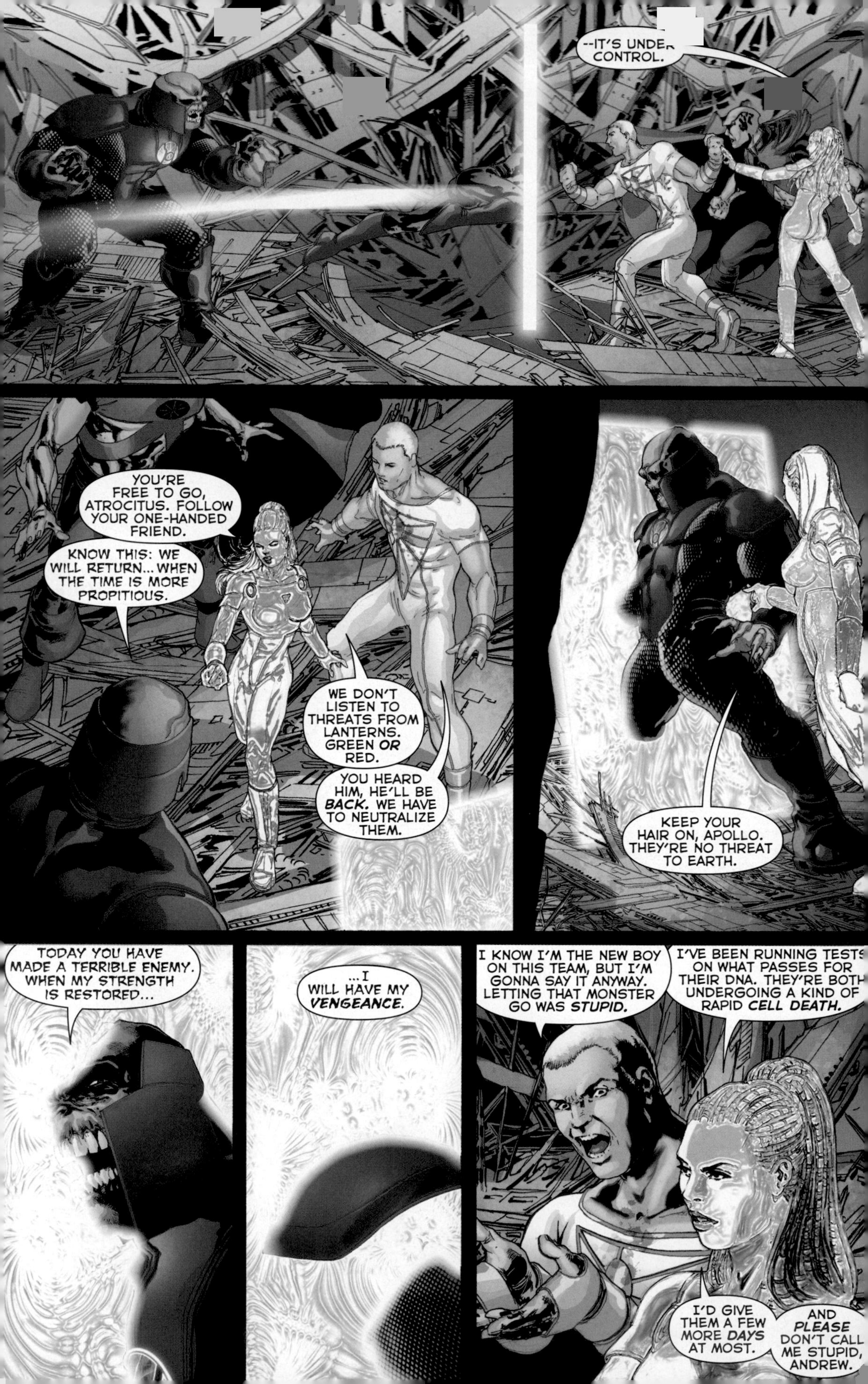
--IT'S UNDER CONTROL.
YOU'RE FREE TO GO, ATROCITUS. FOLLOW YOUR ONE-HANDED FRIEND.
KNOW THIS: WE WILL RETURN...WHEN THE TIME IS MORE PROPITIOUS.
WE DON'T LISTEN TO THREATS FROM LANTERNS. GREEN *OR* RED.
YOU HEARD HIM, HE'LL BE *BACK.* WE HAVE TO NEUTRALIZE THEM.
KEEP YOUR HAIR ON, APOLLO. THEY'RE NO THREAT TO EARTH.
TODAY YOU HAVE MADE A TERRIBLE ENEMY. WHEN MY STRENGTH IS RESTORED...
...I WILL HAVE MY *VENGEANCE.*
I KNOW I'M THE NEW BOY ON THIS TEAM, BUT I'M GONNA SAY IT ANYWAY. LETTING THAT MONSTER GO WAS *STUPID.*
I'VE BEEN RUNNING TESTS ON WHAT PASSES FOR THEIR DNA. THEY'RE BOTH UNDERGOING A KIND OF RAPID *CELL DEATH.*
I'D GIVE THEM A FEW MORE *DAYS* AT MOST.
AND *PLEASE* DON'T CALL ME STUPID, ANDREW.

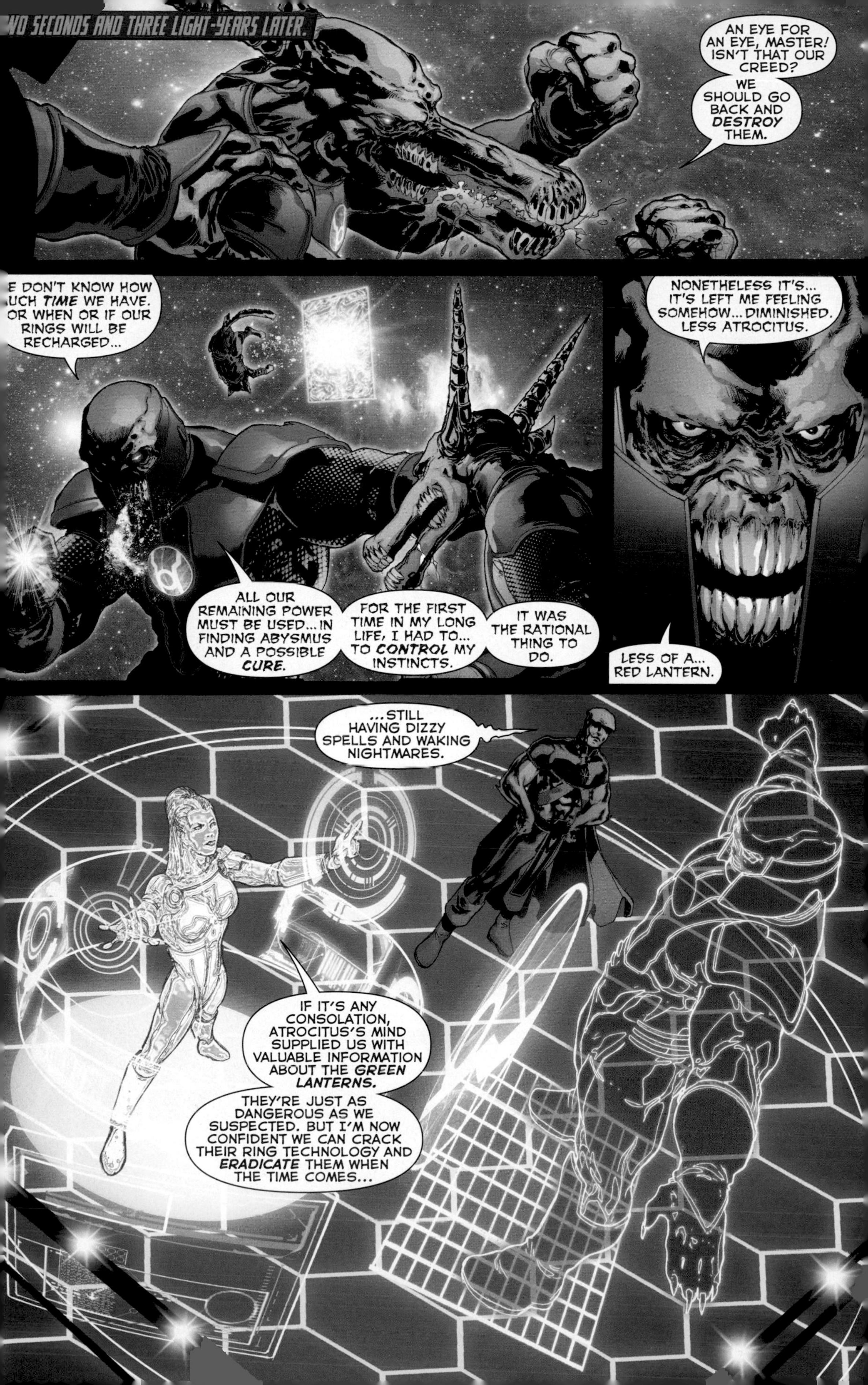
WO SECONDS AND THREE LIGHT-YEARS LATER.
AN EYE FOR AN EYE, MASTER! ISN'T THAT OUR CREED?
WE SHOULD GO BACK AND DESTROY THEM.
E DON'T KNOW HOW UCH TIME WE HAVE. OR WHEN OR IF OUR RINGS WILL BE RECHARGED...
ALL OUR REMAINING POWER MUST BE USED...IN FINDING ABYSMUS AND A POSSIBLE CURE.
FOR THE FIRST TIME IN MY LONG LIFE, I HAD TO... TO CONTROL MY INSTINCTS.
IT WAS THE RATIONAL THING TO DO.
NONETHELESS IT'S... IT'S LEFT ME FEELING SOMEHOW...DIMINISHED. LESS ATROCITUS.
LESS OF A... RED LANTERN.
...STILL HAVING DIZZY SPELLS AND WAKING NIGHTMARES.
IF IT'S ANY CONSOLATION, ATROCITUS'S MIND SUPPLIED US WITH VALUABLE INFORMATION ABOUT THE GREEN LANTERNS.
THEY'RE JUST AS DANGEROUS AS WE SUSPECTED. BUT I'M NOW CONFIDENT WE CAN CRACK THEIR RING TECHNOLOGY AND ERADICATE THEM WHEN THE TIME COMES...

SECTOR 1416.

WE'RE NEARING THE PLANET OF THE STAR SAPPHIRES.

THAT MYSTERIOUS GROUP WHO BLEEZ INSISTS IS RESPONSIBLE FOR OUR LINGERING DEATHS.

THEN IT HAPPENS AGAIN. OF *COURSE* IT DOES.

I'M THE OUTSIDER. THE EASY TARGET.

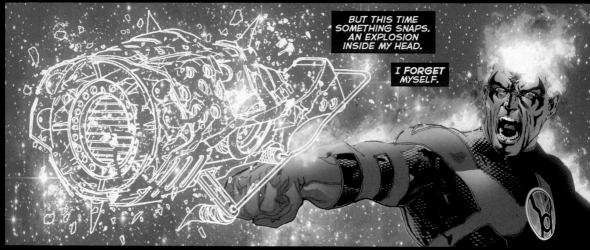

BUT THIS TIME SOMETHING SNAPS. AN EXPLOSION INSIDE MY HEAD.

I FORGET MYSELF.

I FORGET JACK MOORE.

GHHNN!

I BECOME RANKORR.

A RED LANTERN.

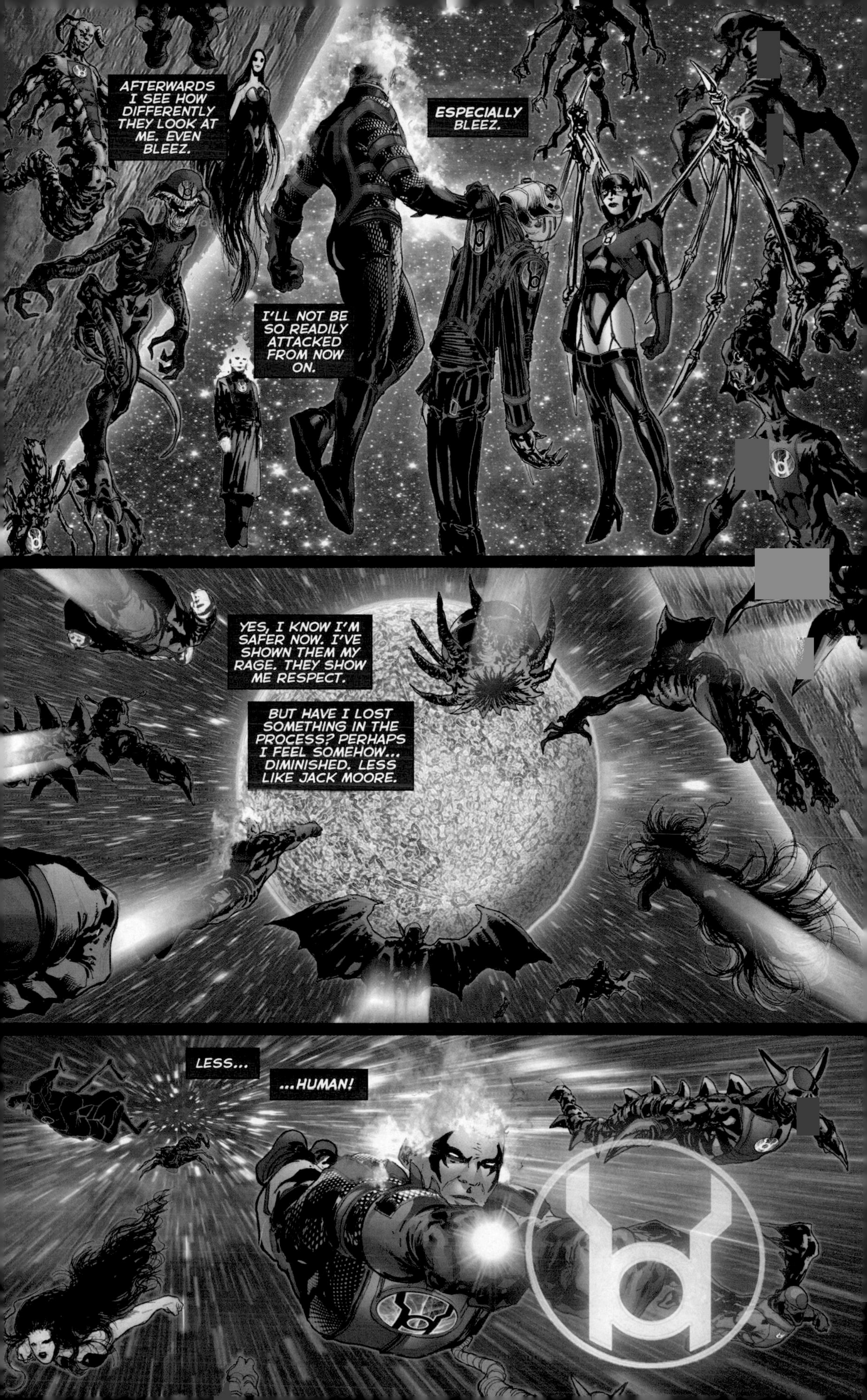
AFTERWARDS I SEE HOW DIFFERENTLY THEY LOOK AT ME. EVEN BLEEZ.
ESPECIALLY BLEEZ.
I'LL NOT BE SO READILY ATTACKED FROM NOW ON.
YES, I KNOW I'M SAFER NOW. I'VE SHOWN THEM MY RAGE. THEY SHOW ME RESPECT.
BUT HAVE I LOST SOMETHING IN THE PROCESS? PERHAPS I FEEL SOMEHOW... DIMINISHED. LESS LIKE JACK MOORE.
LESS...
...HUMAN!

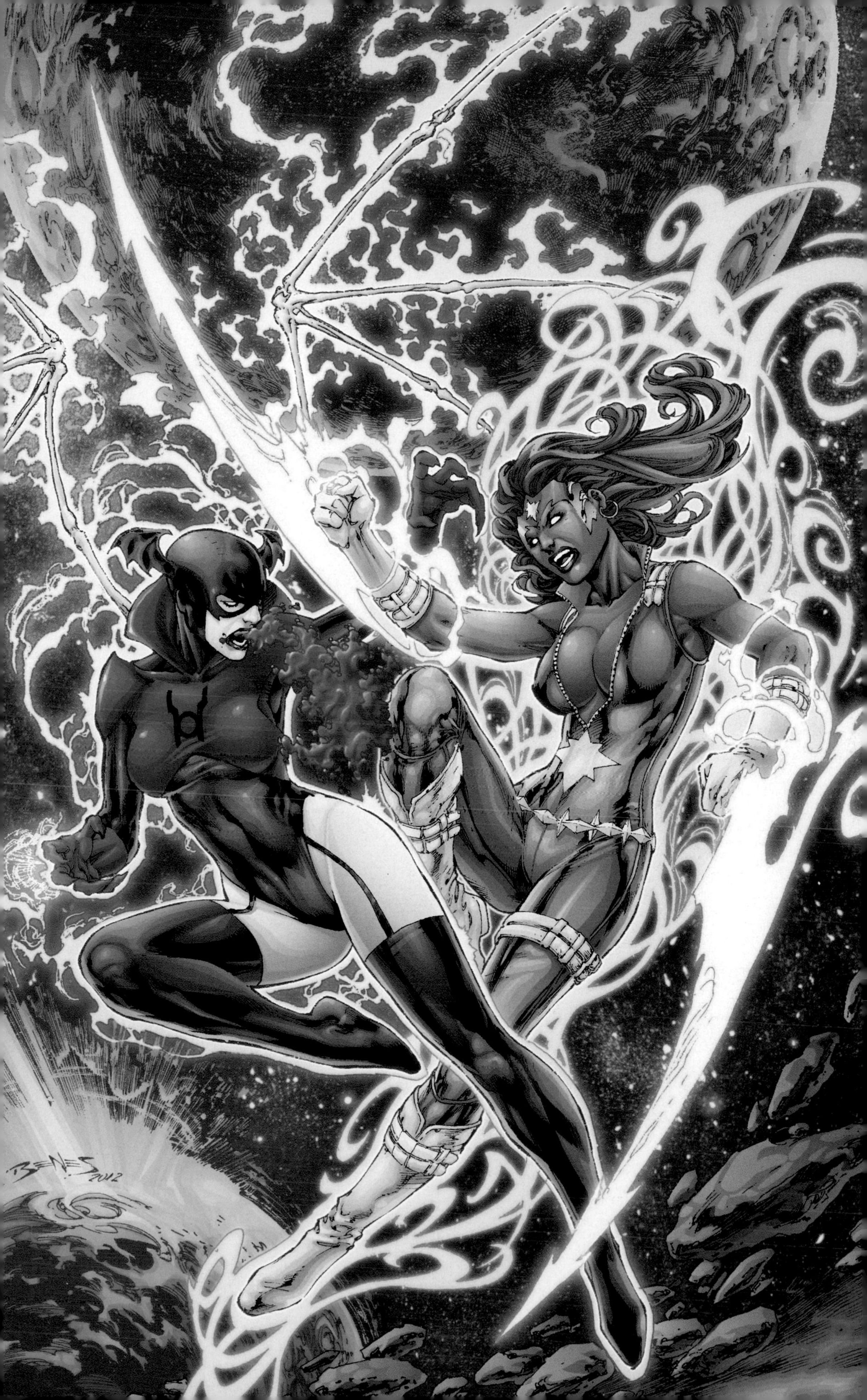
BENES 2012

LOVE AND HATE

PETER MILLIGAN
writer

MIGUEL SEPULVEDA
artist

cover art by ED BENES & NATHAN EYRING

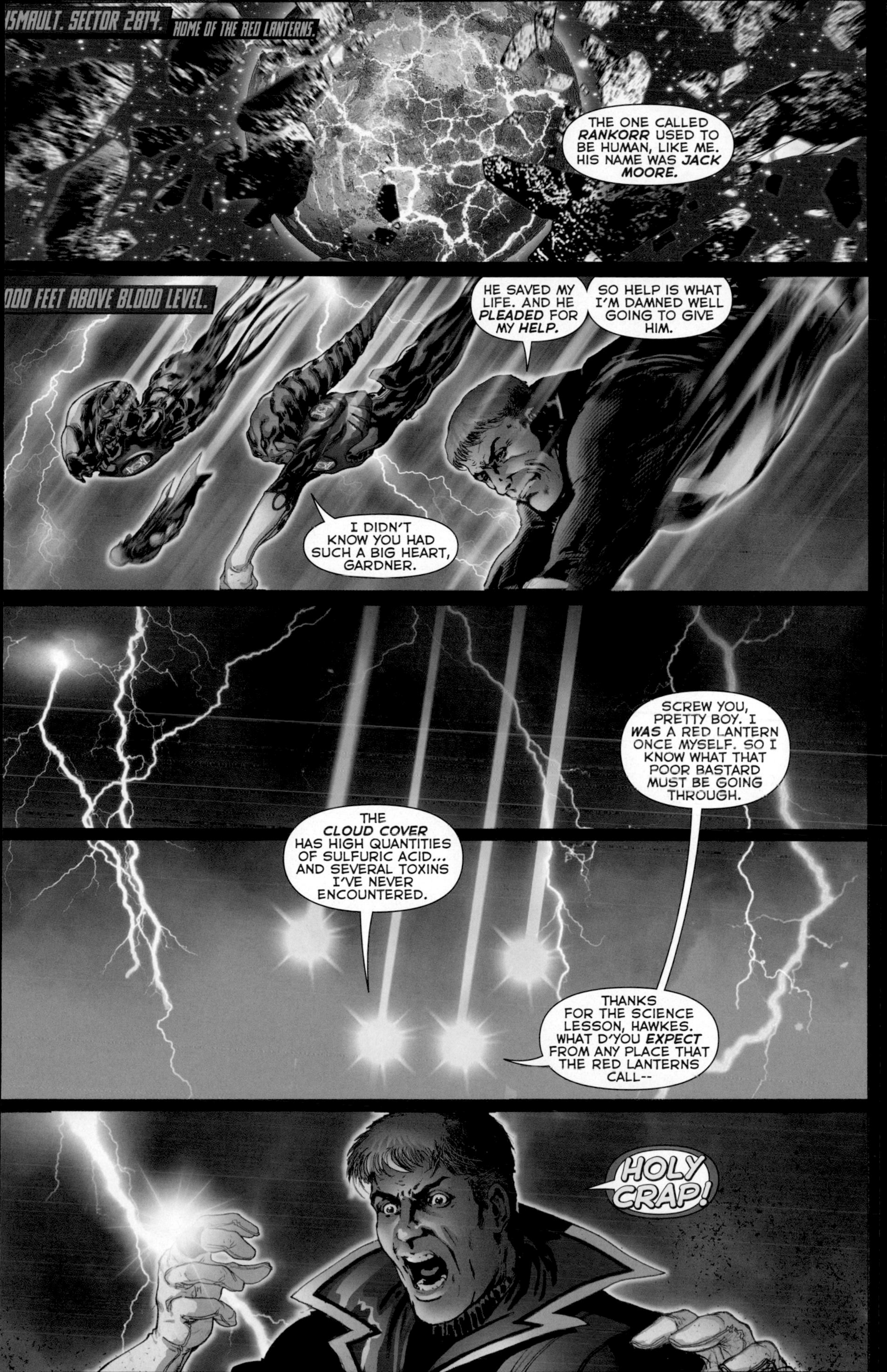

YSMAULT. SECTOR 2814.
HOME OF THE RED LANTERNS.
THE ONE CALLED RANKORR USED TO BE HUMAN, LIKE ME. HIS NAME WAS JACK MOORE.
OOO FEET ABOVE BLOOD LEVEL.
HE SAVED MY LIFE. AND HE PLEADED FOR MY HELP.
SO HELP IS WHAT I'M DAMNED WELL GOING TO GIVE HIM.
I DIDN'T KNOW YOU HAD SUCH A BIG HEART, GARDNER.
SCREW YOU, PRETTY BOY. I WAS A RED LANTERN ONCE MYSELF. SO I KNOW WHAT THAT POOR BASTARD MUST BE GOING THROUGH.
THE CLOUD COVER HAS HIGH QUANTITIES OF SULFURIC ACID... AND SEVERAL TOXINS I'VE NEVER ENCOUNTERED.
THANKS FOR THE SCIENCE LESSON, HAWKES. WHAT D'YOU EXPECT FROM ANY PLACE THAT THE RED LANTERNS CALL--
HOLY CRAP!

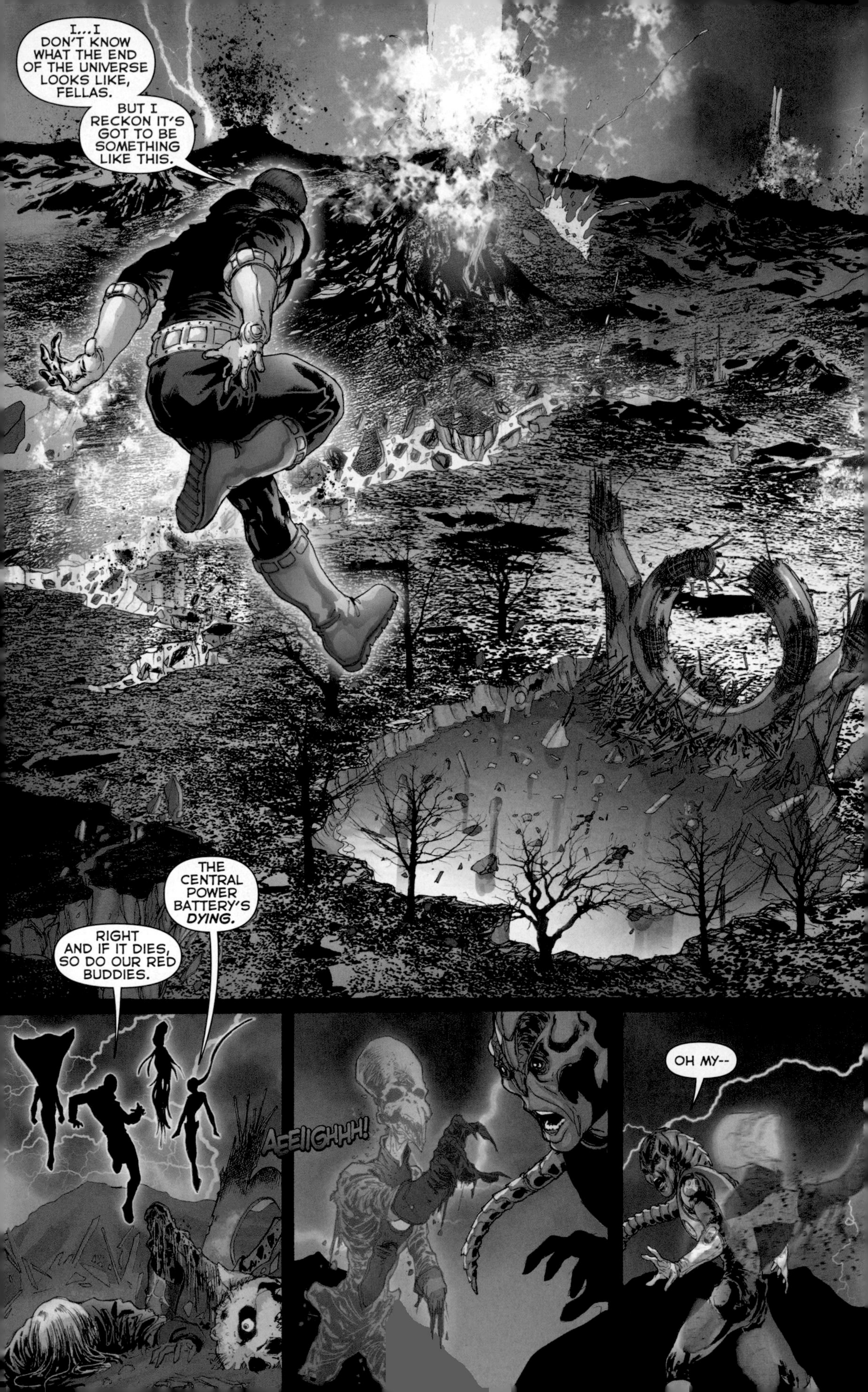
I...I DON'T KNOW WHAT THE END OF THE UNIVERSE LOOKS LIKE, FELLAS.
BUT I RECKON IT'S GOT TO BE SOMETHING LIKE THIS.
THE CENTRAL POWER BATTERY'S *DYING*.
RIGHT AND IF IT DIES, SO DO OUR RED BUDDIES.
AEEIIGHHH!
OH MY--

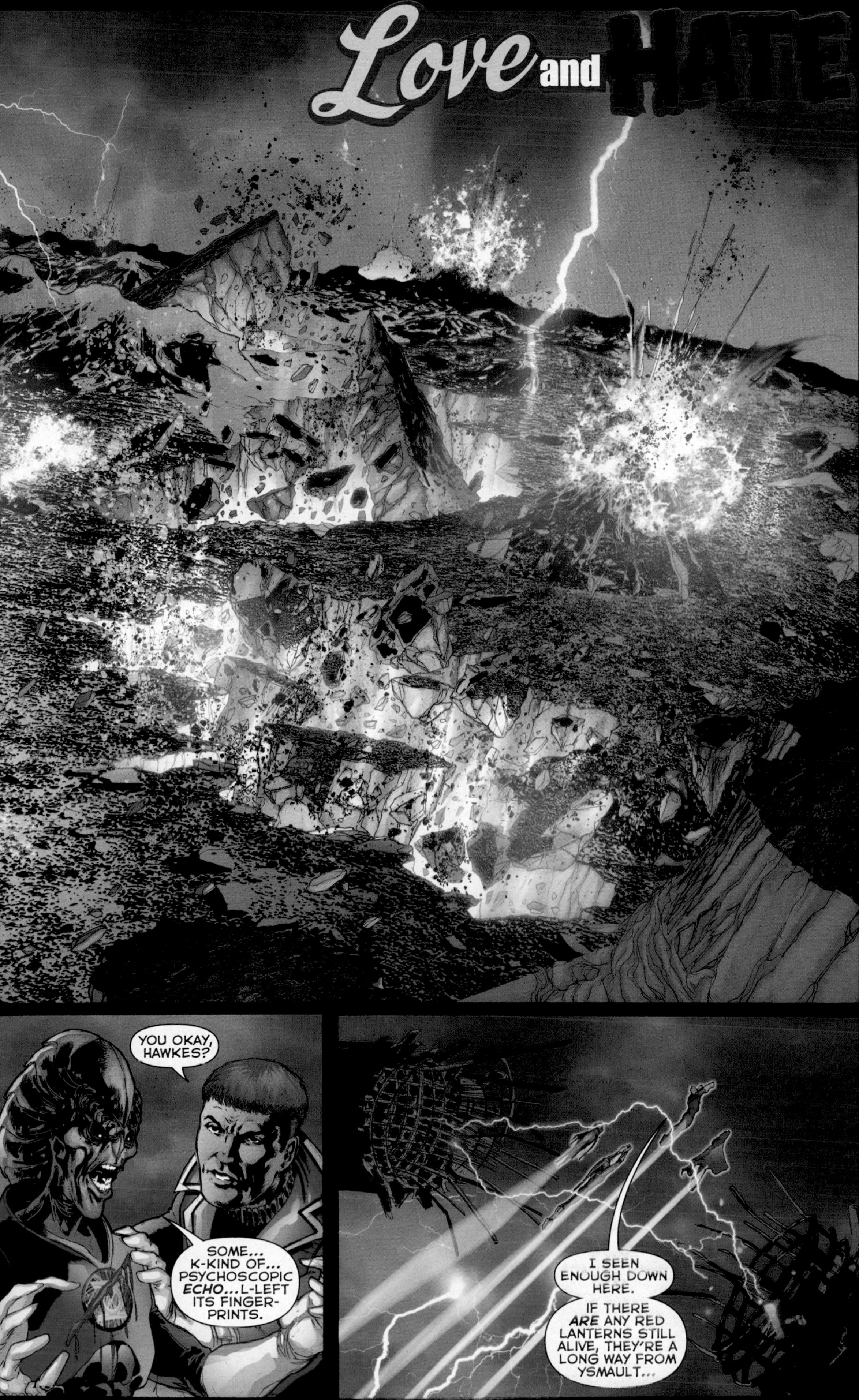
Love and HATE
YOU OKAY, HAWKES?
SOME... K-KIND OF... PSYCHOSCOPIC ECHO... L-LEFT ITS FINGER-PRINTS.
I SEEN ENOUGH DOWN HERE.
IF THERE ARE ANY RED LANTERNS STILL ALIVE, THEY'RE A LONG WAY FROM YSMAULT...

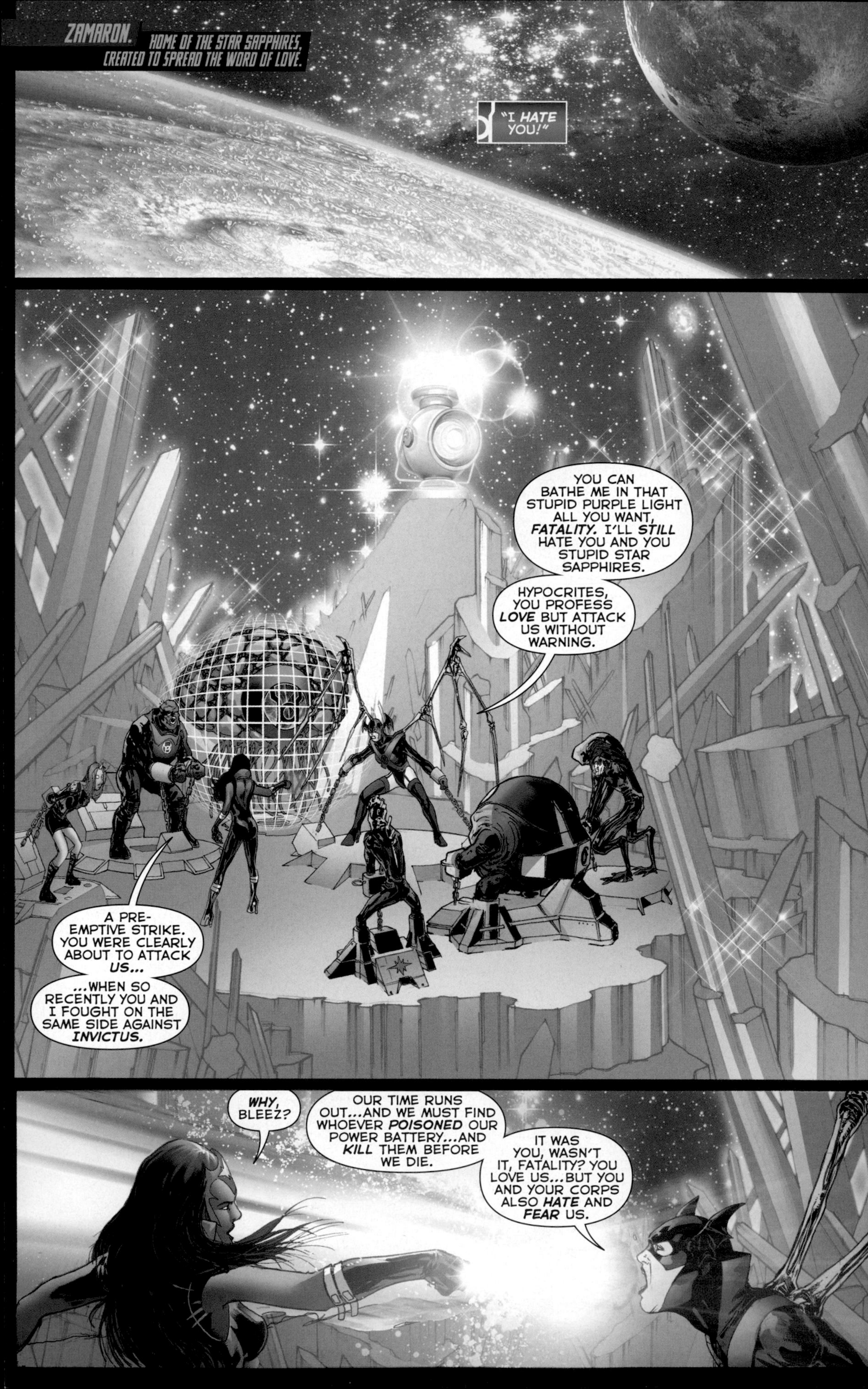
ZAMARON. HOME OF THE STAR SAPPHIRES, CREATED TO SPREAD THE WORD OF LOVE.
"I HATE YOU!"
YOU CAN BATHE ME IN THAT STUPID PURPLE LIGHT ALL YOU WANT, FATALITY. I'LL STILL HATE YOU AND YOU STUPID STAR SAPPHIRES.
HYPOCRITES, YOU PROFESS LOVE BUT ATTACK US WITHOUT WARNING.
A PRE-EMPTIVE STRIKE. YOU WERE CLEARLY ABOUT TO ATTACK US...
...WHEN SO RECENTLY YOU AND I FOUGHT ON THE SAME SIDE AGAINST INVICTUS.
WHY, BLEEZ?
OUR TIME RUNS OUT...AND WE MUST FIND WHOEVER POISONED OUR POWER BATTERY...AND KILL THEM BEFORE WE DIE.
IT WAS YOU, WASN'T IT, FATALITY? YOU LOVE US...BUT YOU AND YOUR CORPS ALSO HATE AND FEAR US.

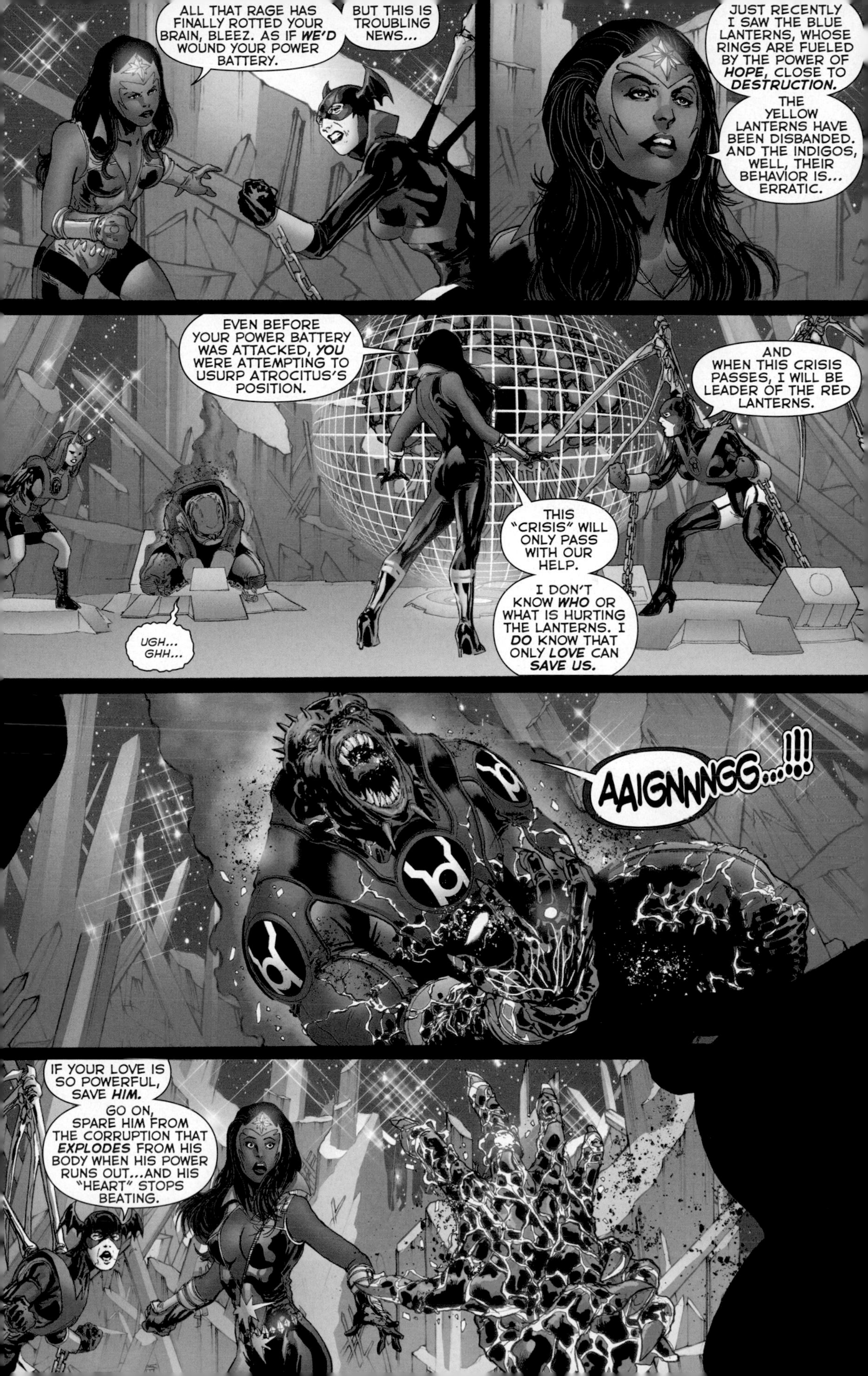
ALL THAT RAGE HAS FINALLY ROTTED YOUR BRAIN, BLEEZ. AS IF WE'D WOUND YOUR POWER BATTERY.
BUT THIS IS TROUBLING NEWS...
JUST RECENTLY I SAW THE BLUE LANTERNS, WHOSE RINGS ARE FUELED BY THE POWER OF HOPE, CLOSE TO DESTRUCTION.
THE YELLOW LANTERNS HAVE BEEN DISBANDED. AND THE INDIGOS, WELL, THEIR BEHAVIOR IS... ERRATIC.
EVEN BEFORE YOUR POWER BATTERY WAS ATTACKED, YOU WERE ATTEMPTING TO USURP ATROCITUS'S POSITION.
AND WHEN THIS CRISIS PASSES, I WILL BE LEADER OF THE RED LANTERNS.
THIS "CRISIS" WILL ONLY PASS WITH OUR HELP.
I DON'T KNOW WHO OR WHAT IS HURTING THE LANTERNS. I DO KNOW THAT ONLY LOVE CAN SAVE US.
UGH... GHH...
AAIGNNNGG...!!!
IF YOUR LOVE IS SO POWERFUL, SAVE HIM.
GO ON, SPARE HIM FROM THE CORRUPTION THAT EXPLODES FROM HIS BODY WHEN HIS POWER RUNS OUT...AND HIS "HEART" STOPS BEATING.

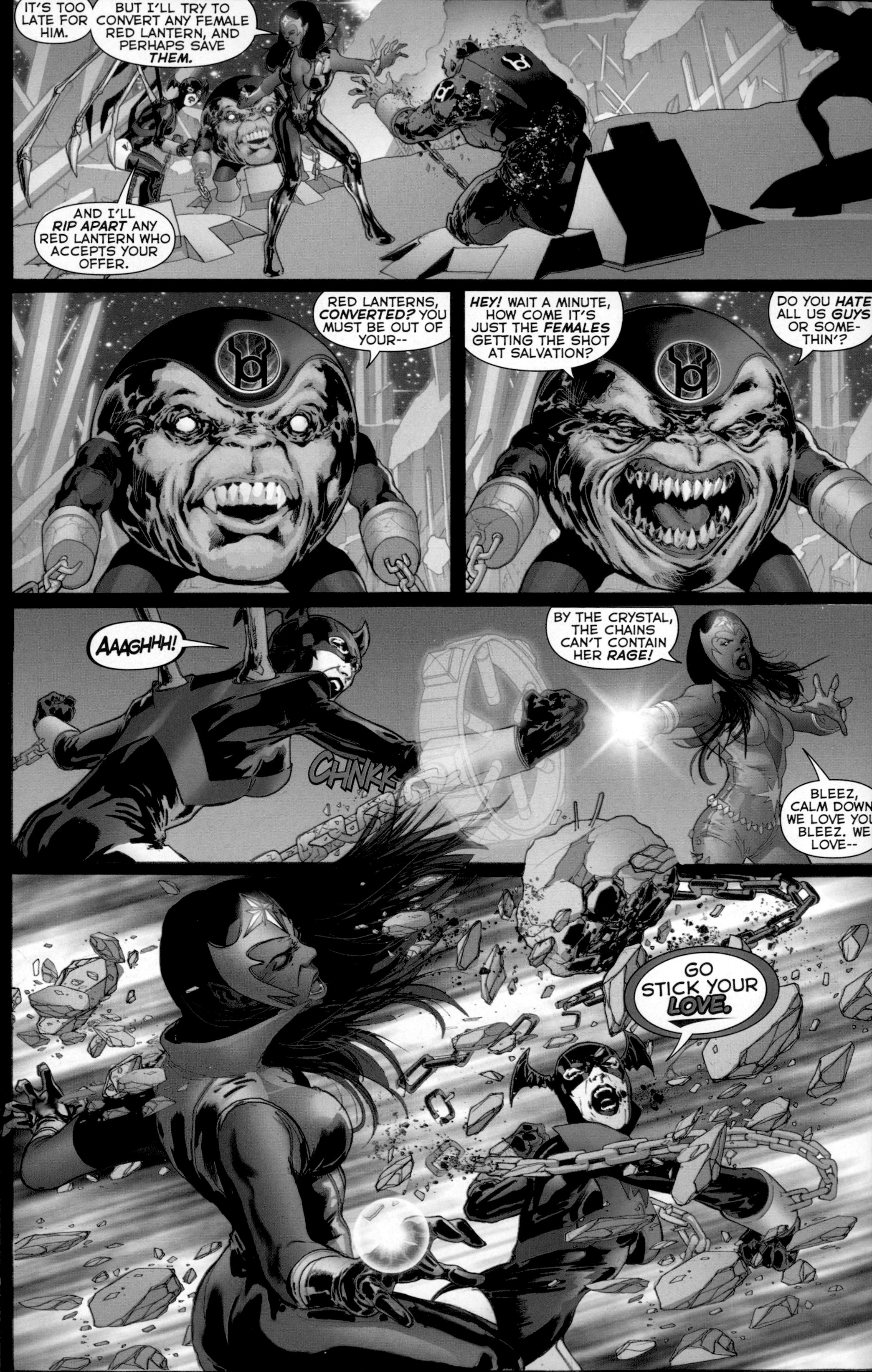
IT'S TOO LATE FOR HIM.
BUT I'LL TRY TO CONVERT ANY FEMALE RED LANTERN, AND PERHAPS SAVE THEM.
AND I'LL RIP APART ANY RED LANTERN WHO ACCEPTS YOUR OFFER.
RED LANTERNS, CONVERTED? YOU MUST BE OUT OF YOUR--
HEY! WAIT A MINUTE, HOW COME IT'S JUST THE FEMALES GETTING THE SHOT AT SALVATION?
DO YOU HATE ALL US GUYS OR SOME-THIN'?
AAAGHHH!
BY THE CRYSTAL, THE CHAINS CAN'T CONTAIN HER RAGE!
CHNKK
BLEEZ, CALM DOWN WE LOVE YOU BLEEZ. WE LOVE--
GO STICK YOUR LOVE.

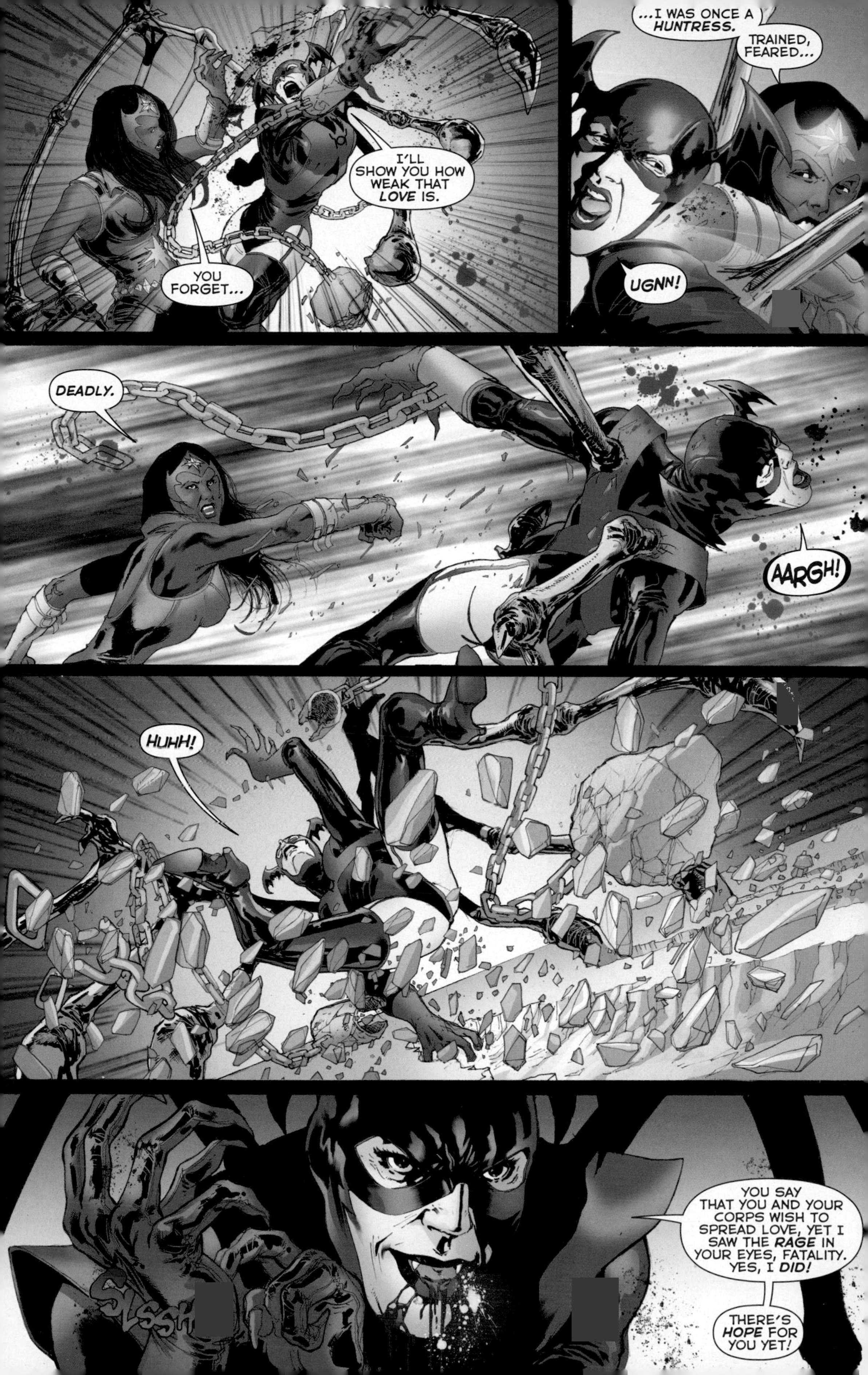
I'LL SHOW YOU HOW WEAK THAT LOVE IS.
YOU FORGET...
...I WAS ONCE A HUNTRESS.
TRAINED, FEARED...
UGNN!
DEADLY.
AARGH!
HUHH!
YOU SAY THAT YOU AND YOUR CORPS WISH TO SPREAD LOVE, YET I SAW THE RAGE IN YOUR EYES, FATALITY. YES, I DID!
THERE'S HOPE FOR YOU YET!
SLSSH

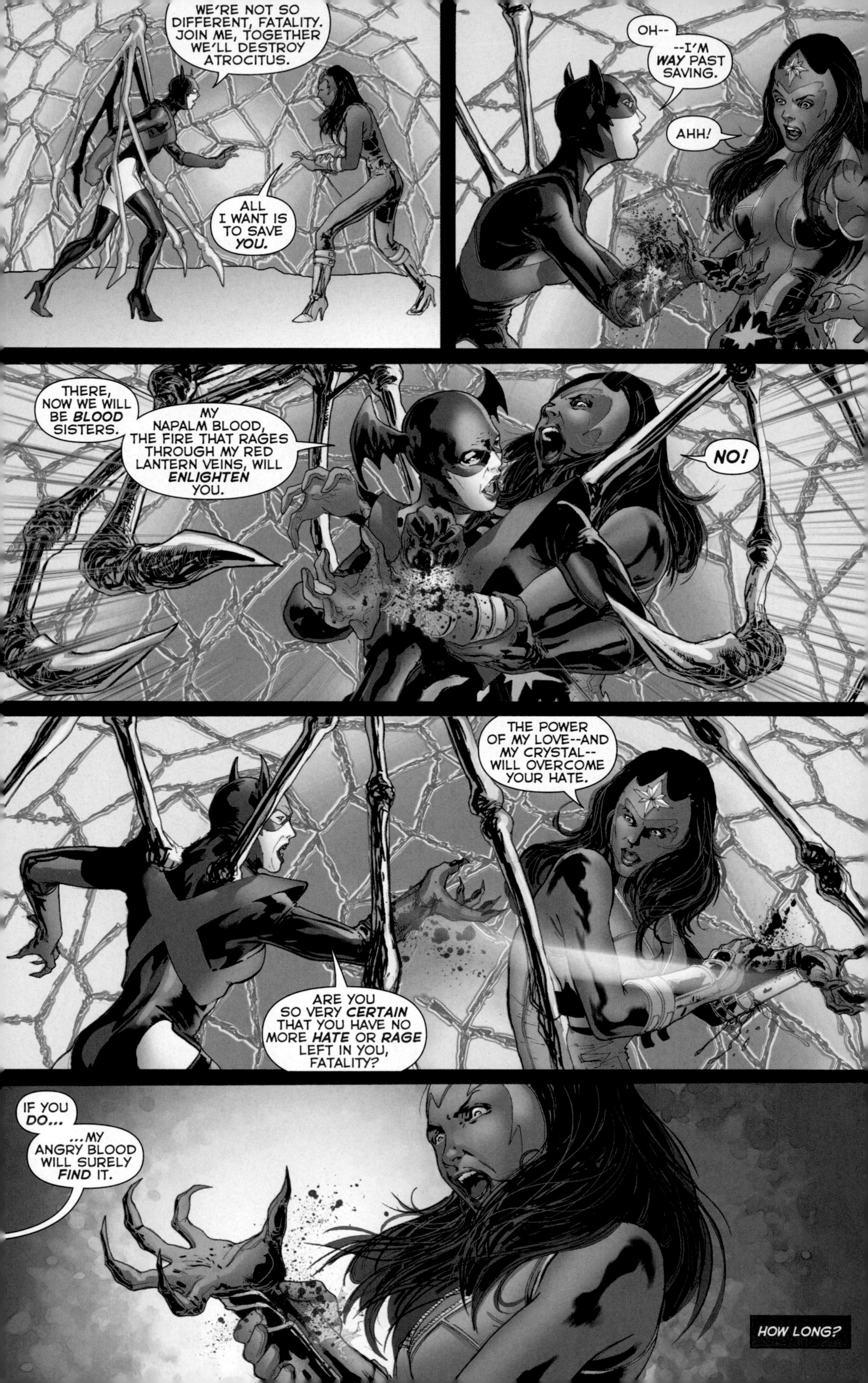

WE'RE NOT SO DIFFERENT, FATALITY. JOIN ME, TOGETHER WE'LL DESTROY ATROCITUS.
ALL I WANT IS TO SAVE YOU.
OH--
--I'M WAY PAST SAVING.
AHH!
THERE, NOW WE WILL BE BLOOD SISTERS.
MY NAPALM BLOOD, THE FIRE THAT RAGES THROUGH MY RED LANTERN VEINS, WILL ENLIGHTEN YOU.
NO!
THE POWER OF MY LOVE--AND MY CRYSTAL--WILL OVERCOME YOUR HATE.
ARE YOU SO VERY CERTAIN THAT YOU HAVE NO MORE HATE OR RAGE LEFT IN YOU, FATALITY?
IF YOU DO...
...MY ANGRY BLOOD WILL SURELY FIND IT.
HOW LONG?

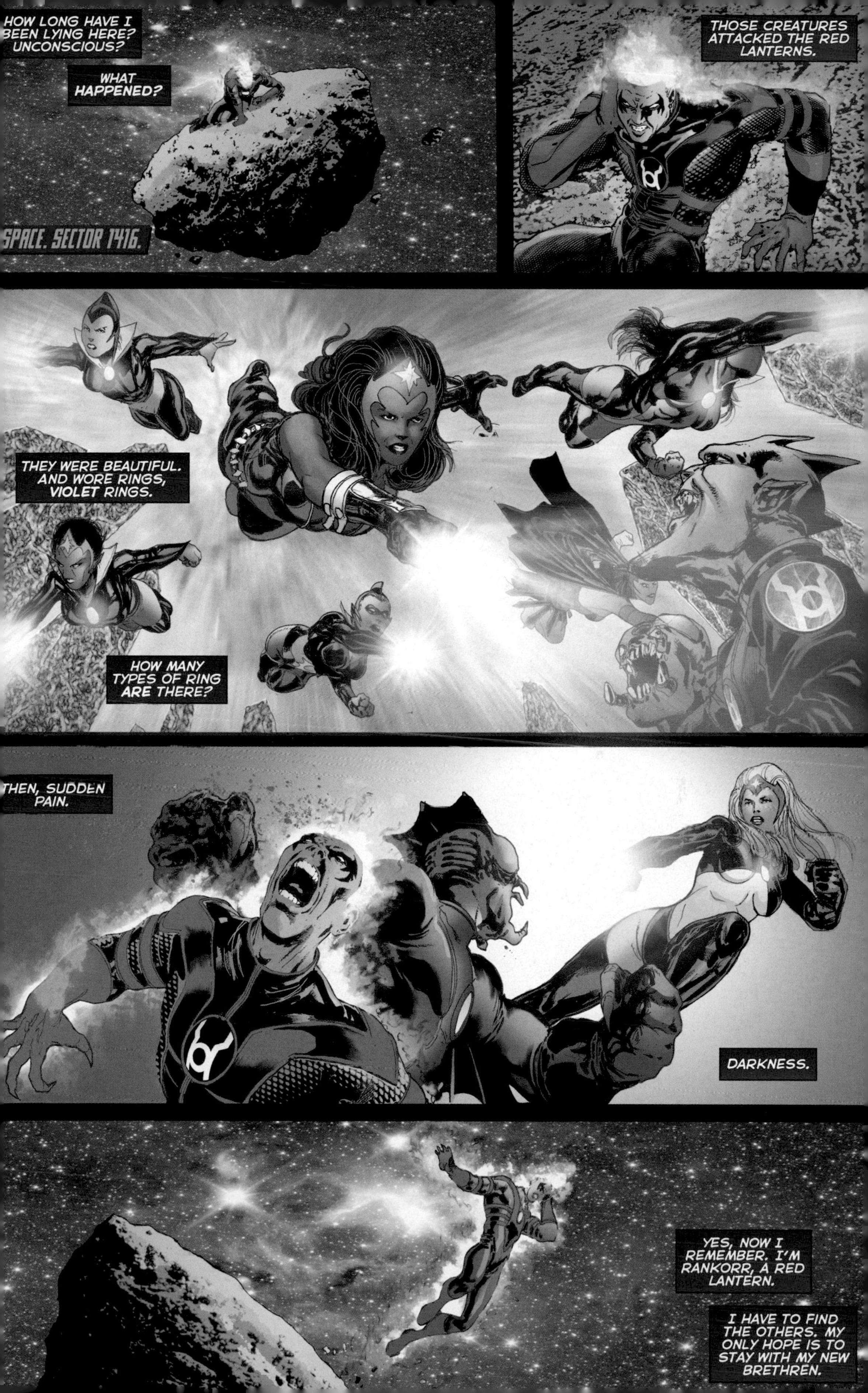
HOW LONG HAVE I BEEN LYING HERE? UNCONSCIOUS?
WHAT HAPPENED?
SPACE. SECTOR 1416.
THOSE CREATURES ATTACKED THE RED LANTERNS.
THEY WERE BEAUTIFUL. AND WORE RINGS, VIOLET RINGS.
HOW MANY TYPES OF RING ARE THERE?
THEN, SUDDEN PAIN.
DARKNESS.
YES, NOW I REMEMBER. I'M RANKORR, A RED LANTERN.
I HAVE TO FIND THE OTHERS. MY ONLY HOPE IS TO STAY WITH MY NEW BRETHREN.

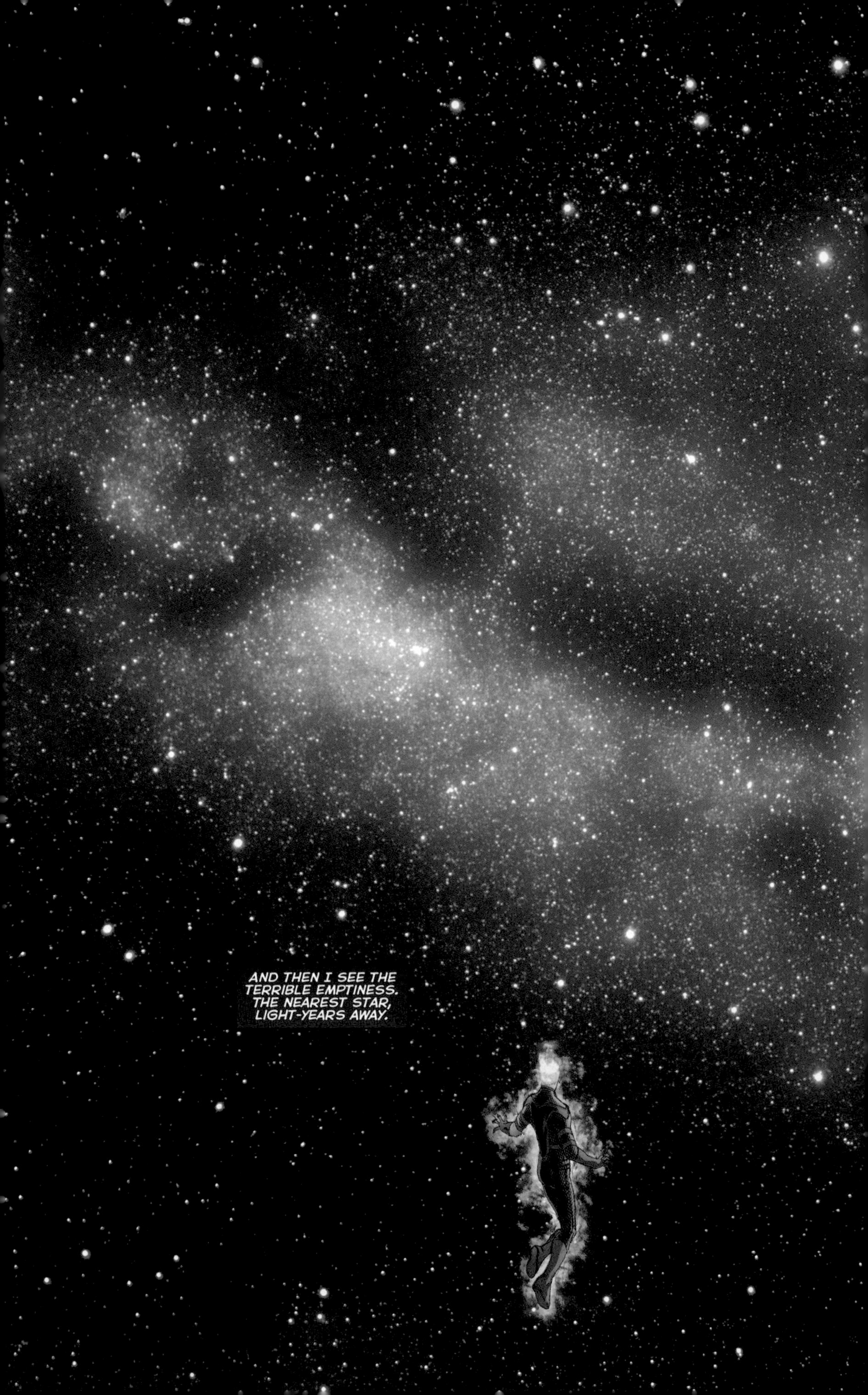
AND THEN I SEE THE TERRIBLE EMPTINESS. THE NEAREST STAR, LIGHT-YEARS AWAY.

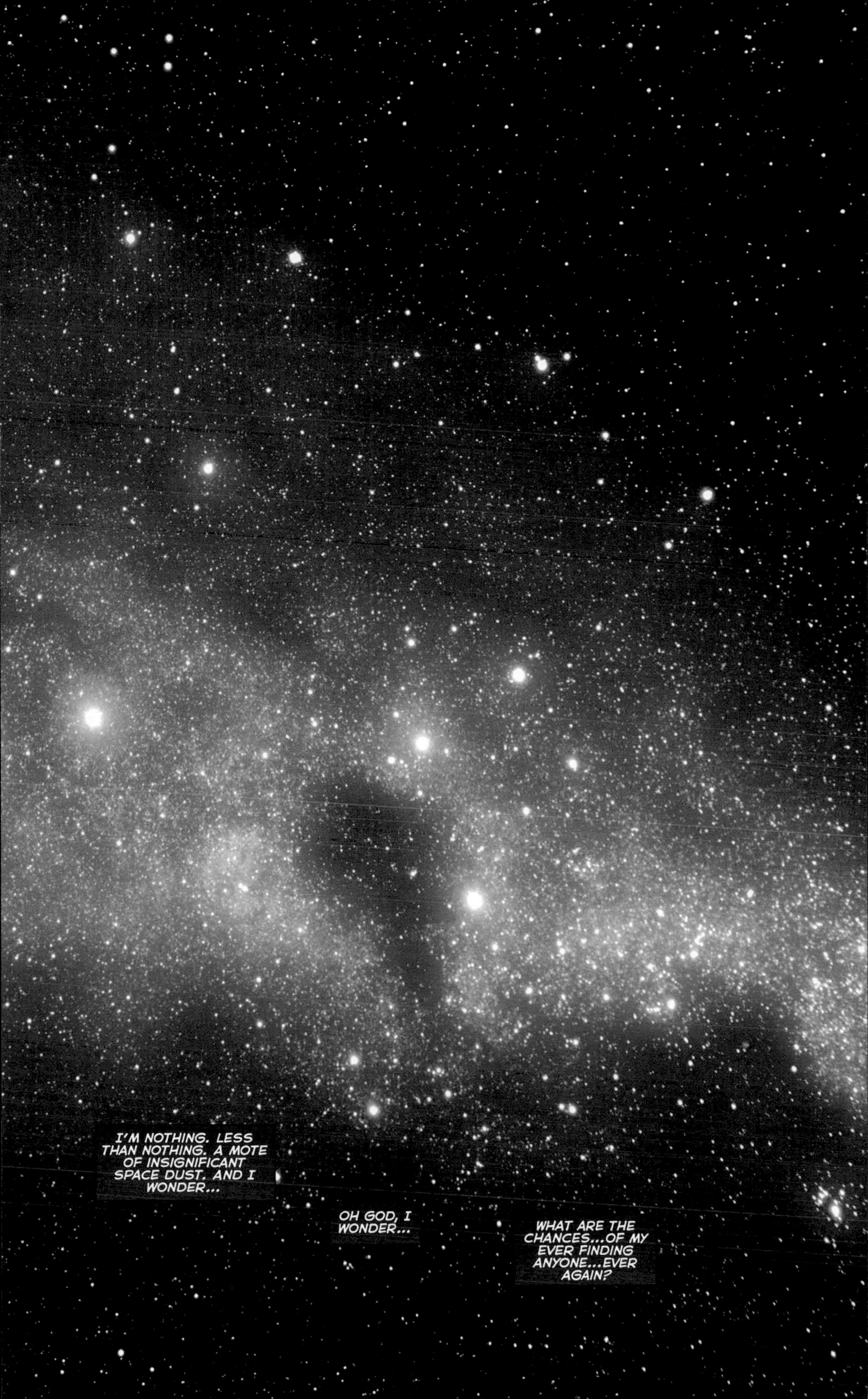
I'M NOTHING. LESS THAN NOTHING. A MOTE OF INSIGNIFICANT SPACE DUST. AND I WONDER...
OH GOD, I WONDER...
WHAT ARE THE CHANCES...OF MY EVER FINDING ANYONE...EVER AGAIN?

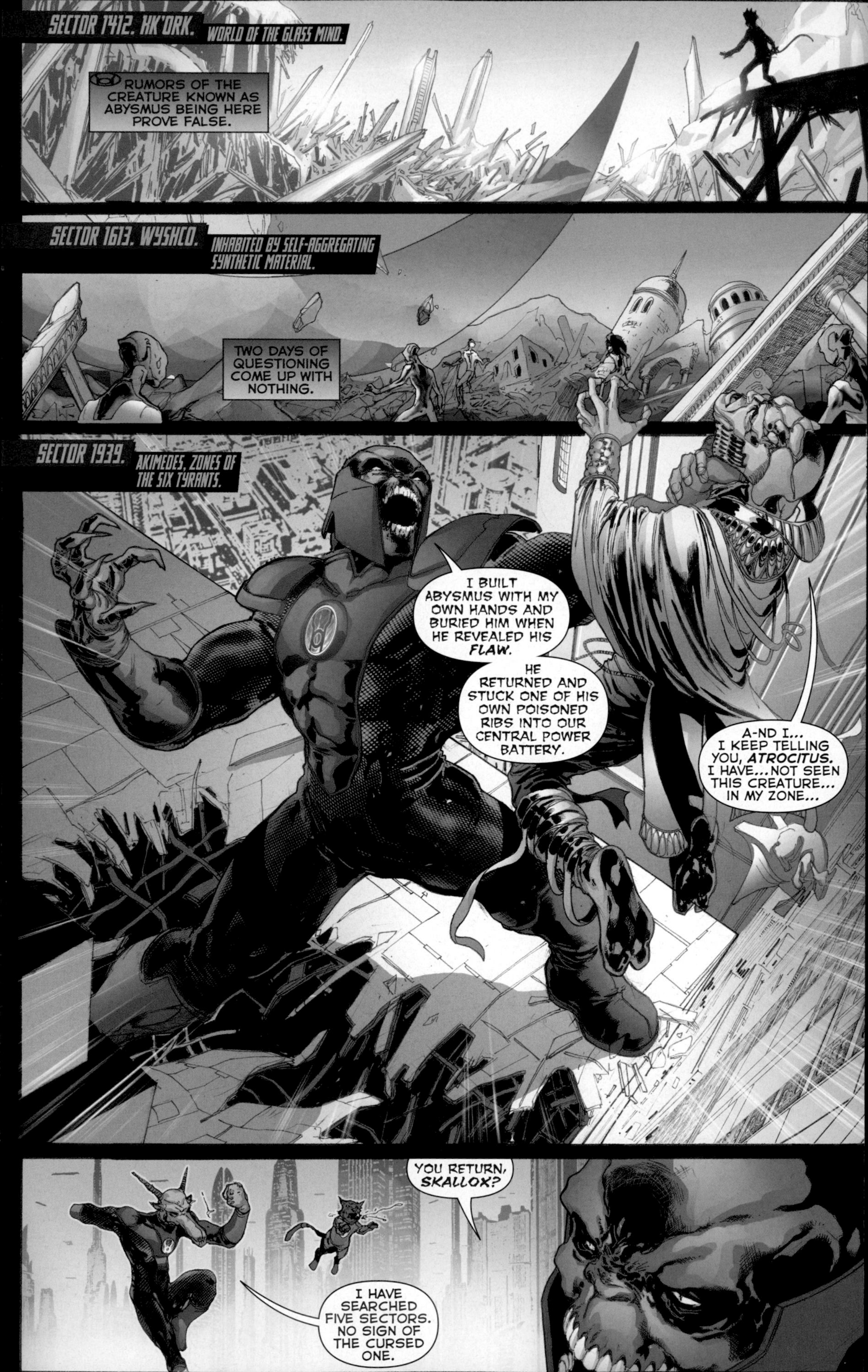
SECTOR 1412. HK'ORK.
WORLD OF THE GLASS MIND.
RUMORS OF THE CREATURE KNOWN AS ABYSMUS BEING HERE PROVE FALSE.
SECTOR 1613. WYSHCO.
INHABITED BY SELF-AGGREGATING SYNTHETIC MATERIAL.
TWO DAYS OF QUESTIONING COME UP WITH NOTHING.
SECTOR 1939.
AKIMEDES, ZONES OF THE SIX TYRANTS.
I BUILT ABYSMUS WITH MY OWN HANDS AND BURIED HIM WHEN HE REVEALED HIS FLAW.
HE RETURNED AND STUCK ONE OF HIS OWN POISONED RIBS INTO OUR CENTRAL POWER BATTERY.
A-ND I... I KEEP TELLING YOU, ATROCITUS. I HAVE...NOT SEEN THIS CREATURE... IN MY ZONE...
YOU RETURN, SKALLOX?
I HAVE SEARCHED FIVE SECTORS. NO SIGN OF THE CURSED ONE.

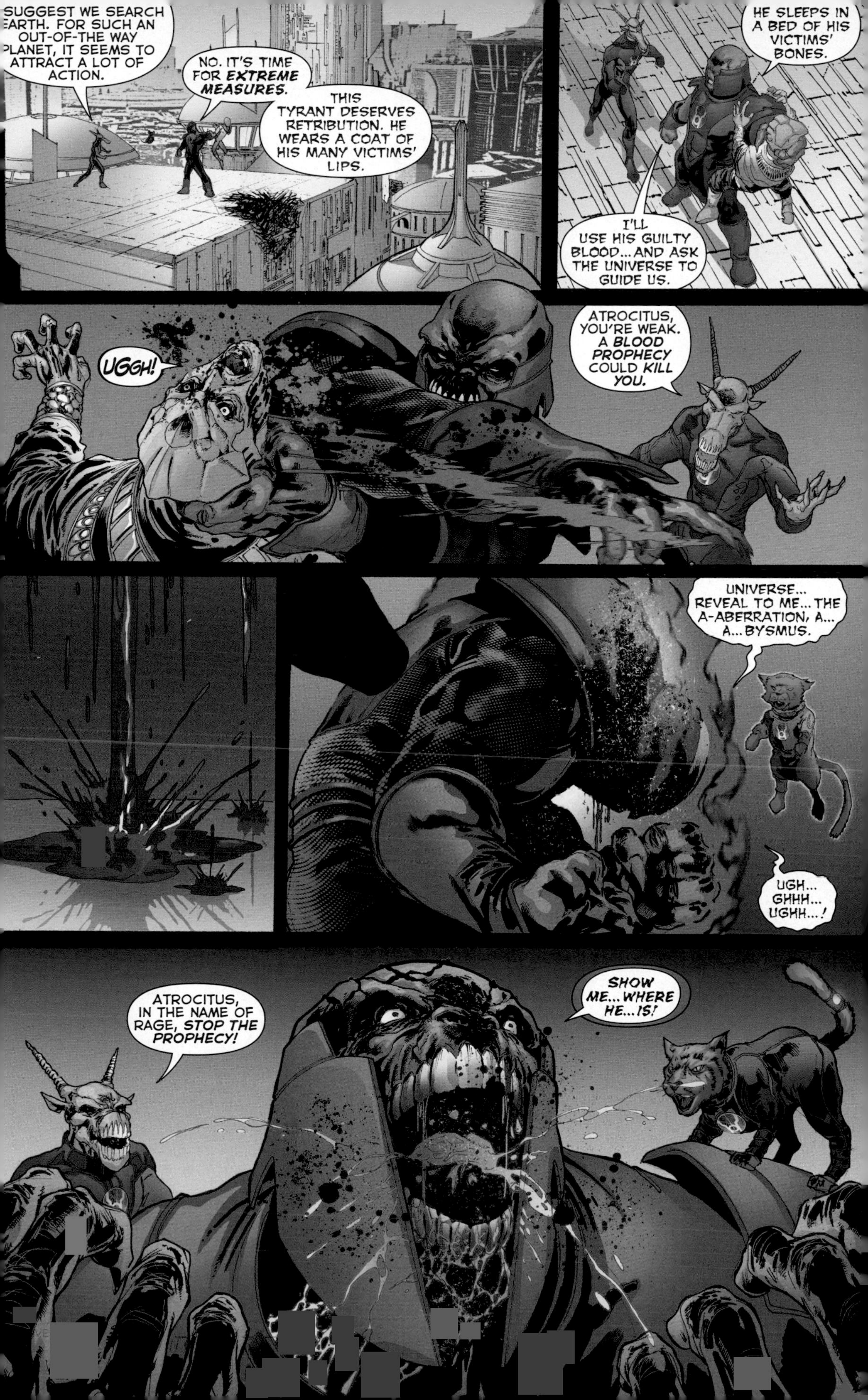
SUGGEST WE SEARCH EARTH. FOR SUCH AN OUT-OF-THE WAY PLANET, IT SEEMS TO ATTRACT A LOT OF ACTION.
NO. IT'S TIME FOR EXTREME MEASURES.
THIS TYRANT DESERVES RETRIBUTION. HE WEARS A COAT OF HIS MANY VICTIMS' LIPS.
HE SLEEPS IN A BED OF HIS VICTIMS' BONES.
I'LL USE HIS GUILTY BLOOD... AND ASK THE UNIVERSE TO GUIDE US.
UGGH!
ATROCITUS, YOU'RE WEAK. A BLOOD PROPHECY COULD KILL YOU.
UNIVERSE... REVEAL TO ME... THE A-ABERRATION, A... A... BYSMUS.
UGH... GHHH... UGHH...!
ATROCITUS, IN THE NAME OF RAGE, STOP THE PROPHECY!
SHOW ME... WHERE HE... IS!

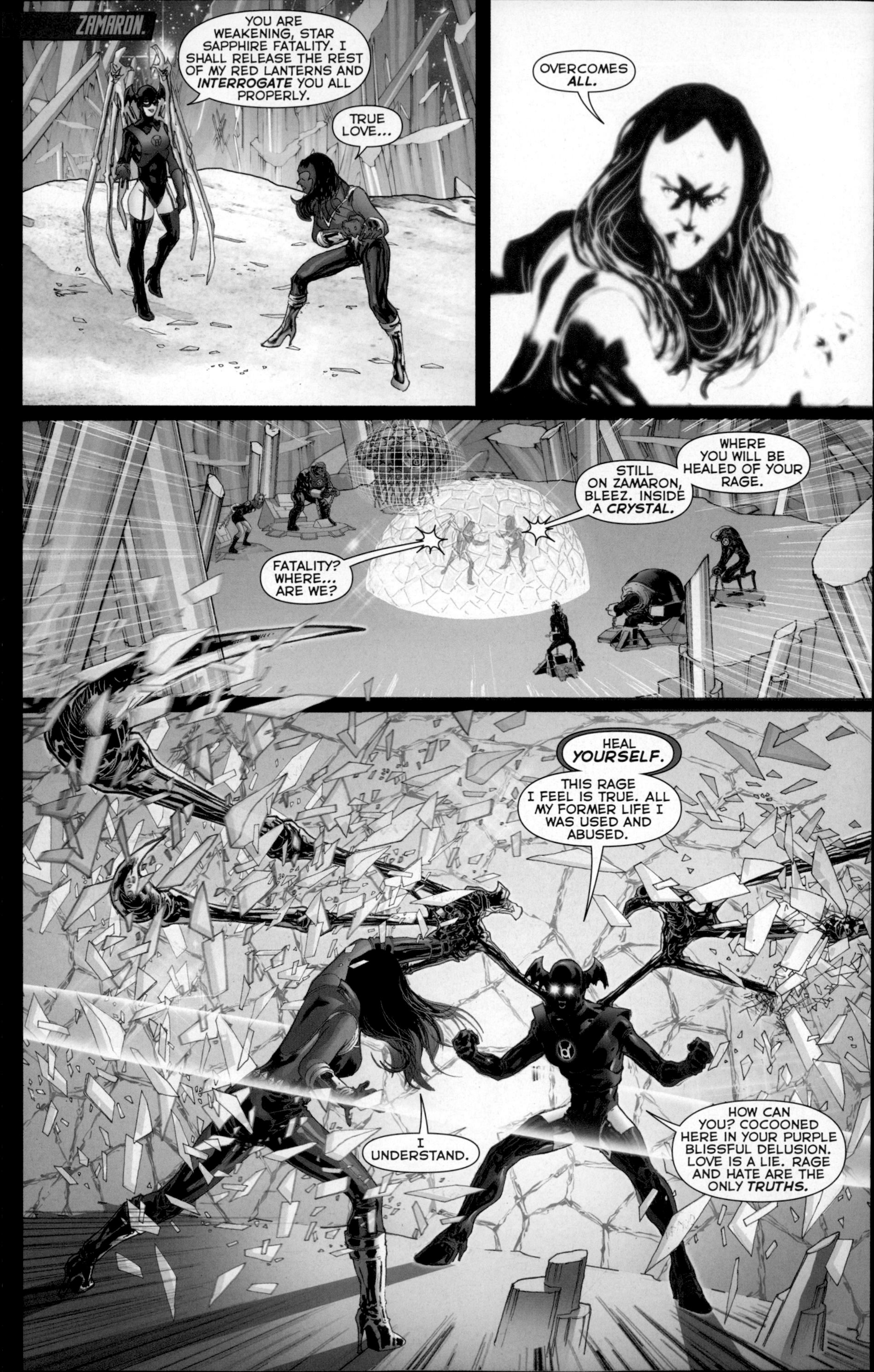
ZAMARON.
YOU ARE WEAKENING, STAR SAPPHIRE FATALITY. I SHALL RELEASE THE REST OF MY RED LANTERNS AND *INTERROGATE* YOU ALL PROPERLY.
TRUE LOVE...
OVERCOMES *ALL.*
FATALITY? WHERE... ARE WE?
STILL ON ZAMARON, BLEEZ. INSIDE A *CRYSTAL.*
WHERE YOU WILL BE HEALED OF YOUR RAGE.
HEAL *YOURSELF.*
THIS RAGE I FEEL IS TRUE. ALL MY FORMER LIFE I WAS USED AND ABUSED.
I UNDERSTAND.
HOW CAN YOU? COCOONED HERE IN YOUR PURPLE BLISSFUL DELUSION. LOVE IS A LIE. RAGE AND HATE ARE THE ONLY *TRUTHS.*

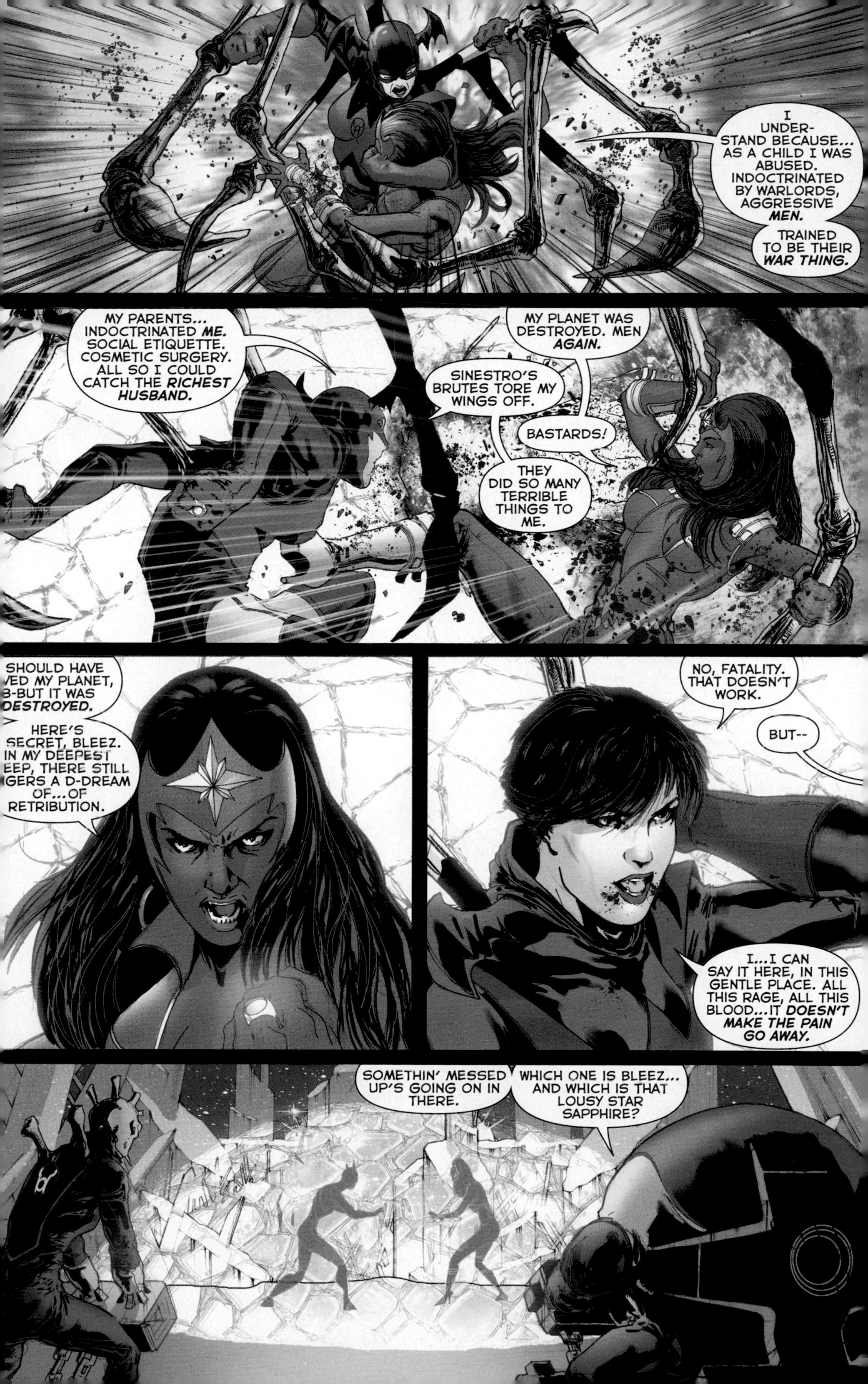
I UNDER-STAND BECAUSE... AS A CHILD I WAS ABUSED. INDOCTRINATED BY WARLORDS, AGGRESSIVE MEN.
TRAINED TO BE THEIR WAR THING.
MY PARENTS... INDOCTRINATED ME. SOCIAL ETIQUETTE. COSMETIC SURGERY. ALL SO I COULD CATCH THE RICHEST HUSBAND.
MY PLANET WAS DESTROYED. MEN AGAIN.
SINESTRO'S BRUTES TORE MY WINGS OFF.
BASTARDS!
THEY DID SO MANY TERRIBLE THINGS TO ME.
SHOULD HAVE VED MY PLANET, B-BUT IT WAS DESTROYED.
HERE'S SECRET, BLEEZ. IN MY DEEPEST EEP, THERE STILL IGERS A D-DREAM OF...OF RETRIBUTION.
NO, FATALITY. THAT DOESN'T WORK.
BUT--
I...I CAN SAY IT HERE, IN THIS GENTLE PLACE. ALL THIS RAGE, ALL THIS BLOOD...IT DOESN'T MAKE THE PAIN GO AWAY.
SOMETHIN' MESSED UP'S GOING ON IN THERE.
WHICH ONE IS BLEEZ... AND WHICH IS THAT LOUSY STAR SAPPHIRE?

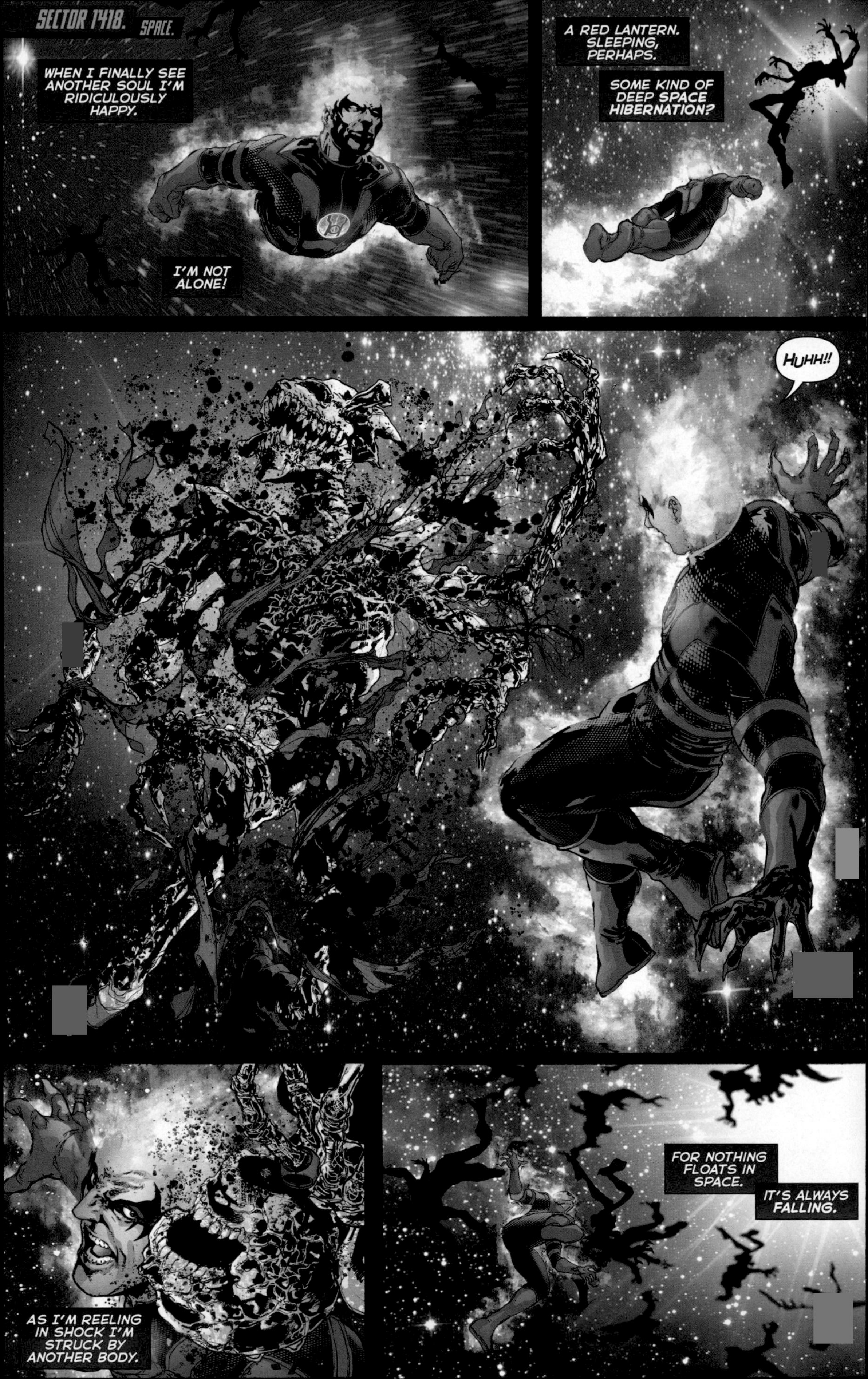
SECTOR 1418.
SPACE.
WHEN I FINALLY SEE ANOTHER SOUL I'M RIDICULOUSLY HAPPY.
I'M NOT ALONE!
A RED LANTERN. SLEEPING, PERHAPS.
SOME KIND OF DEEP SPACE HIBERNATION?
HUHH!!
AS I'M REELING IN SHOCK I'M STRUCK BY ANOTHER BODY.
FOR NOTHING FLOATS IN SPACE.
IT'S ALWAYS FALLING.

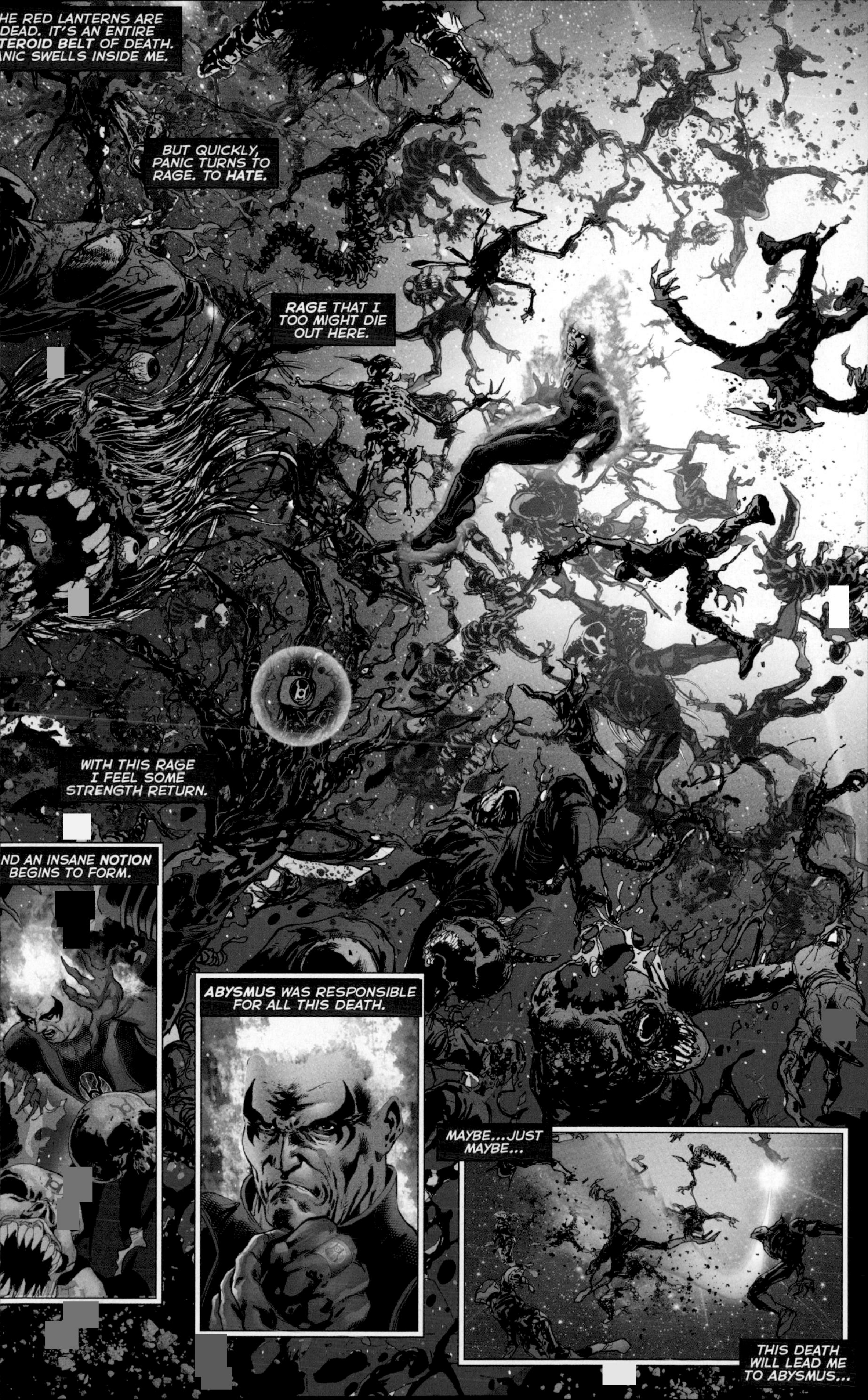
HE RED LANTERNS ARE DEAD. IT'S AN ENTIRE TEROID BELT OF DEATH. ANIC SWELLS INSIDE ME.
BUT QUICKLY, PANIC TURNS TO RAGE. TO HATE.
RAGE THAT I TOO MIGHT DIE OUT HERE.
WITH THIS RAGE I FEEL SOME STRENGTH RETURN.
ND AN INSANE NOTION BEGINS TO FORM.
ABYSMUS WAS RESPONSIBLE FOR ALL THIS DEATH.
MAYBE...JUST MAYBE...
THIS DEATH WILL LEAD ME TO ABYSMUS...

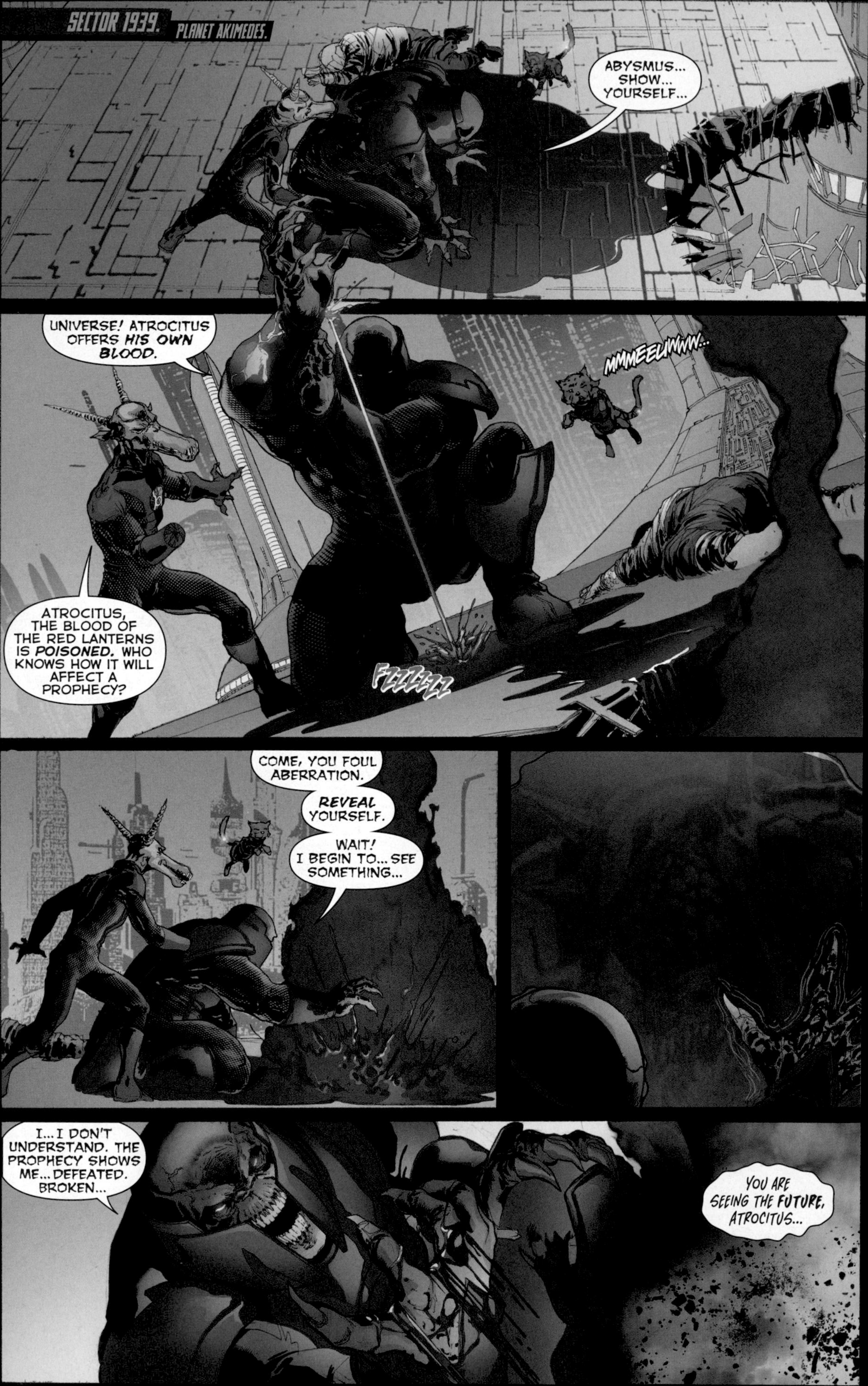
SECTOR 1939.
PLANET AKIMEDES.
ABYSMUS... SHOW... YOURSELF...
UNIVERSE! ATROCITUS OFFERS HIS OWN BLOOD.
MMMEEUWWW...
ATROCITUS, THE BLOOD OF THE RED LANTERNS IS POISONED. WHO KNOWS HOW IT WILL AFFECT A PROPHECY?
FZZZZZZZ
COME, YOU FOUL ABERRATION.
REVEAL YOURSELF.
WAIT! I BEGIN TO... SEE SOMETHING...
I... I DON'T UNDERSTAND. THE PROPHECY SHOWS ME... DEFEATED. BROKEN...
YOU ARE SEEING THE FUTURE, ATROCITUS...

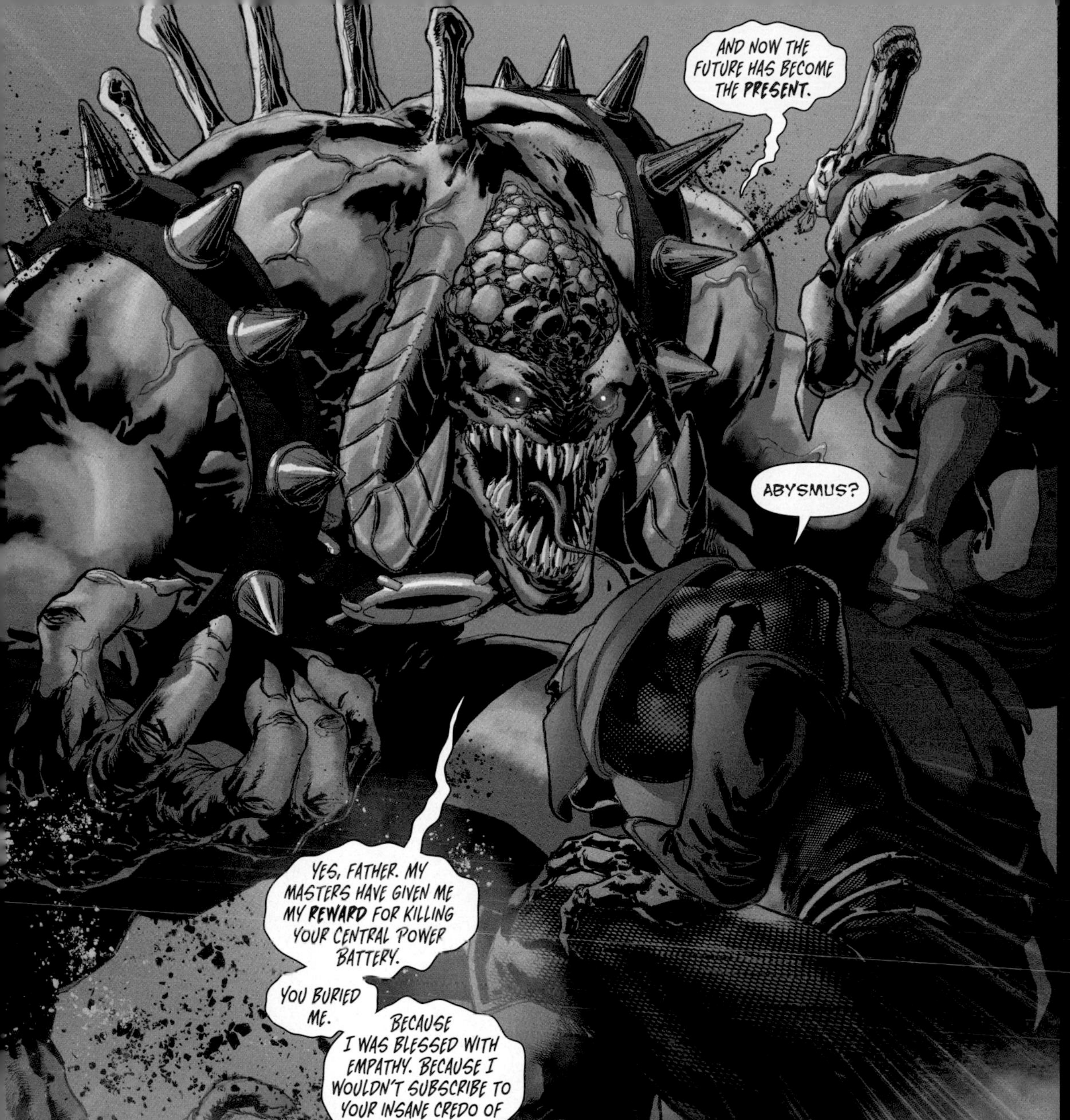
AND NOW THE FUTURE HAS BECOME THE PRESENT.
ABYSMUS?
YES, FATHER. MY MASTERS HAVE GIVEN ME MY REWARD FOR KILLING YOUR CENTRAL POWER BATTERY.
YOU BURIED ME.
BECAUSE I WAS BLESSED WITH EMPATHY. BECAUSE I WOULDN'T SUBSCRIBE TO YOUR INSANE CREDO OF REVENGE...

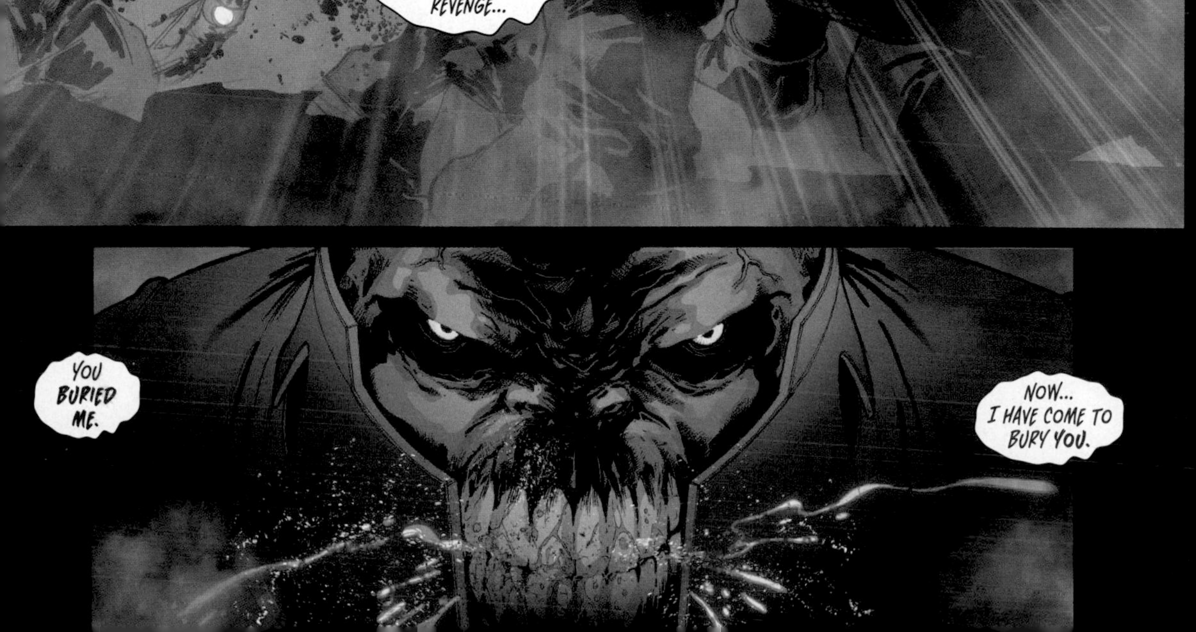
YOU BURIED ME.
NOW... I HAVE COME TO BURY YOU.

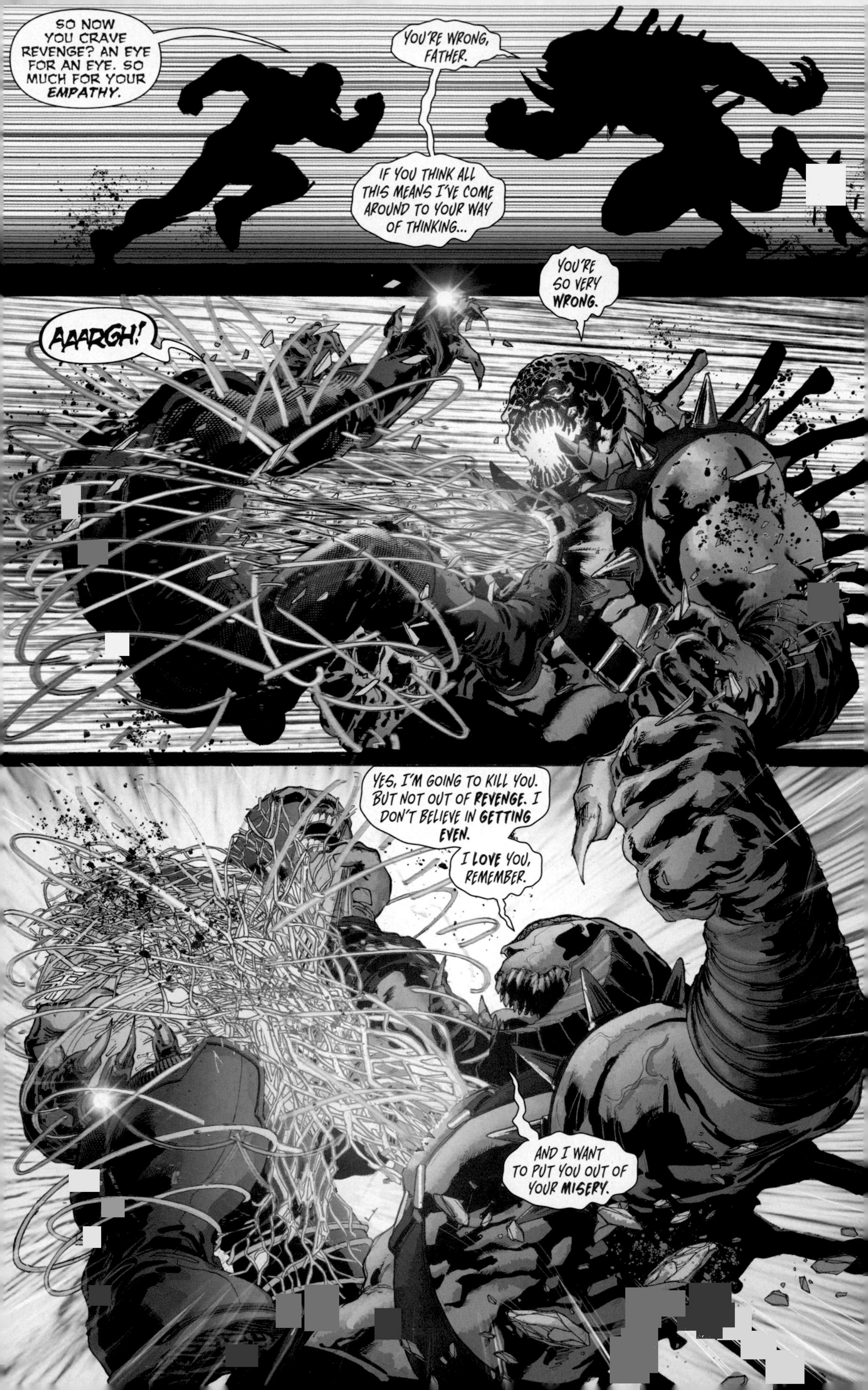
SO NOW YOU CRAVE REVENGE? AN EYE FOR AN EYE. SO MUCH FOR YOUR EMPATHY.
YOU'RE WRONG, FATHER.
IF YOU THINK ALL THIS MEANS I'VE COME AROUND TO YOUR WAY OF THINKING...
YOU'RE SO VERY WRONG.
AAARGH!
YES, I'M GOING TO KILL YOU. BUT NOT OUT OF REVENGE. I DON'T BELIEVE IN GETTING EVEN.
I LOVE YOU, REMEMBER.
AND I WANT TO PUT YOU OUT OF YOUR MISERY.

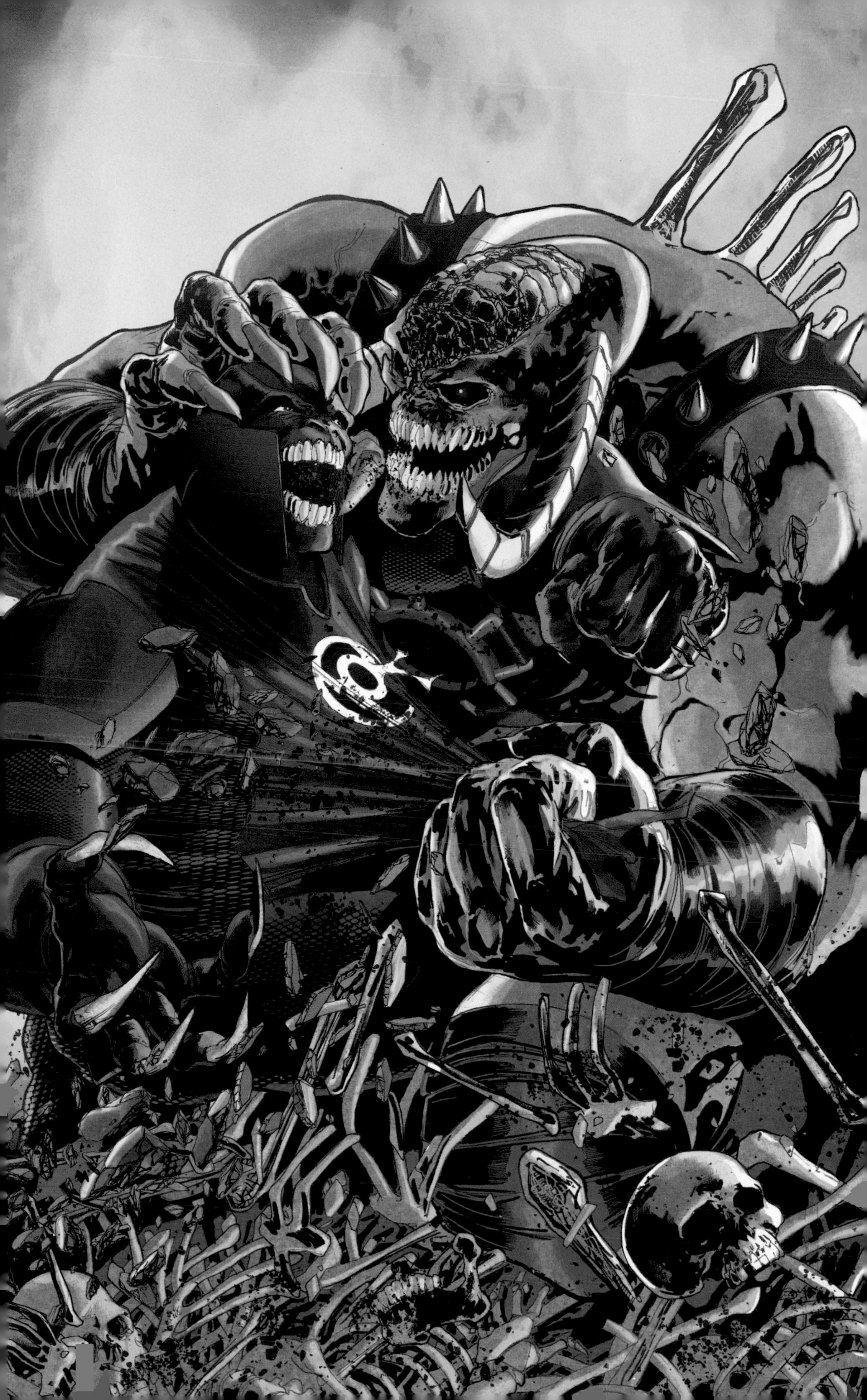

NECTAR

PETER MILLIGAN
writer

MIGUEL SEPULVEDA
artist

cover art by MIGUEL SEPULVEDA & RAIN BEREDO

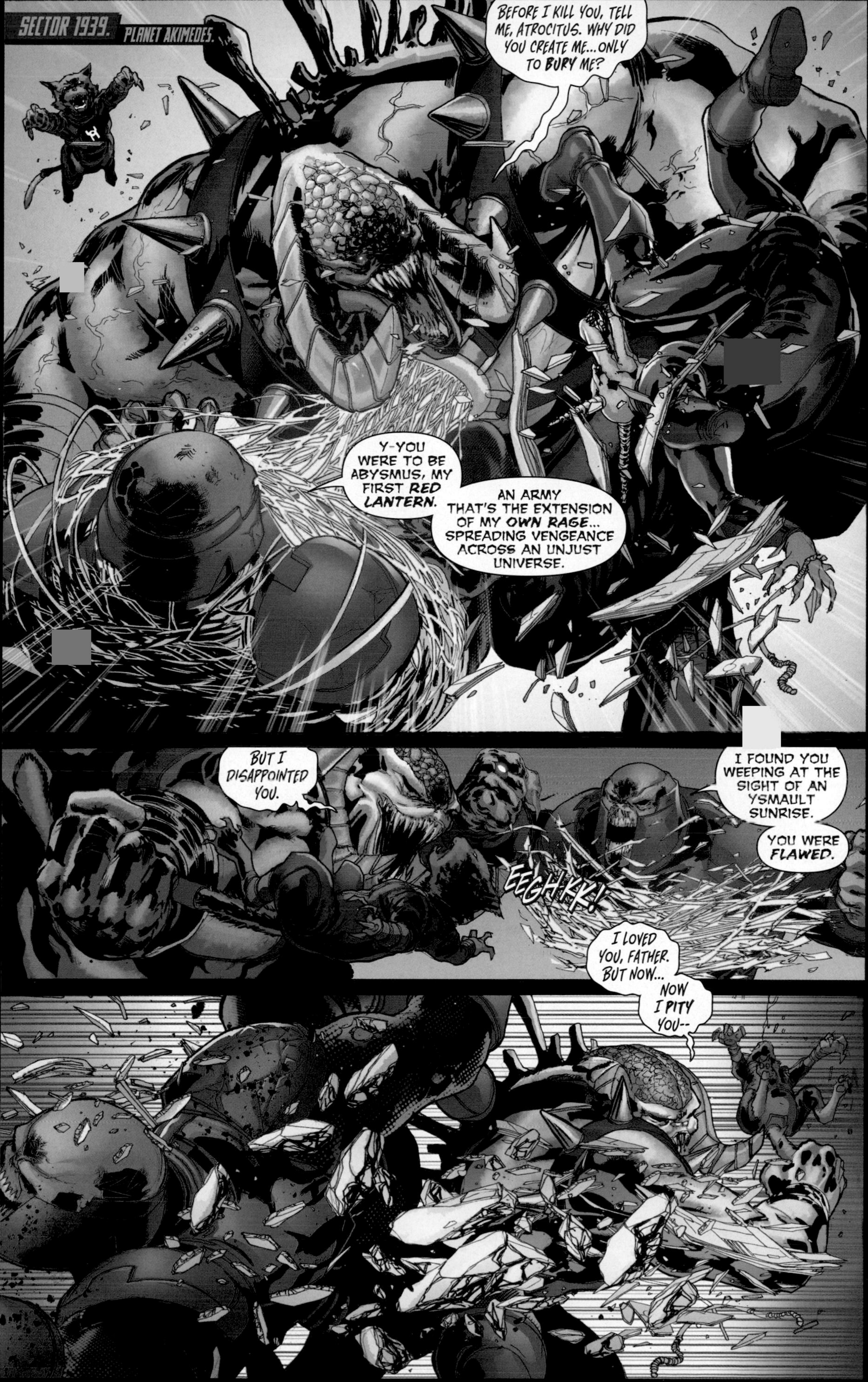
SECTOR 1939.
PLANET AKIMEDES.
BEFORE I KILL YOU, TELL ME, ATROCITUS. WHY DID YOU CREATE ME...ONLY TO BURY ME?
Y-YOU WERE TO BE ABYSMUS, MY FIRST RED LANTERN.
AN ARMY THAT'S THE EXTENSION OF MY OWN RAGE... SPREADING VENGEANCE ACROSS AN UNJUST UNIVERSE.
BUT I DISAPPOINTED YOU.
I FOUND YOU WEEPING AT THE SIGHT OF AN YSMAULT SUNRISE.
YOU WERE FLAWED.
EEGHKK!
I LOVED YOU, FATHER. BUT NOW...
NOW I PITY YOU--

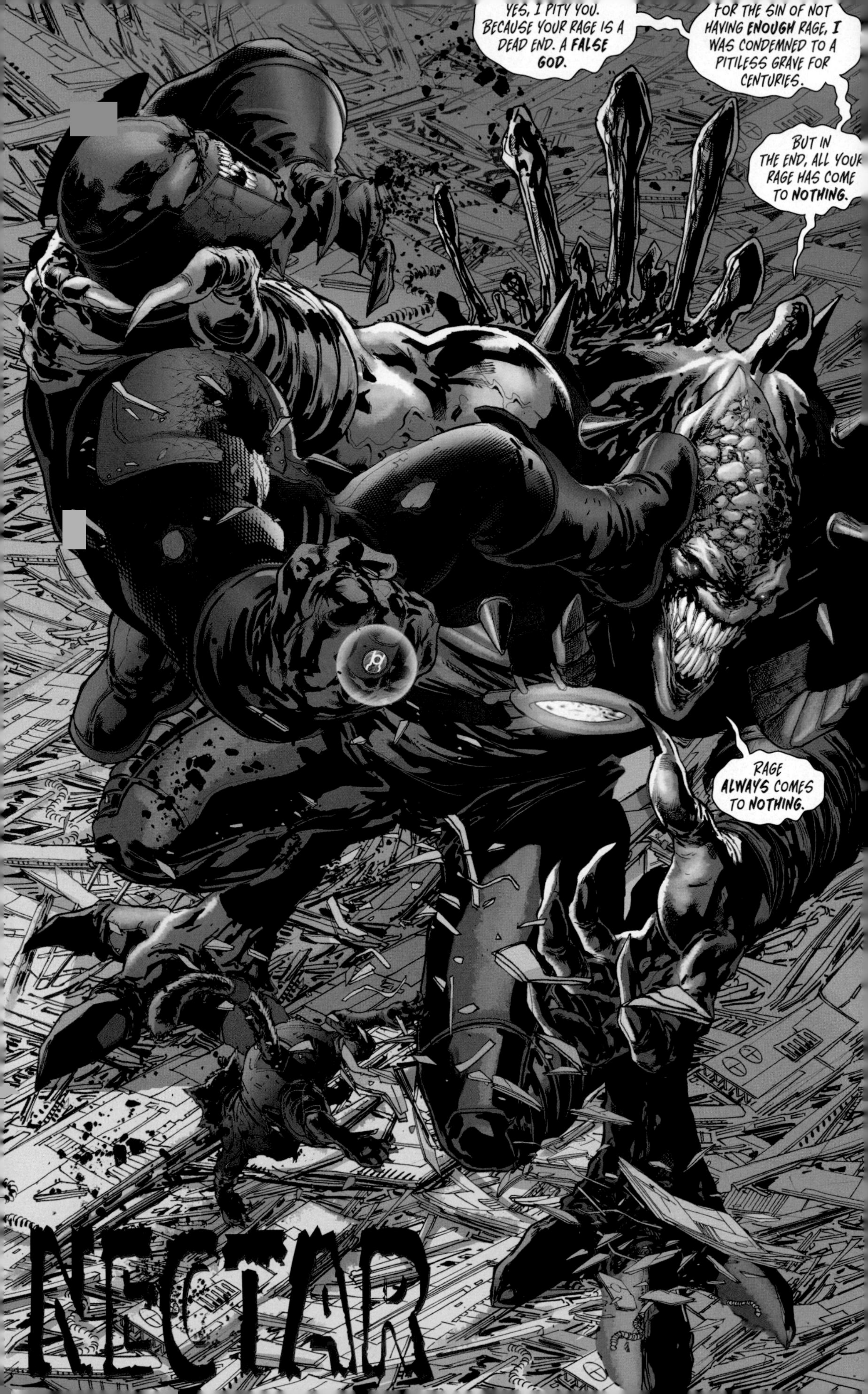
YES, I PITY YOU. BECAUSE YOUR RAGE IS A DEAD END. A **FALSE GOD.**
FOR THE SIN OF NOT HAVING **ENOUGH** RAGE, I WAS CONDEMNED TO A PITILESS GRAVE FOR CENTURIES.
BUT IN THE END, ALL YOUR RAGE HAS COME TO **NOTHING.**
RAGE **ALWAYS** COMES TO **NOTHING.**
NECTAR

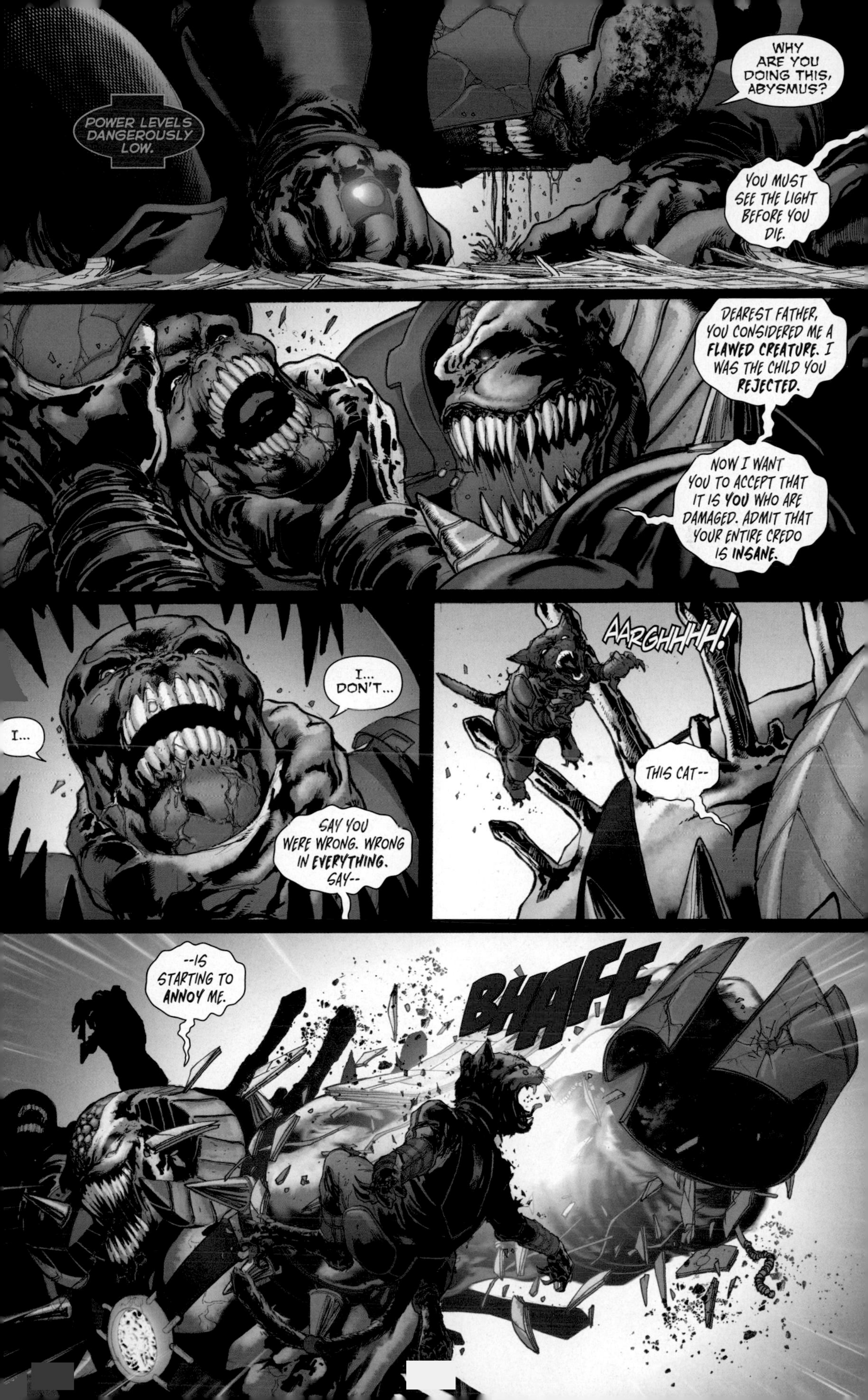
POWER LEVELS DANGEROUSLY LOW.
WHY ARE YOU DOING THIS, ABYSMUS?
YOU MUST SEE THE LIGHT BEFORE YOU DIE.
DEAREST FATHER, YOU CONSIDERED ME A FLAWED CREATURE. I WAS THE CHILD YOU REJECTED.
NOW I WANT YOU TO ACCEPT THAT IT IS YOU WHO ARE DAMAGED. ADMIT THAT YOUR ENTIRE CREDO IS INSANE.
I...
I... DON'T...
SAY YOU WERE WRONG. WRONG IN EVERYTHING. SAY--
AARGHHHH!
THIS CAT--
--IS STARTING TO ANNOY ME.
BHAFF

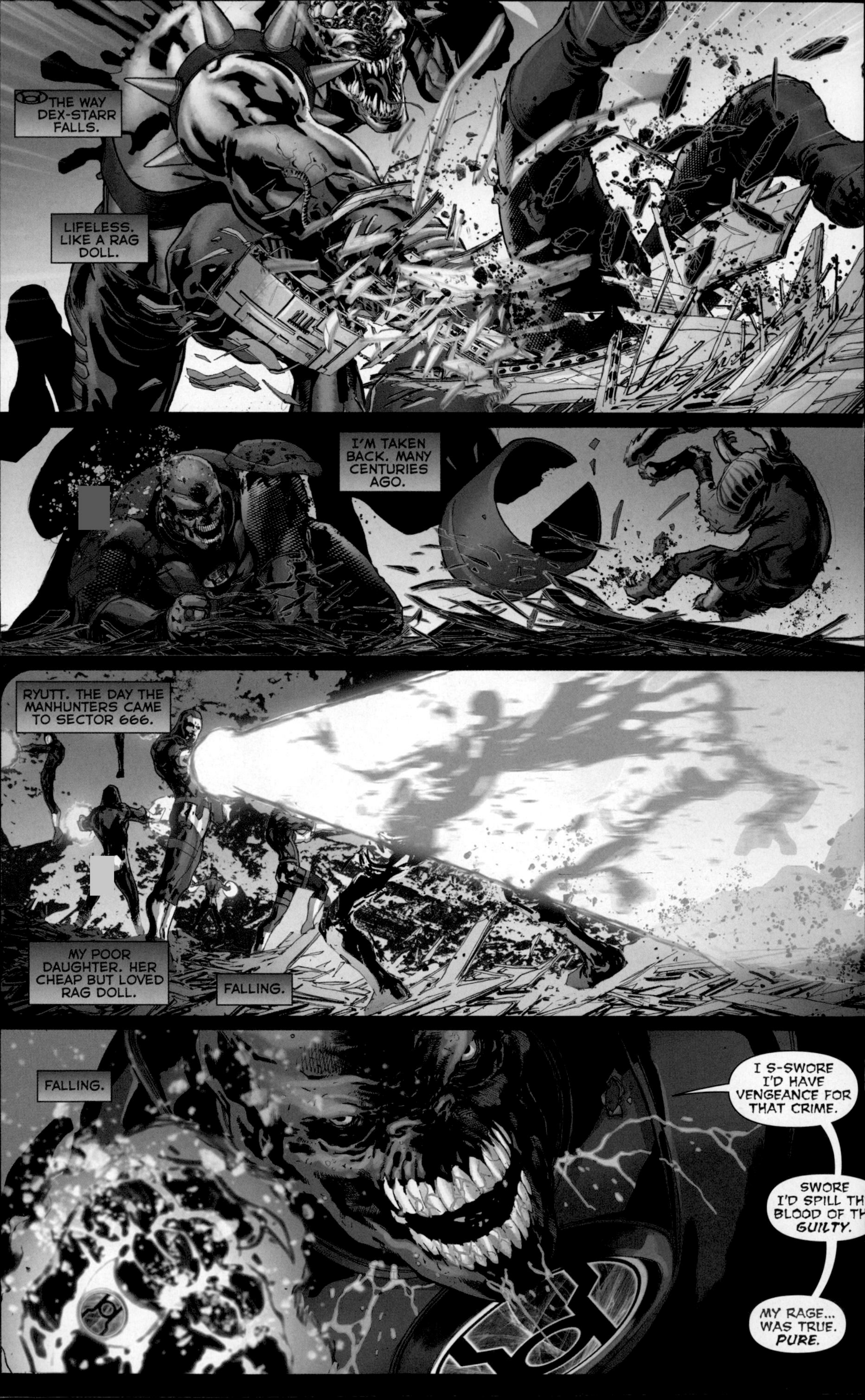
THE WAY DEX-STARR FALLS.
LIFELESS. LIKE A RAG DOLL.
I'M TAKEN BACK. MANY CENTURIES AGO.
RYUTT. THE DAY THE MANHUNTERS CAME TO SECTOR 666.
MY POOR DAUGHTER. HER CHEAP BUT LOVED RAG DOLL.
FALLING.
FALLING.
I S-SWORE I'D HAVE VENGEANCE FOR THAT CRIME.
SWORE I'D SPILL TH BLOOD OF TH *GUILTY*.
MY RAGE... WAS TRUE. *PURE*.

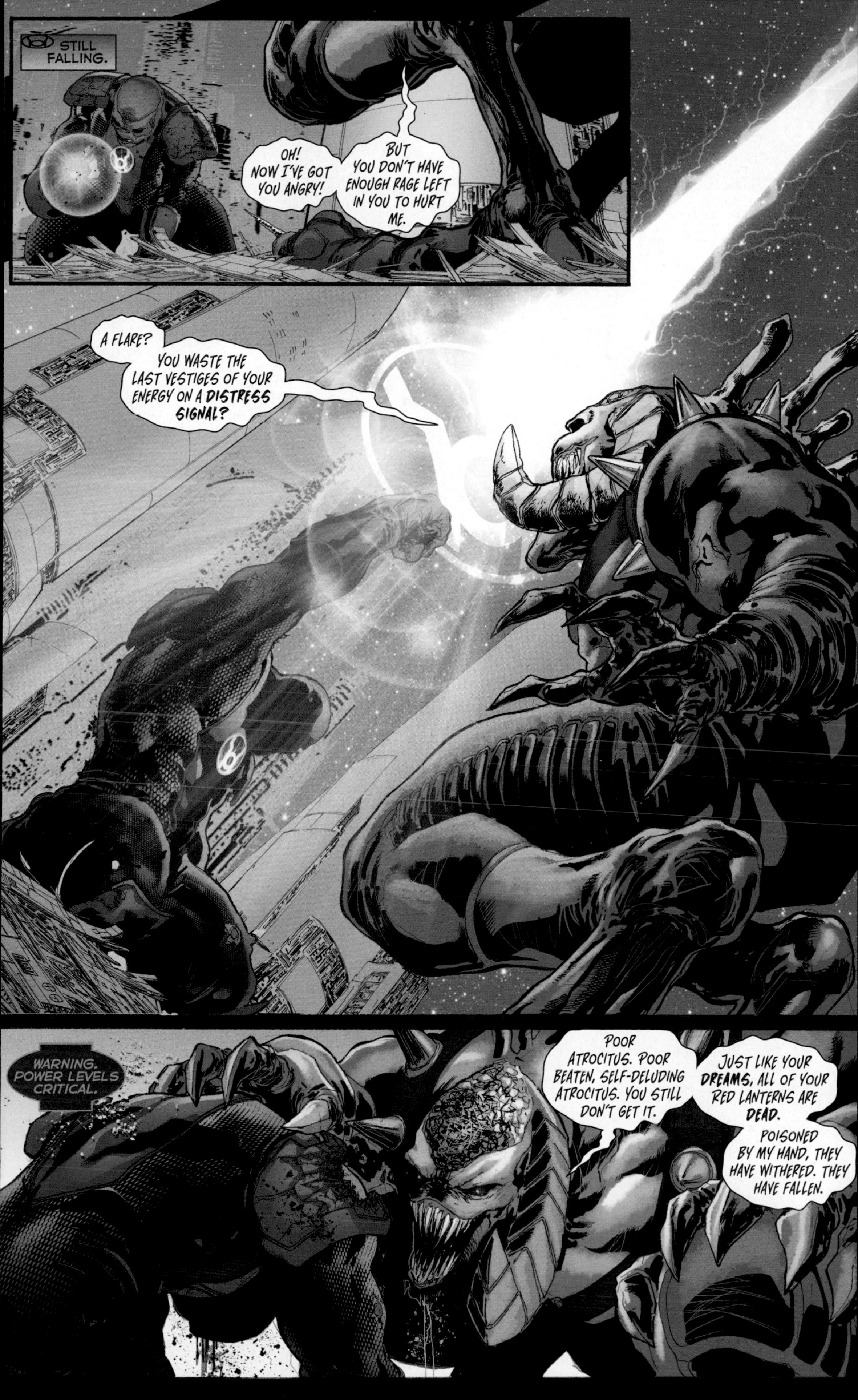
STILL FALLING.
OH! NOW I'VE GOT YOU ANGRY!
BUT YOU DON'T HAVE ENOUGH RAGE LEFT IN YOU TO HURT ME.
A FLARE? YOU WASTE THE LAST VESTIGES OF YOUR ENERGY ON A DISTRESS SIGNAL?
WARNING. POWER LEVELS CRITICAL.
POOR ATROCITUS. POOR BEATEN, SELF-DELUDING ATROCITUS. YOU STILL DON'T GET IT.
JUST LIKE YOUR DREAMS, ALL OF YOUR RED LANTERNS ARE DEAD.
POISONED BY MY HAND, THEY HAVE WITHERED. THEY HAVE FALLEN.

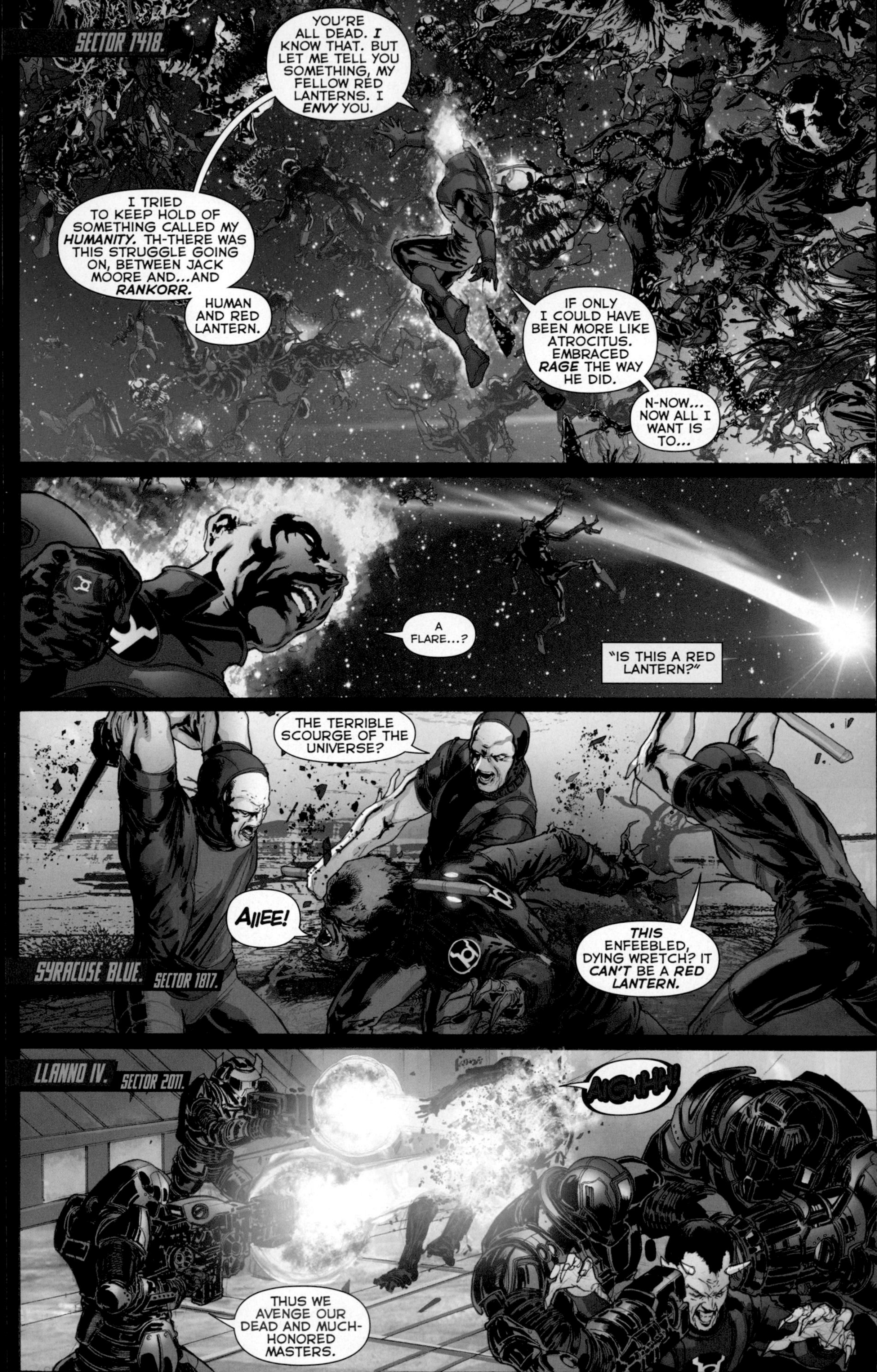
SECTOR 1418.
YOU'RE ALL DEAD. I KNOW THAT. BUT LET ME TELL YOU SOMETHING, MY FELLOW RED LANTERNS. I ENVY YOU.
I TRIED TO KEEP HOLD OF SOMETHING CALLED MY HUMANITY. TH-THERE WAS THIS STRUGGLE GOING ON, BETWEEN JACK MOORE AND...AND RANKORR.
HUMAN AND RED LANTERN.
IF ONLY I COULD HAVE BEEN MORE LIKE ATROCITUS. EMBRACED RAGE THE WAY HE DID.
N-NOW... NOW ALL I WANT IS TO...
A FLARE...?
"IS THIS A RED LANTERN?"
THE TERRIBLE SCOURGE OF THE UNIVERSE?
AIIEE!
THIS ENFEEBLED, DYING WRETCH? IT CAN'T BE A RED LANTERN.
SYRACUSE BLUE. SECTOR 1817.
LLANNO IV. SECTOR 2011.
AIGHHH!
THUS WE AVENGE OUR DEAD AND MUCH-HONORED MASTERS.

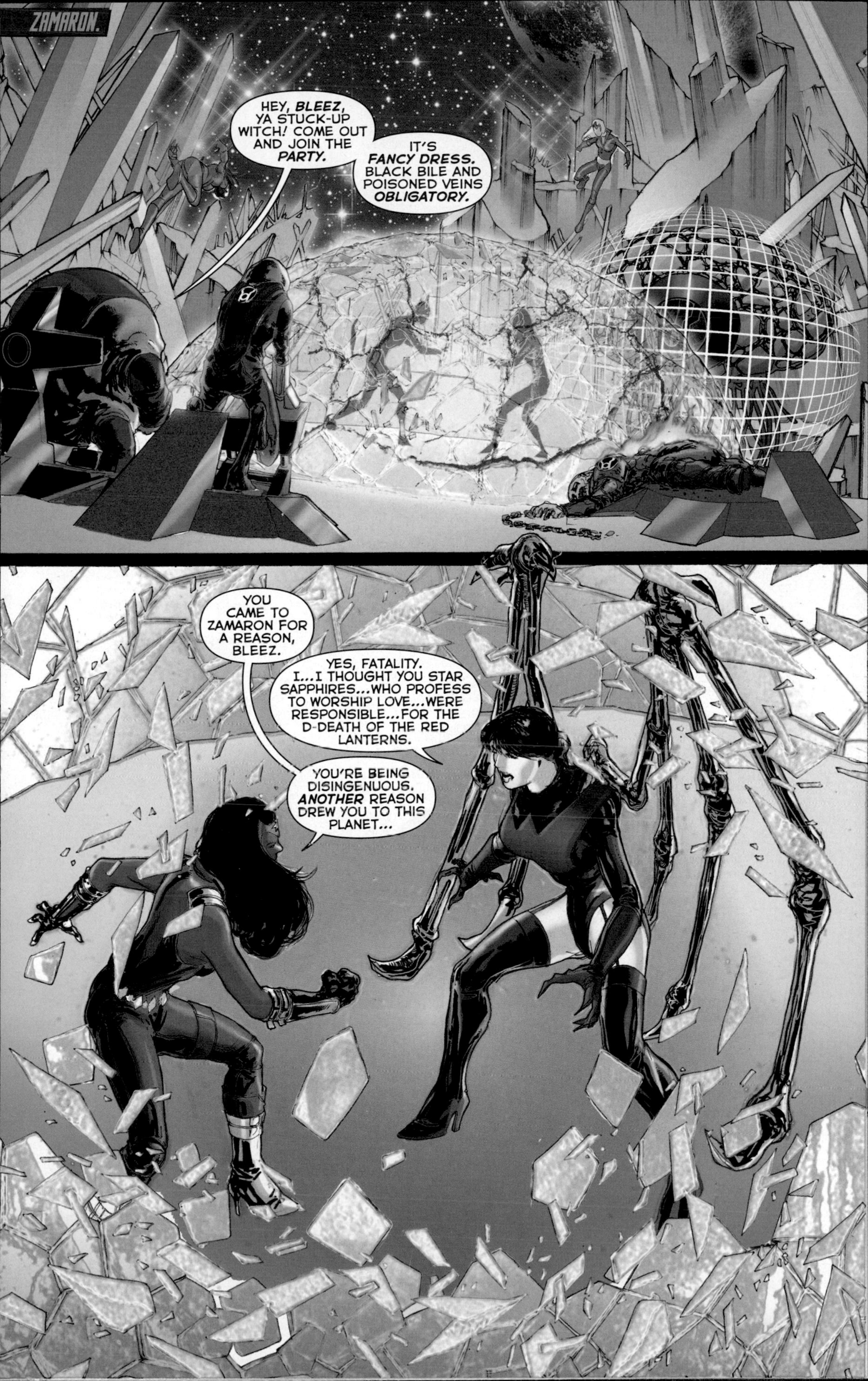
ZAMARON.
HEY, BLEEZ, YA STUCK-UP WITCH! COME OUT AND JOIN THE PARTY.
IT'S FANCY DRESS. BLACK BILE AND POISONED VEINS OBLIGATORY.
YOU CAME TO ZAMARON FOR A REASON, BLEEZ.
YES, FATALITY. I...I THOUGHT YOU STAR SAPPHIRES...WHO PROFESS TO WORSHIP LOVE...WERE RESPONSIBLE...FOR THE D-DEATH OF THE RED LANTERNS.
YOU'RE BEING DISINGENUOUS. ANOTHER REASON DREW YOU TO THIS PLANET...

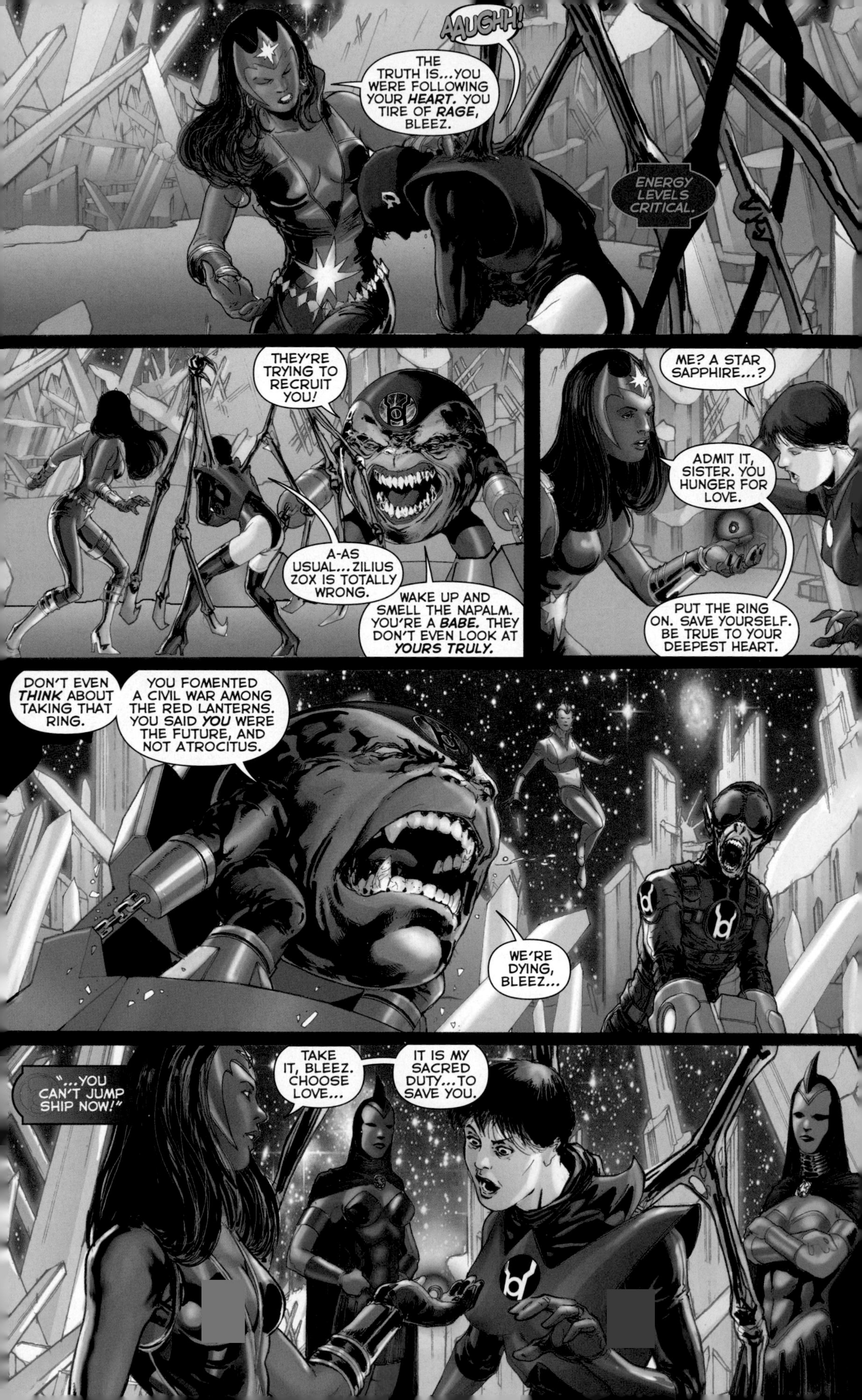
THE TRUTH IS...YOU WERE FOLLOWING YOUR HEART. YOU TIRE OF RAGE, BLEEZ.
AAUGHH!
ENERGY LEVELS CRITICAL.
THEY'RE TRYING TO RECRUIT YOU!
A-AS USUAL...ZILIUS ZOX IS TOTALLY WRONG.
WAKE UP AND SMELL THE NAPALM. YOU'RE A BABE. THEY DON'T EVEN LOOK AT YOURS TRULY.
ME? A STAR SAPPHIRE...?
ADMIT IT, SISTER. YOU HUNGER FOR LOVE.
PUT THE RING ON. SAVE YOURSELF. BE TRUE TO YOUR DEEPEST HEART.
DON'T EVEN THINK ABOUT TAKING THAT RING.
YOU FOMENTED A CIVIL WAR AMONG THE RED LANTERNS. YOU SAID YOU WERE THE FUTURE, AND NOT ATROCITUS.
WE'RE DYING, BLEEZ...
"...YOU CAN'T JUMP SHIP NOW!"
TAKE IT, BLEEZ. CHOOSE LOVE...
IT IS MY SACRED DUTY...TO SAVE YOU.

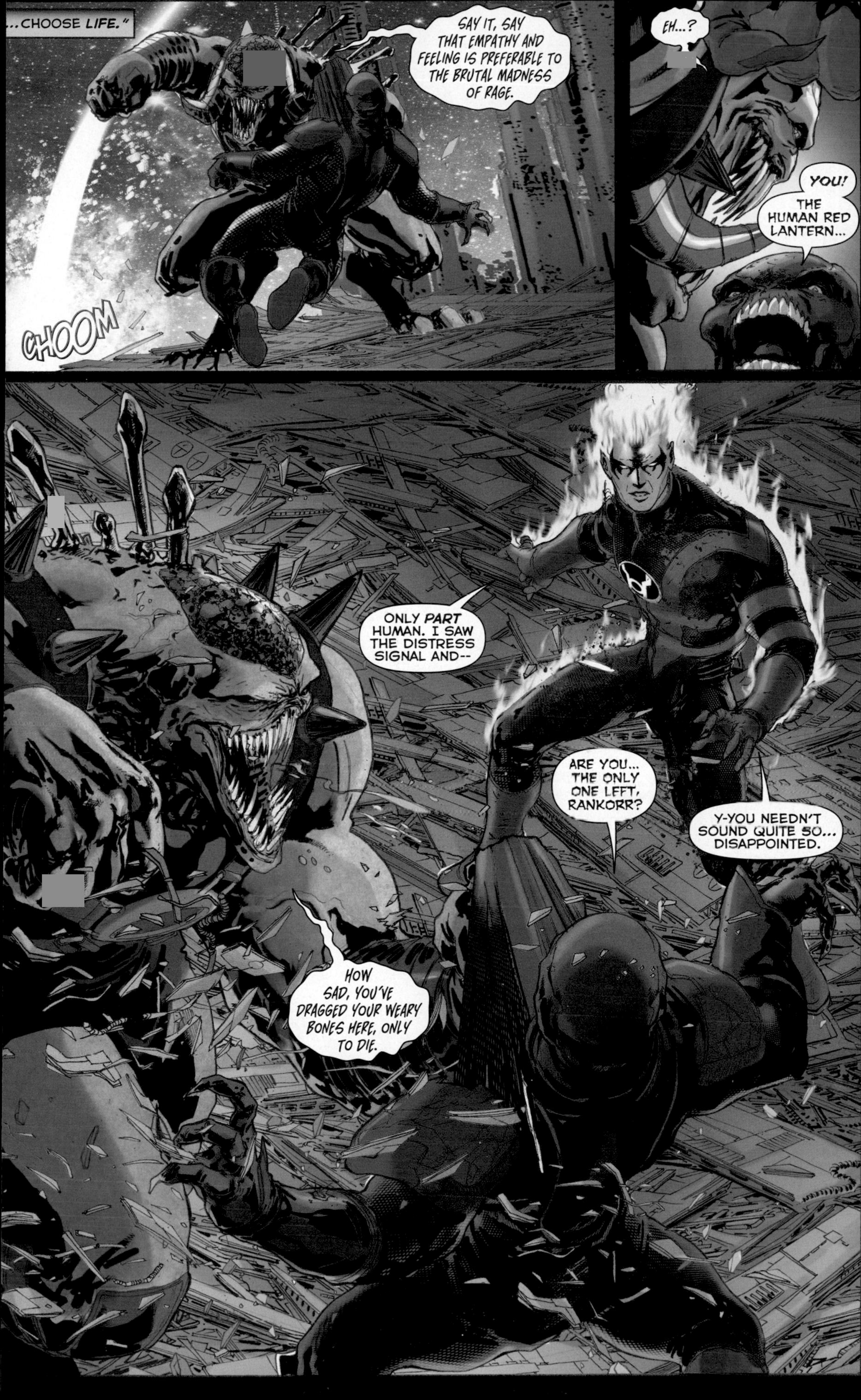
...CHOOSE *LIFE*."
SAY IT, SAY THAT EMPATHY AND FEELING IS PREFERABLE TO THE BRUTAL MADNESS OF RAGE.
CHOOM
EH...?
YOU! THE HUMAN RED LANTERN...
ONLY *PART* HUMAN. I SAW THE DISTRESS SIGNAL AND--
HOW SAD, YOU'VE DRAGGED YOUR WEARY BONES HERE, ONLY TO DIE.
ARE YOU... THE ONLY ONE LEFT, RANKORR?
Y-YOU NEEDN'T SOUND QUITE SO... DISAPPOINTED.

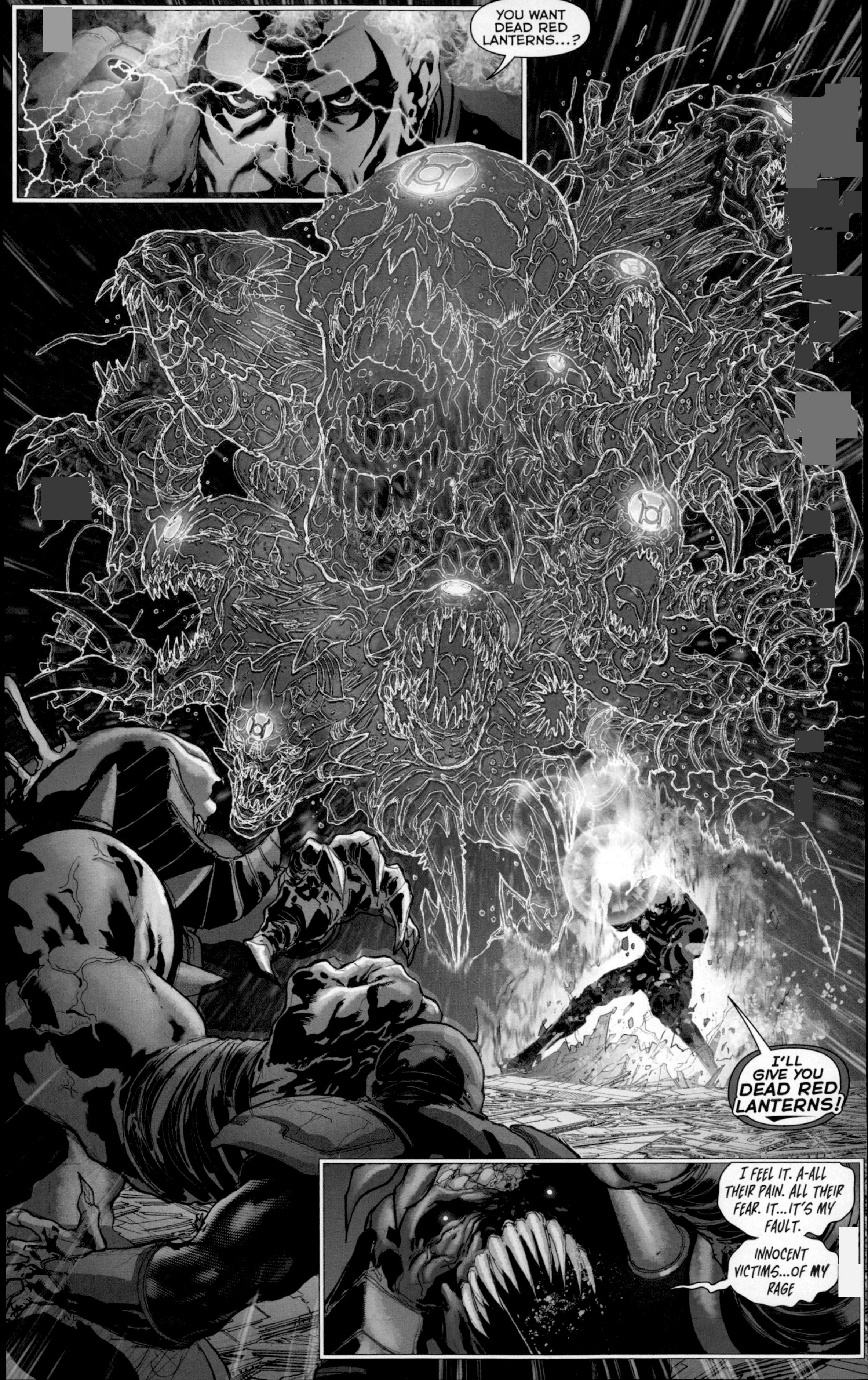
YOU WANT DEAD RED LANTERNS...?
I'LL GIVE YOU DEAD RED LANTERNS!
I FEEL IT. A-ALL THEIR PAIN. ALL THEIR FEAR. IT...IT'S MY FAULT.
INNOCENT VICTIMS...OF MY RAGE

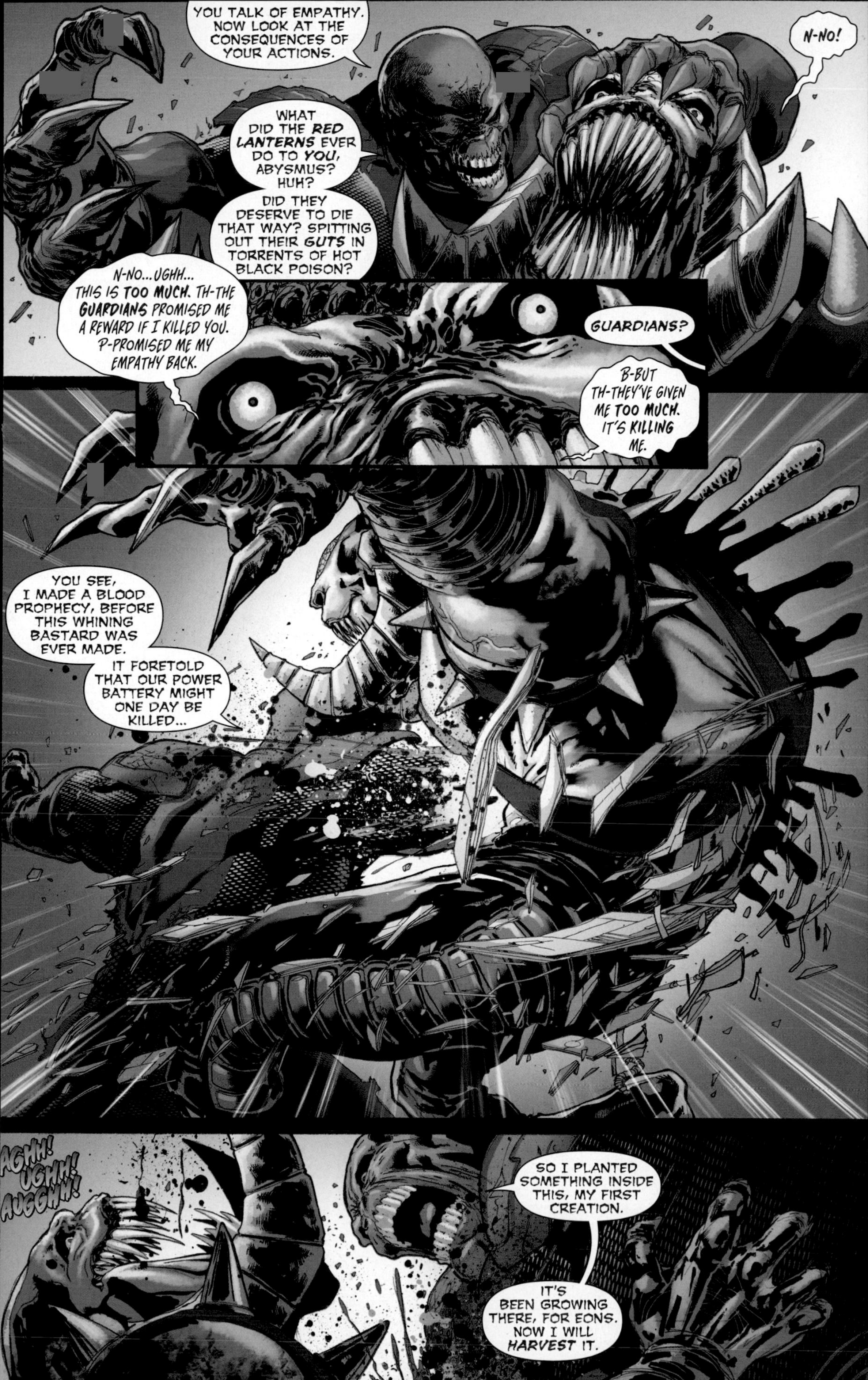
YOU TALK OF EMPATHY. NOW LOOK AT THE CONSEQUENCES OF YOUR ACTIONS.
N-NO!
WHAT DID THE RED LANTERNS EVER DO TO YOU, ABYSMUS? HUH?
DID THEY DESERVE TO DIE THAT WAY? SPITTING OUT THEIR GUTS IN TORRENTS OF HOT BLACK POISON?
N-NO...UGHH... THIS IS TOO MUCH. TH-THE GUARDIANS PROMISED ME A REWARD IF I KILLED YOU. P-PROMISED ME MY EMPATHY BACK.
GUARDIANS?
B-BUT TH-THEY'VE GIVEN ME TOO MUCH. IT'S KILLING ME.
YOU SEE, I MADE A BLOOD PROPHECY, BEFORE THIS WHINING BASTARD WAS EVER MADE.
IT FORETOLD THAT OUR POWER BATTERY MIGHT ONE DAY BE KILLED...
AGHH! UGHH! AUGGHH!
SO I PLANTED SOMETHING INSIDE THIS, MY FIRST CREATION.
IT'S BEEN GROWING THERE, FOR EONS. NOW I WILL HARVEST IT.

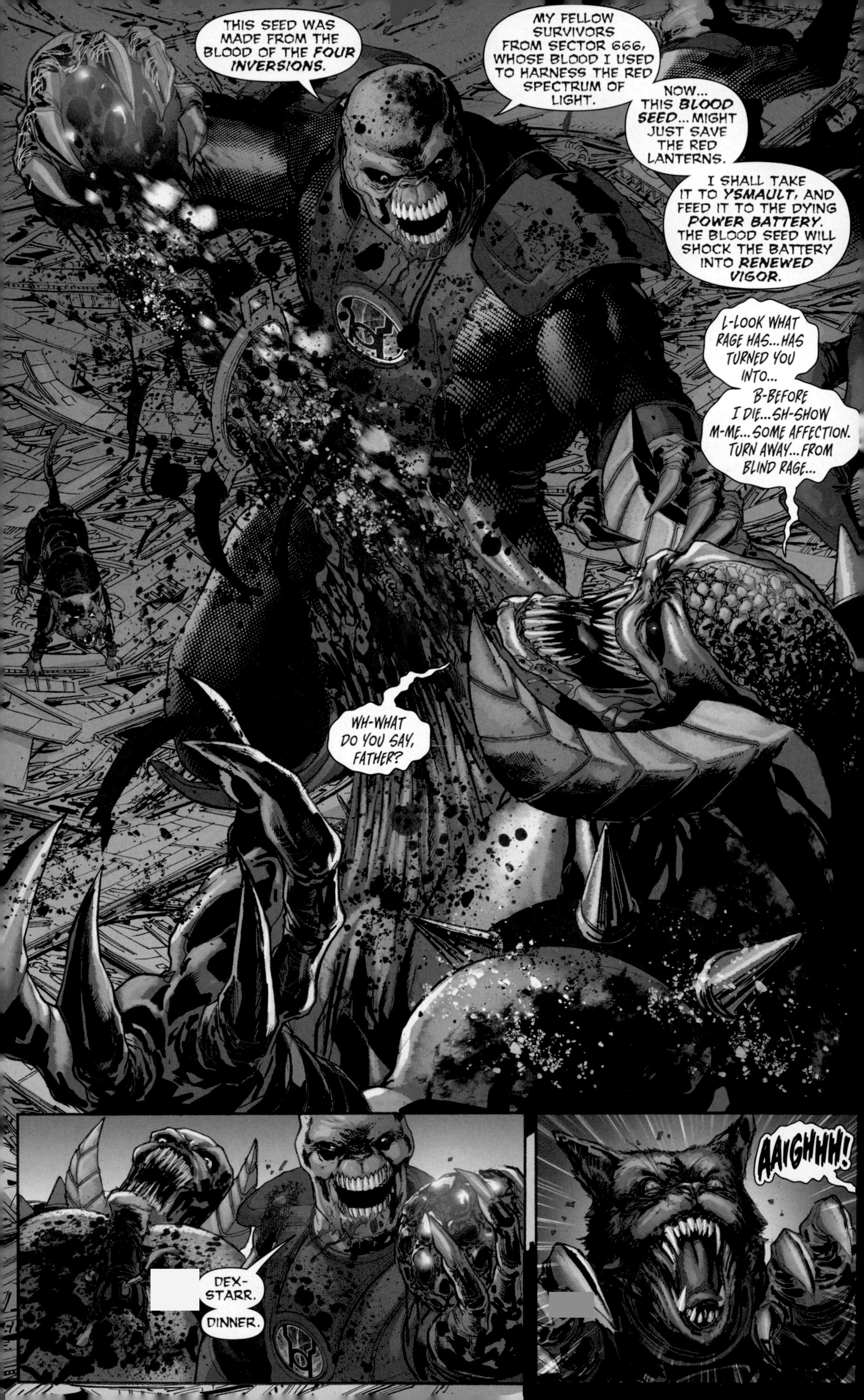
THIS SEED WAS MADE FROM THE BLOOD OF THE FOUR INVERSIONS.
MY FELLOW SURVIVORS FROM SECTOR 666, WHOSE BLOOD I USED TO HARNESS THE RED SPECTRUM OF LIGHT.
NOW... THIS BLOOD SEED... MIGHT JUST SAVE THE RED LANTERNS.
I SHALL TAKE IT TO YSMAULT, AND FEED IT TO THE DYING POWER BATTERY. THE BLOOD SEED WILL SHOCK THE BATTERY INTO RENEWED VIGOR.
L-LOOK WHAT RAGE HAS...HAS TURNED YOU INTO...
B-BEFORE I DIE...SH-SHOW M-ME...SOME AFFECTION. TURN AWAY...FROM BLIND RAGE...
WH-WHAT DO YOU SAY, FATHER?
DEX-STARR.
DINNER.
AAIGHHH!

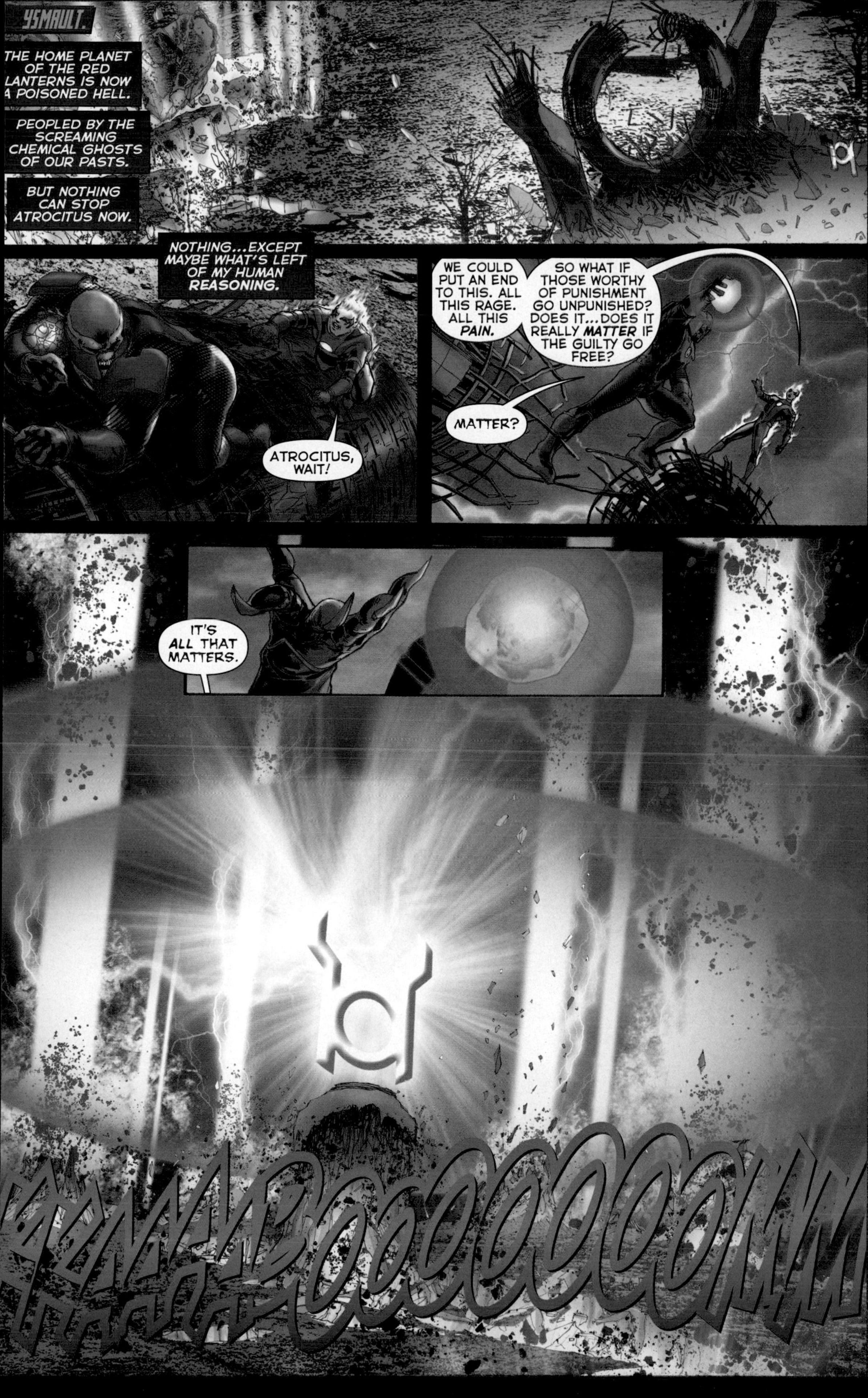
YSMAULT.
THE HOME PLANET OF THE RED LANTERNS IS NOW A POISONED HELL.
PEOPLED BY THE SCREAMING CHEMICAL GHOSTS OF OUR PASTS.
BUT NOTHING CAN STOP ATROCITUS NOW.
NOTHING...EXCEPT MAYBE WHAT'S LEFT OF MY HUMAN REASONING.
ATROCITUS, WAIT!
WE COULD PUT AN END TO THIS. ALL THIS RAGE. ALL THIS PAIN.
SO WHAT IF THOSE WORTHY OF PUNISHMENT GO UNPUNISHED? DOES IT...DOES IT REALLY MATTER IF THE GUILTY GO FREE?
MATTER?
IT'S ALL THAT MATTERS.

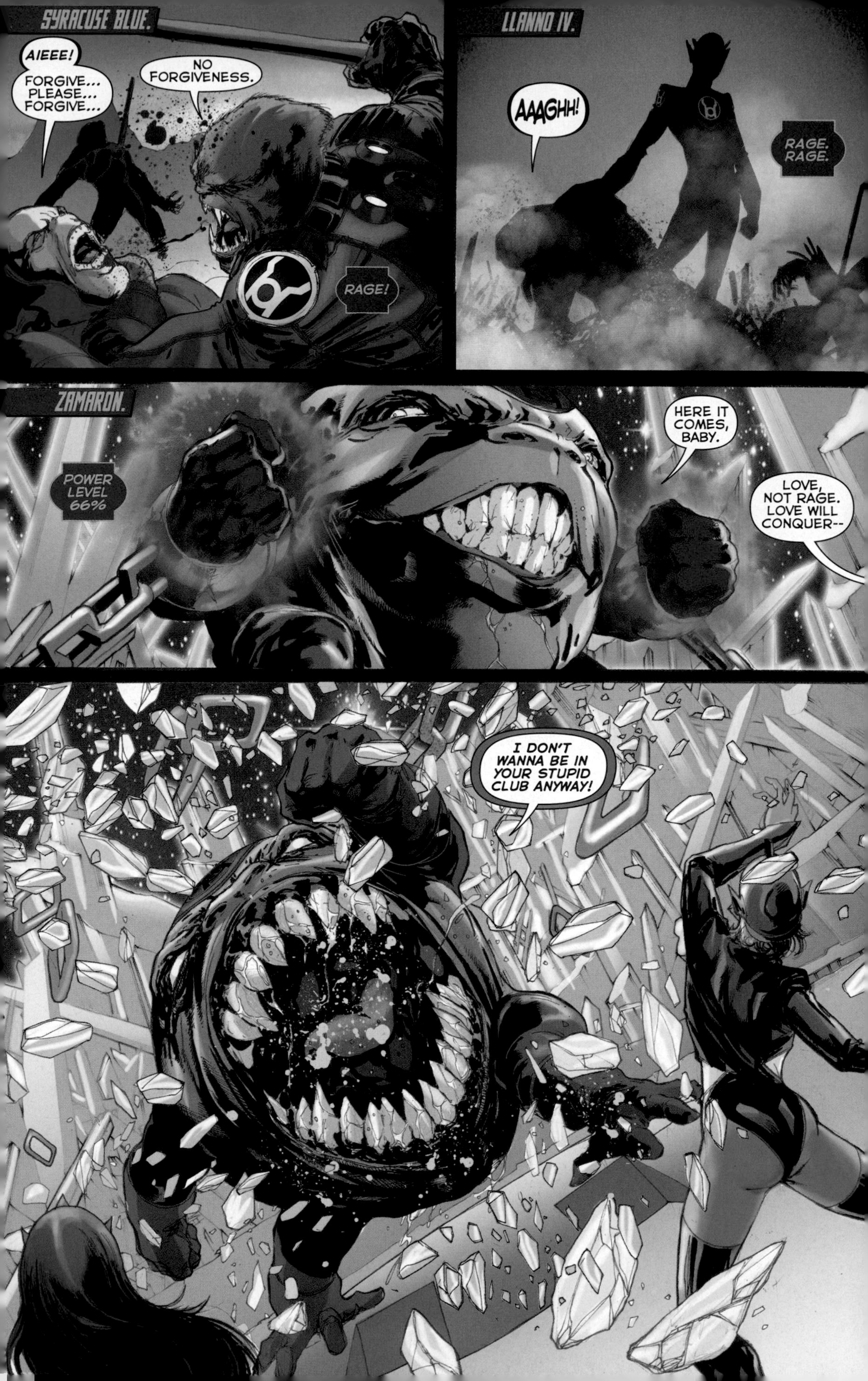
SYRACUSE BLUE.
AIEEE!
FORGIVE... PLEASE... FORGIVE...
NO FORGIVENESS.
RAGE!
LLANNO IV.
AAAGHH!
RAGE. RAGE.
ZAMARON.
POWER LEVEL 66%
HERE IT COMES, BABY.
LOVE, NOT RAGE. LOVE WILL CONQUER--
I DON'T WANNA BE IN YOUR STUPID CLUB ANYWAY!

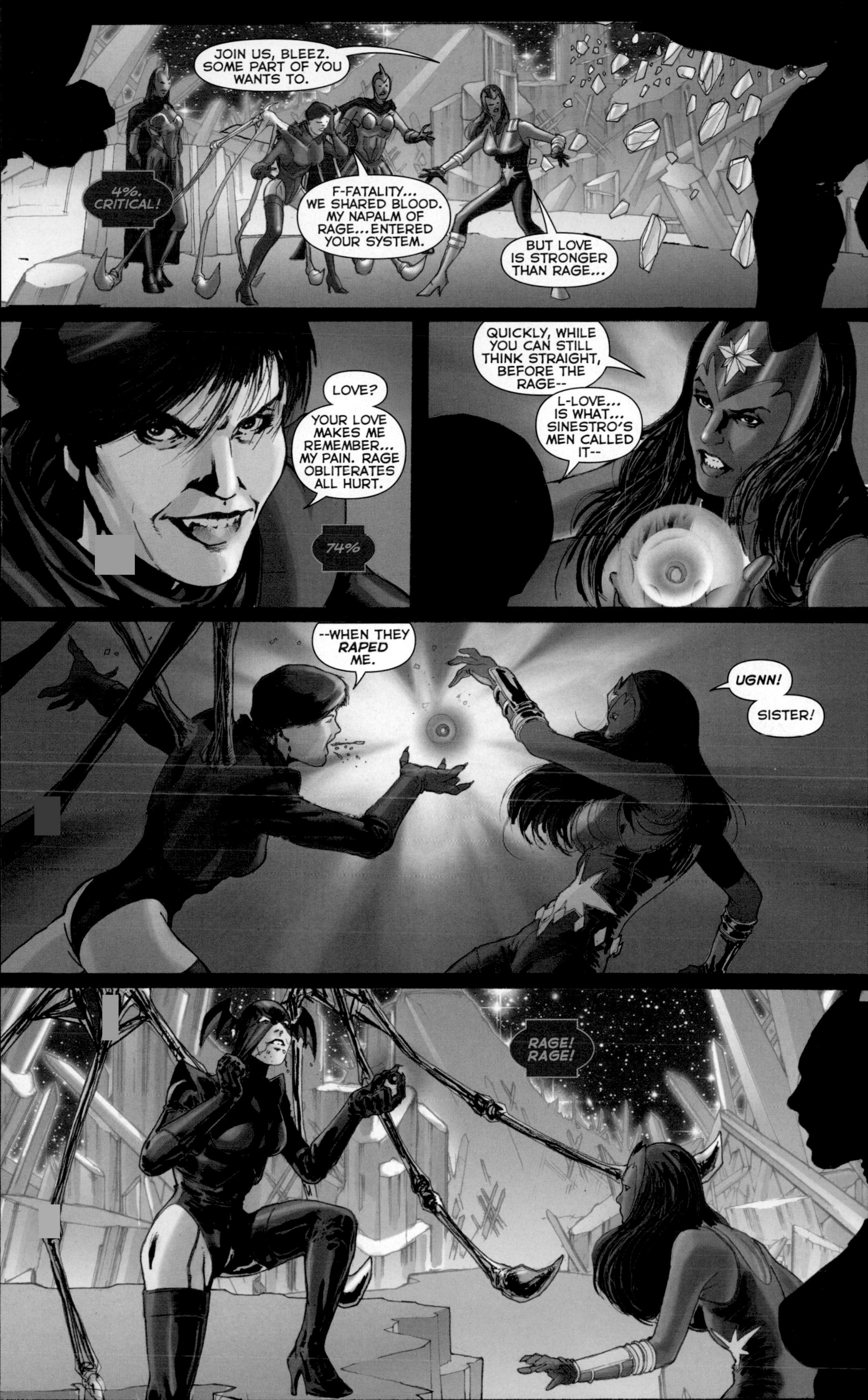
JOIN US, BLEEZ. SOME PART OF YOU WANTS TO.
4%. CRITICAL!
F-FATALITY... WE SHARED BLOOD. MY NAPALM OF RAGE...ENTERED YOUR SYSTEM.
BUT LOVE IS STRONGER THAN RAGE...
LOVE?
YOUR LOVE MAKES ME REMEMBER... MY PAIN. RAGE OBLITERATES ALL HURT.
74%
QUICKLY, WHILE YOU CAN STILL THINK STRAIGHT, BEFORE THE RAGE--
L-LOVE... IS WHAT... SINESTRO'S MEN CALLED IT--
--WHEN THEY *RAPED* ME.
UGNN!
SISTER!
RAGE! RAGE!

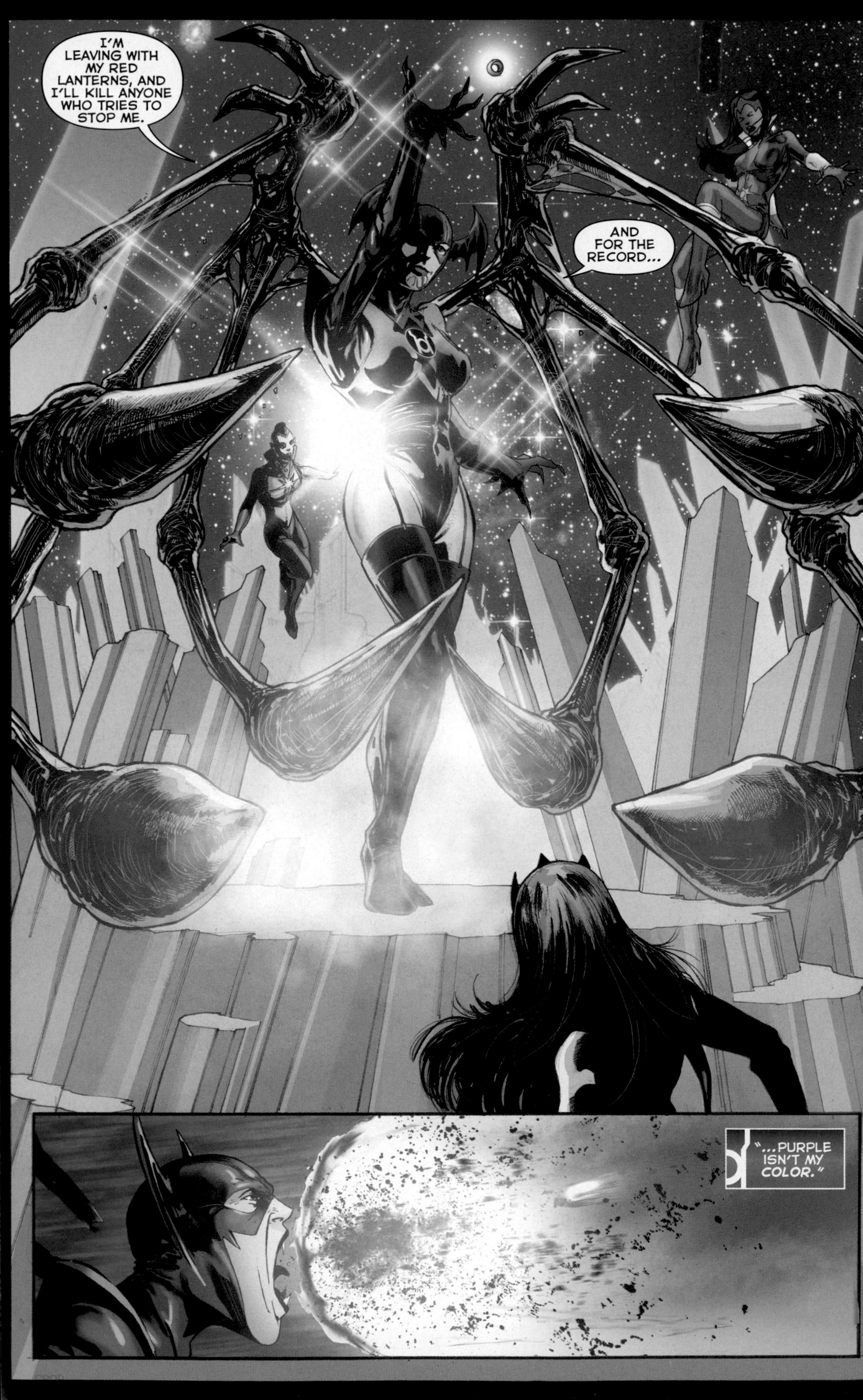
I'M LEAVING WITH MY RED LANTERNS, AND I'LL KILL ANYONE WHO TRIES TO STOP ME.
AND FOR THE RECORD...
"...PURPLE ISN'T MY COLOR."

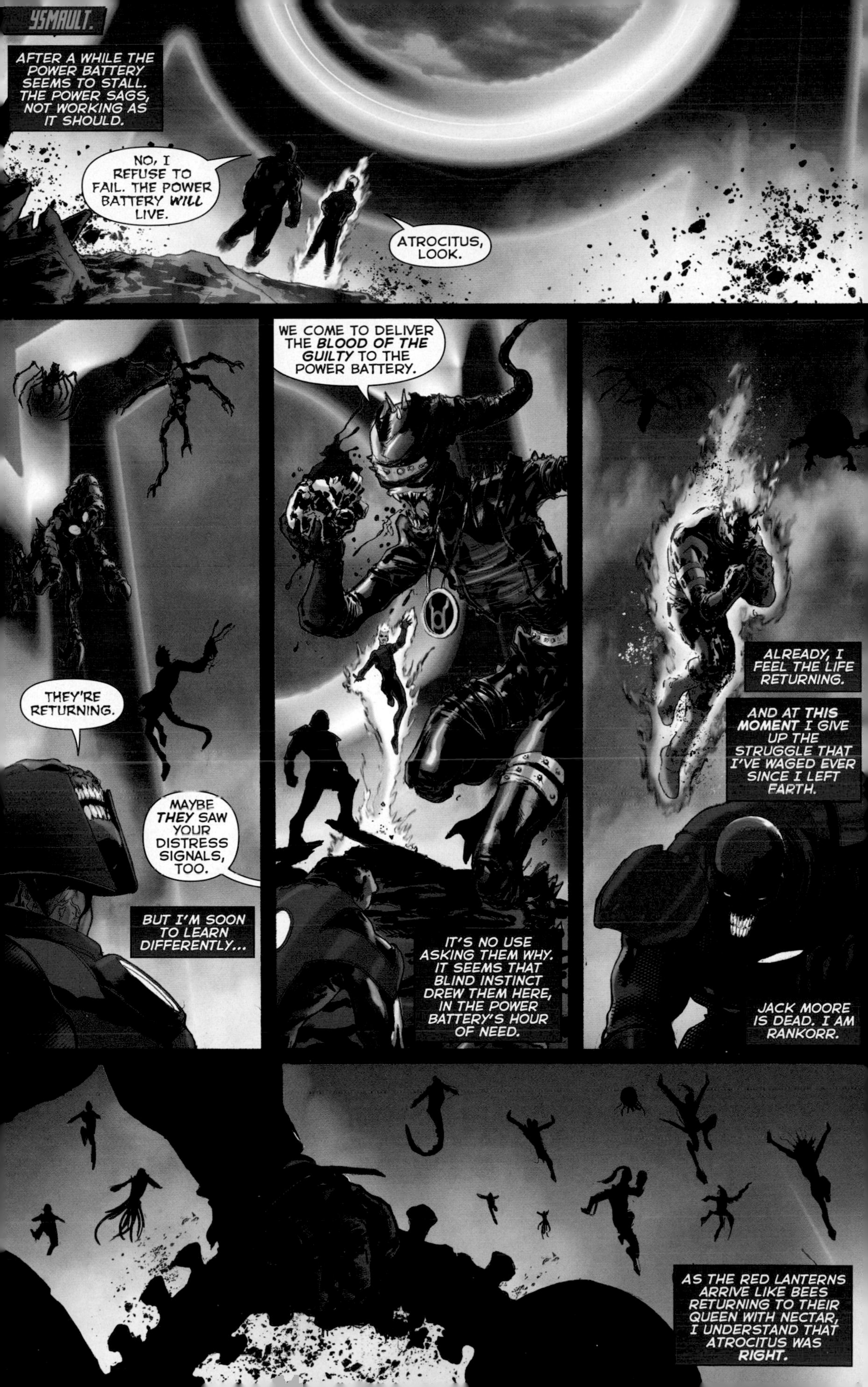
YSMAULT.
AFTER A WHILE THE POWER BATTERY SEEMS TO STALL. THE POWER SAGS, NOT WORKING AS IT SHOULD.
NO, I REFUSE TO FAIL. THE POWER BATTERY *WILL* LIVE.
ATROCITUS, LOOK.
THEY'RE RETURNING.
MAYBE *THEY* SAW YOUR DISTRESS SIGNALS, TOO.
BUT I'M SOON TO LEARN DIFFERENTLY...
WE COME TO DELIVER THE *BLOOD OF THE GUILTY* TO THE POWER BATTERY.
IT'S NO USE ASKING THEM WHY. IT SEEMS THAT BLIND INSTINCT DREW THEM HERE, IN THE POWER BATTERY'S HOUR OF NEED.
ALREADY, I FEEL THE LIFE RETURNING.
AND AT **THIS MOMENT** I GIVE UP THE STRUGGLE THAT I'VE WAGED EVER SINCE I LEFT EARTH.
JACK MOORE IS DEAD. I AM RANKORR.
AS THE RED LANTERNS ARRIVE LIKE BEES RETURNING TO THEIR QUEEN WITH NECTAR, I UNDERSTAND THAT ATROCITUS WAS **RIGHT**.

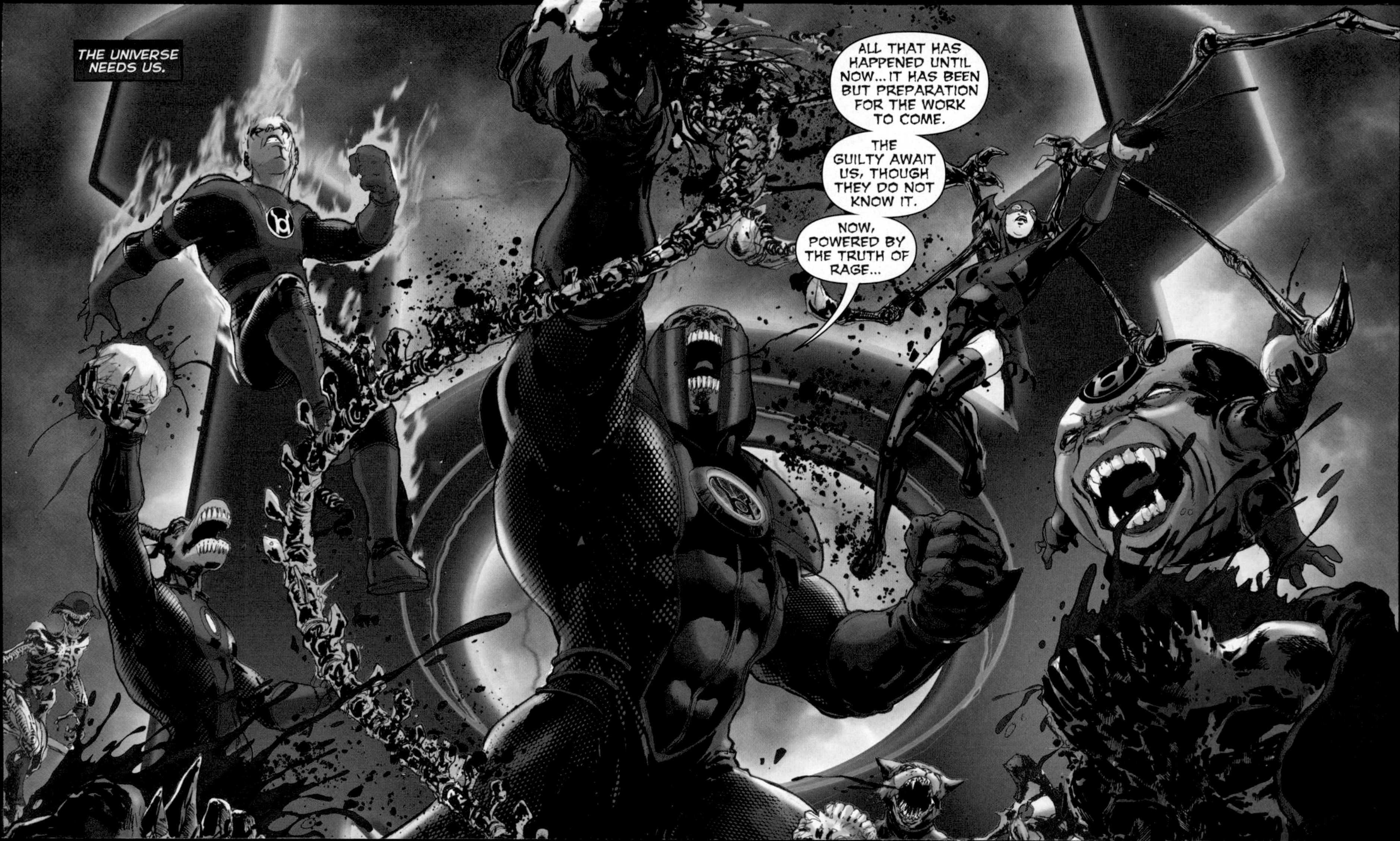
THE UNIVERSE NEEDS US.
ALL THAT HAS HAPPENED UNTIL NOW...IT HAS BEEN BUT PREPARATION FOR THE WORK TO COME.
THE GUILTY AWAIT US, THOUGH THEY DO NOT KNOW IT.
NOW, POWERED BY THE TRUTH OF RAGE...

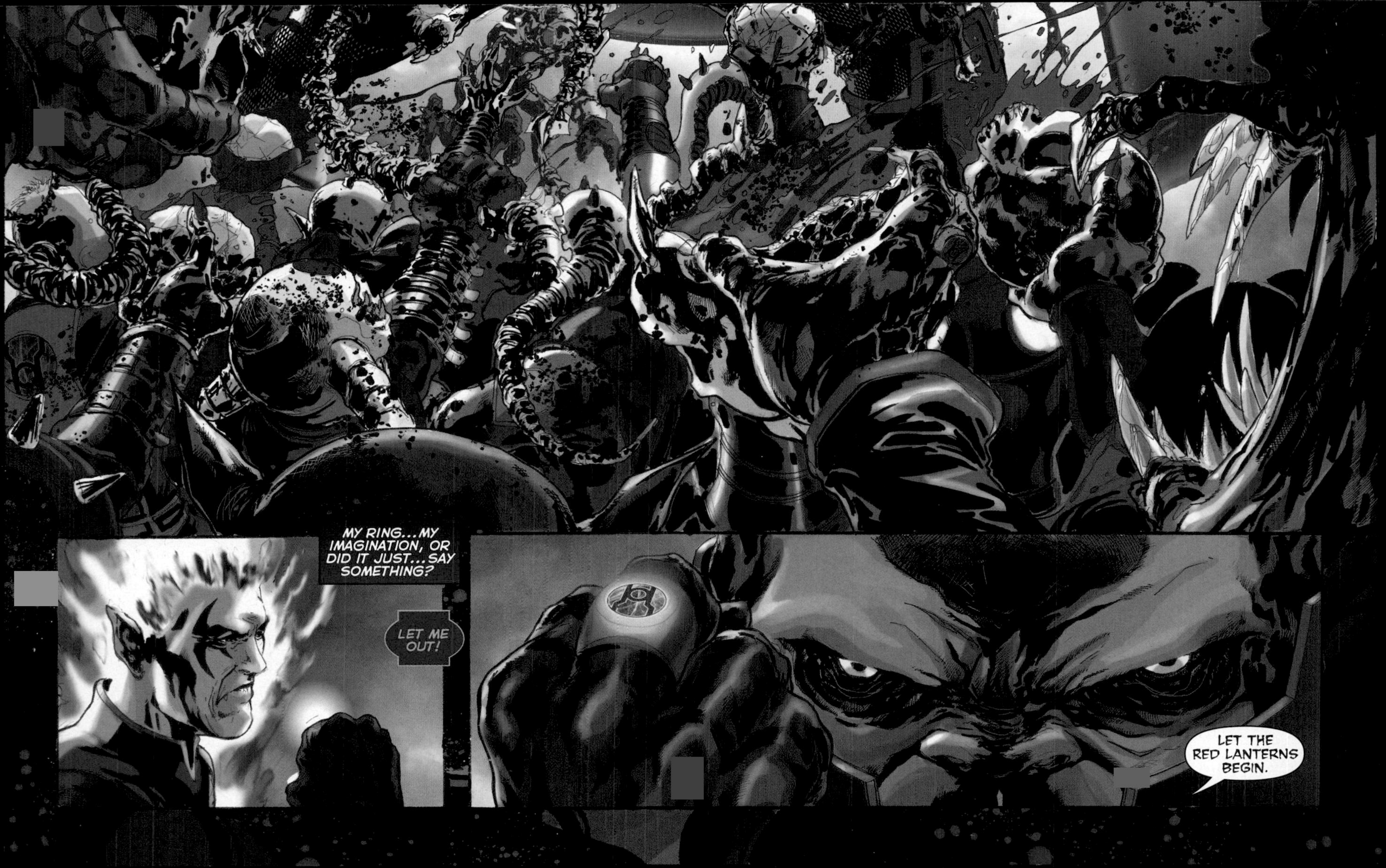
MY RING...MY IMAGINATION, OR DID IT JUST...SAY SOMETHING?
LET ME OUT!
LET THE RED LANTERNS BEGIN.

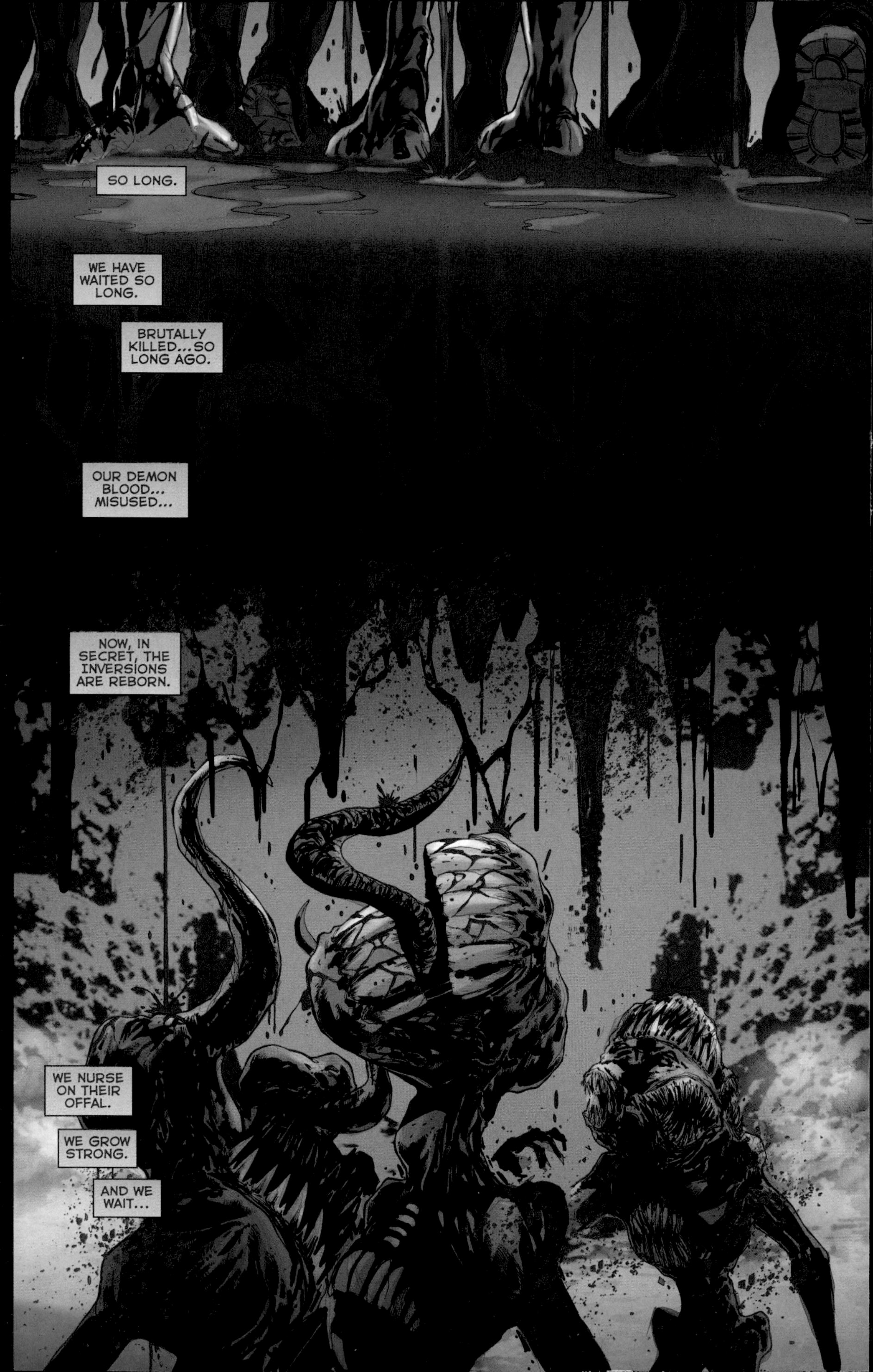
SO LONG.
WE HAVE WAITED SO LONG.
BRUTALLY KILLED...SO LONG AGO.
OUR DEMON BLOOD... MISUSED...
NOW, IN SECRET, THE INVERSIONS ARE REBORN.
WE NURSE ON THEIR OFFAL.
WE GROW STRONG.
AND WE WAIT...

DC COMICS™

START AT THE BEGINNING!

GREEN LANTERN
VOLUME 1: SINESTRO

**GREEN LANTERN
CORPS VOLUME 1:
FEARSOME**

**RED LANTERNS
VOLUME 1:
BLOOD AND RAGE**

**GREEN LANTERN:
NEW GUARDIANS
VOLUME 1:
THE RING BEARER**

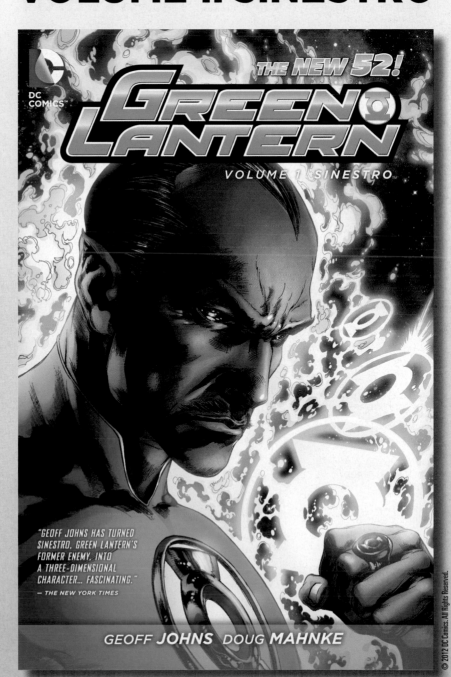

"GEOFF JOHNS HAS TURNED
SINESTRO, GREEN LANTERN'S
FORMER ENEMY, INTO
A THREE-DIMENSIONAL
CHARACTER... FASCINATING."
— THE NEW YORK TIMES

GEOFF **JOHNS** DOUG **MAHNKE**

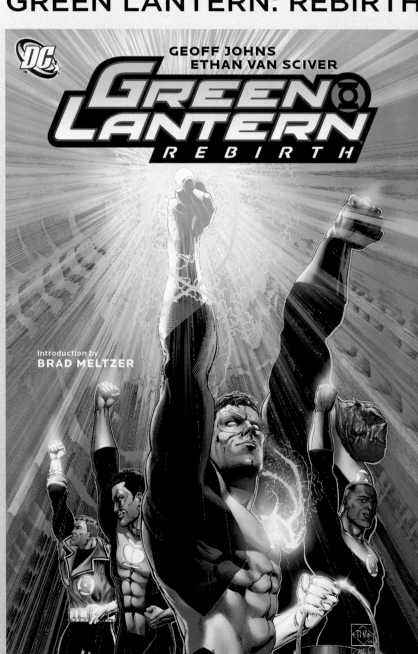

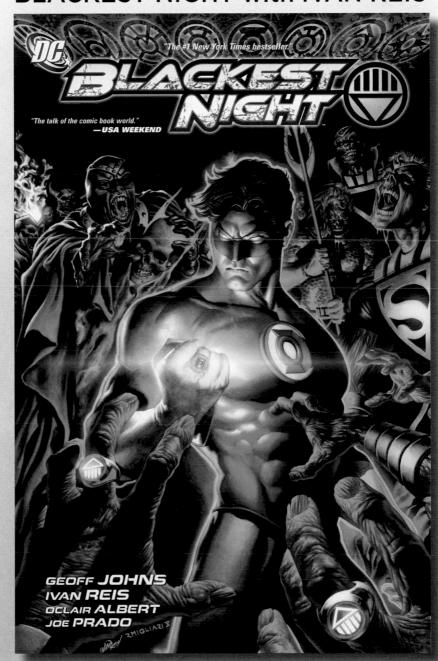